Developing Critical Thinking

Developing Critical Thinking

From Theory to Classroom Practice

Edited by
Fernando Naiditch

ROWMAN & LITTLEFIELD
Lanham • Boulder • New York • London

Published by Rowman & Littlefield
A wholly owned subsidiary of The Rowman & Littlefield Publishing Group, Inc.
4501 Forbes Boulevard, Suite 200, Lanham, Maryland 20706
www.rowman.com

Unit A, Whitacre Mews, 26-34 Stannary Street, London SE11 4AB

British Library Cataloguing in Publication Information Available

Library of Congress Cataloging-in-Publication Data
Names: Naiditch, Fernando, editor.
Title: Developing critical thinking : from theory to classroom practice / edited by
    Fernando Naiditch.
Description: Lanham : Rowman & Littlefield, a wholly owned subsidiary of
    The Rowman & Littlefield Publishing Group, Inc., [2016]
Identifiers: LCCN 2016031774 (print) | LCCN 2016045273 (ebook) |
    ISBN 9781475818925 (cloth : alk. paper) | ISBN 9781475818932 (pbk. : alk.
    paper) | ISBN 9781475818949 (Electronic)
Subjects: LCSH: Critical thinking–Study and teaching.
Classification: LCC LB1590.3 .D46 2016 (print) | LCC LB1590.3 (ebook) |
    DDC 370.15/2–dc23
LC record available at https://lccn.loc.gov/2016031774

Printed in the United States of America

Contents

Acknowledgments

Teaching and learning are collaborative endeavors. It is the nature of my work and also a personal belief that knowledge is built collectively, and that it is advanced by people coming together in action that promotes transformation and leads to change.

My deepest gratitude:

To the colleagues whose contributions are featured in this book.

To the graduate assistants whose dedication is much appreciated—Vani Apanosian, Gregory Gallet, and Brian Hoesly.

To my family whose unconditional love and support has made me a stronger and better person.

To the many students and teachers whose stories are shared on these pages.

Everyone involved in this project has brought expertise to the conversation, an immeasurable passion for education, and a firm conviction in the power of teachers as agents of change.

Their original ideas and innovative pedagogy have helped shape the vision of critical thinking developed in this book.

Introduction

Teaching and Learning Critical Thinking

Fernando Naiditch

This book is about understanding the concept of critical thinking in action, that is, what it means in terms of pedagogical practices in the classroom. Critical thinking skills can be taught and the best approach to teaching them is by understanding the subskills involved in critical thinking and by providing students with plenty of opportunities to practice and develop these subskills in the classroom.

In order to practice critical thinking, students need to be on task in the classroom and engaged in activities that speak to them, that is, the curriculum has to be tailored to adapt to the students and not the other way around. Students learn best when they can relate to content, so the most effective classroom practices will encourage students to use their background knowledge and culture to relate to what they are being presented with. Classroom practices and approaches that validate students' experiences and build on what they bring to class engage them in more meaningful ways and are more likely to have a long-term effect on students.

Teachers also need to think of classroom practices that will enable students to find their voices. Giving them a voice will also lead them to learn to listen to other students' voices and consider that a classroom is a diverse environment where everyone has different ideas, perspectives, and ways of seeing and interpreting the world.

Teaching practices that encourage critical thinking skills expose students to a variety of sources, information, and points of view. Of course there is a lot of information out there and students need to be able to discern between the sources they use and understand how reliable and solid they are, but that comes with time and practice. As students develop critical thinking, they also learn to understand conflicting information and to deal with it in a more mature and responsible way.

The role of the teacher is to be open and accepting to the fact that there is more than one possible way of doing and looking at things; thus encouraging differences in the ways students think and express their thoughts. A teacher is many times referred to as a facilitator of learning. This means being able to guide students through the process of reaching their own conclusions based on what they researched, read, and discussed.

Needless to say, students' opinions, conclusions, and ideas need to be informed and well supported by appropriate literature. While guiding students, then, the teacher needs to constantly engage them in questioning—both by asking questions himself and by encouraging students to ask questions. Learning develops as students explore their curiosity through questions, problem-solving, and inquiry. Critical thinking permeates all of these cognitive processes as a tool, a way of approaching tasks, interacting and dialoguing with content and materials.

The chapters in this book present different approaches to the teaching of critical thinking and introduce pedagogical strategies and instructional practices that encourage students to think critically.

Chapter 1 presents an overview of critical thinking with definitions and examples. The term critical thinking is so widely used in the field of education that sometimes people assume that its understanding is universal. However, critical thinking can take different meanings and uses depending on the way it is understood and implemented as a teaching tool and instructional practice. In order to plan for a pedagogy that encourages and develops students' ability to relate to content, classroom materials, and each other in critical and responsible ways, chapter 1 elaborates on this book's approach to the term.

In chapter 2, Olivier Michaud describes how philosophy can be used even with students at a very young age to develop critical thinking skills. The practice of philosophy is usually associated with big existential questions—who we are, what our purpose in life is, and the very meaning of life and nature of reality. Philosophy is also associated with moral and ethical dilemmas we face in life and society, issues of right versus wrong, societal and personal values, systems of belief and attitudes.

While engaging in the practice of philosophy, students are developing larger critical thinking skills, especially the ones related to learning to ask questions and developing arguments. The critical thinking skills developed in philosophy are mostly of the analytical nature, that is, students engage in a detailed investigation of structural elements of a problem. In order to get to a conclusion, they need to learn to separate fact from fiction, and look deeply into what they are studying by identifying and separating its constituent elements.

In the program called Philosophy for Children, young learners are asked to engage in a collective process of asking and answering questions based on a story they have been told. In doing so, they learn to search for answers and justify them using the facts provided in the story, develop arguments, and communicate them effectively.

In chapter 3, Elizabeth Quintero describes her work with teachers, student teachers, and children and families in developing a pedagogy that is based on participation of all stakeholders, respect for multiple sources of knowledge, and the responsibility for transformative action.

While educating prospective early childhood and elementary school teachers, Elizabeth develops her students' critical thinking skills by engaging them in a process that supports students' multiple languages and cultures, and that recognizes ways that multiple knowledge sources, identities, and language forms can contribute to the formation of new relationships and meanings in all aspects of learning.

The process uses critical pedagogy and critical literacy as a framework for integrated curriculum. The pre-service teachers are pushed to connect early childhood and child and family development theoretical information to a context of critical theory, and they do so by participating in problem-posing activities in which they use multicultural children's literature, interviews of community members, and educational research to give them background information to approach participant observation in schools and early childhood programs. Then, they begin planning and implementing participatory curriculum in their teaching contexts.

The work is based on the notion of funds of knowledge, that is, "historically accumulated and culturally developed bodies of knowledge and skills essential for household or individual functioning and well-being" (Moll, Amanti, Neff & Gonzalez, 1992, p. 133). By coming to know their students and their families in new ways, teachers begin to see that the households of their students contain rich cultural and cognitive resources and that these resources can and should be used in their classroom as part of curriculum to provide culturally responsive and meaningful lessons that tap into students' prior knowledge.

In chapter 4, Jean Ann Slusarczyk and Lucy Villaluz describe a project that involved a whole school community in order to address bullying. Recent statistics on school bullying reveal that bullying has become an epidemic in the United States (Conn, 2004). An average of about 160,000 children miss school every day out of fear of being bullied which translates into about one in seven students in grades kindergarten through twelfth who is either a bully or has been a victim of bullying (Barzelon, 2013). A study by Bradshaw, Sawyer & O'Brennan (2007) showed that in one month about 49 percent of children in grades 4–12 reported being bullied by other students at school, whereas 30.8 percent reported bullying others during that time.

School bullying is now at the center of every educational discussion and policy decision (Swearer, Espelage, & Napolitano, 2009). In 2014, the

Centers for Disease Control and the Department of Education released the first federal uniform definition of bullying. The definition includes unwanted aggressive behavior, observed or perceived power imbalance, and repetition of behaviors or high likelihood of repetition. It also acknowledges that youth can be bullied or can bully others both directly (in the presence of a targeted youth) and indirectly (bullying not directly communicated to a targeted youth, such as spreading rumors). The federal definition includes four types of bullying: physical, verbal, relational (e.g., efforts to harm the reputation or relationships of the targeted youth), and damage to property (see stopbullying.gov for additional information).

The state of New Jersey has been a leader in the establishment of a strong statutory, regulatory policy and program framework to support the prevention, remediation, and reporting of bullying in schools. The HIB (Harassment, Intimidation and Bullying) policy that came into effect in 2011 has changed the way educators understand and respond to bullying both on and off school grounds.

In order to address this challenge, a group of educators at Franklin Elementary School in Bloomfield partnered with Montclair State University to develop an anti-bullying educational program named *Promoting Respect through Collaboration* (PRTC) with the purpose of fostering collaboration among all school stakeholders, including students, faculty, parents, community members, and higher education partners in order to advance the conversation about bullying and to work toward creating a healthy school environment that encourages collaboration, respect, and a strong sense of community.

The chapter describes the results of this partnership and focuses on the curriculum and activities developed with the community, specifically those that helped elementary school students develop critical thinking skills. The curriculum developed for this program had a critical lens through which all the lessons and materials were developed. Students were confronted with their own school situations and were asked to come up with novel and creative solutions to respond to the conflicts they had identified as bullying in the school. Students were prompted to look critically at their actions and words to understand that they have consequences, and how they contribute to creating a more positive school climate.

In chapter 5, Mark Russo makes use of his years of experience as a mathematics teacher to describe how a math classroom can become a place of constant critical thinking practice. Many high school students in senior elective classes do not consider mathematics class to be useful for their lives, nor do they learn much while they are enrolled in the course. After trying for years to adjust the way he taught these courses, he wondered whether the problem wasn't so much the pedagogy as it was the content itself.

How could a teacher expect students who had performed poorly in previous algebra courses to get excited about a similar college algebra course, especially when the content had little to no significance for their lives? With this question in mind, Mark decided to sculpt a course that was based entirely on mathematics that related to students' lives or future goals. Since he was unsure exactly what type of mathematics to cover, he decided to invite students to co-construct the course with him. The result was a yearlong practitioner action research project that investigated the impact of co-construction on students' attitudes and achievement in mathematics.

Co-construction is a process where students work alongside the teacher to jointly plan units, lessons, and assessments. After struggling through some of the tensions that resulted in this renegotiation of power, Mark found that this process had a significant impact on the teaching and learning that took place in the classroom. The co-construction process impacted students' attitudes by giving them a real voice in what they studied and how they studied it, it impacted student learning by increasing the level of student engagement, and it impacted the teacher's own understanding of what it means to teach mathematics, as he reconsidered how power relations, classroom culture, and individual choice impact the day-to-day interactions in the classroom.

In chapter 6, I explore the contributions of critical pedagogy to the teaching of reading and discuss an approach that helps learners move beyond the level of comprehension and use what they have learned in reading toward engaging in some kind of social action. This chapter was initially published in the journal *Critical Questions in Education* as an article. Given the feedback I received from teachers who have adapted the approach in their classrooms, I decided to include it in this book, especially because reading is an essential skill for life and learning to read critically is essential for participating and engaging in the life of a society and in citizenship.

It is argued that, for reading to be effective and purposeful for both teachers and students, there needs to be a concrete connection between the text and the real world, and that this connection can be achieved through encouraging social action.

Reading has been used in classrooms both as a tool for language development and as a way of supplementing and extending content area knowledge. In order to develop the ability to read, learners need to be taught not only to understand what is presented in a text (comprehension), but to activate their previous knowledge, make comparisons and connections (analysis), and create new knowledge (synthesis).

The critical approach to the teaching of reading that I developed involved having students search for multiple possible interpretations and encouraged differences in the way readers relate to a text. Equally important, learning to read a text critically requires developing an awareness of how the themes that students read can lead to individual and collective transformation.

This chapter is particularly useful for teachers who are searching for instructional strategies to help their students develop critical thinking skills. I describe the different skills and subskills involved in reading and relating to a text in detail and I also describe the steps that teachers can take to develop pedagogical strategies and classroom activities that focus on critical thinking. Reading is an essential skill for every learner at every age, content area, and grade level. Therefore, the example described in the chapter can be translated to any classroom and topic. By following the suggested course of action and by integrating a subskill approach to teaching reading, teachers can build up their students' ability to read critically and to transform what they have read into some kind of action—a project or an activity—that can engage other students and affect the larger community.

In chapter 7, Mark Alter and Joan Rosenberg identify current concerns and strategies with regard to instructional programming for students with special needs. At its most fundamental level, the process of teaching students with disabilities involves assessing the students' behavioral and academic repertoire, translating the information into objectives that will guide instruction, goals and strategies; as well as evaluating and assessing the effects of the decision of what and how to teach.

When a special education teacher designs and implements this process, there are potential learning trajectories and obstacles. This is why they argue for collaboration in the process of educating students with special needs. Teachers must think critically about instruction and act collaboratively, which means that all decisions that may affect a student's life both inside and outside the classroom should be taken by a group of stakeholders that knows the child well, understands the needs of that particular student, and is well versed in the different approaches to educating students with different types of needs.

Inclusion or inclusive education is at the heart of the discussion since the Individuals with Disabilities Education Act (IDEA) was mandated in 1975. There is a growing consensus that educating students with special needs in the general education classes is beneficial for students academically, socially, and psychologically; and that the benefits will extend beyond the school years and translate into a student's future life in society.

The chapter advocates for assigning students with disabilities to general education classrooms, but cautions that in order to do so, a strong support system, adequate services, and a solid administrative structure are needed to meet the needs of these students. One of the questions at the center of this discussion is whether there is a common body of knowledge that teachers of students with disabilities should have to be able to teach these students effectively. Many teachers do not feel adequately prepared or feel that they lack the skills needed to address and meet the needs of students with disabilities.

Schools need to think critically and creatively in order to prepare teachers to work with students with special needs, and work collaboratively to provide teachers and students with the appropriate tools, resources, and adaptations.

In chapter 8, Bettina Steren dos Santos, Carla Spagnolo, and Caroline Buker focus on the role of creativity and motivation in the classroom as necessary elements of critical thinking. Being a teacher in times of standardized testing and Common Core Standards requires teachers to develop a new set of skills and differentiated dispositions that go beyond the traditional view of pedagogical content knowledge (Schulman, 1987). Given the new set of requirements and demands on teachers, how does one remain motivated and approach the teaching profession as a creative endeavor? In the chapter, they focus on the relationships between active and creative methodologies and the motivational theory of self-determination. The idea of innovation and creativity in the classroom is based on Design Thinking (Brown, 2009) and comes from global firm IDEO and the Center for Innovations in Learning at Stanford University.

Five steps are described to introduce creative and critical thinking in the classroom: empathize, define, ideate, prototype, and test. By following these steps, teaching becomes an action of problematizing in the classroom and, therefore, engages students in taking an active role in their learning process by developing critical thinking strategies and processes to tackle classroom tasks. In the chapter, they explore how Design Thinking can become part of the curriculum and contribute to enriching classroom experiences by transforming the classroom in a space of critical teaching, learning and thinking.

In chapter 9, I describe a yearlong project developed with student teachers (pre-service English as a foreign language teachers) placed in public schools that served poor populations living in Brazilian *favelas* (shanty towns). The chapter focuses on one particular student teacher—Maria—and her challenges and successes while learning to navigate the world of a low socioeconomic urban school where poverty and even violence prevailed. Like many of the student teachers in her cohort, Maria understood how difficult it was both for her and her students to be there in that "pretend" school environment, a room with broken windows, not enough chairs or desks for everyone, no supplies at all.

In one of her lessons Maria was confronted with questions from the students that she had not anticipated and may not have been ready or prepared to face. The scenario described in this chapter made the student teachers question the purposes of education in a democratic society and forced them to understand the socioeconomic, political, and historical implications of what they do in the classroom. I describe how we transformed students' questions into curriculum and invite the reader to question who decides what is appropriate or necessary for a certain grade level or student population, and what the bases are for developing curriculum. My student teacher faced the challenge of learning how to become a classroom teacher while also learning to develop curriculum, to take charge of the education of the students she was teaching, to empower her students, and to assess her responsibility as an educator.

The chapter uses the example of second language education as an opportunity to develop teachers who are critical and able to understand the student population they teach—their needs and specific life circumstances. I focus on the importance of using a community's funds of knowledge as the basis for the curriculum and on using students' life stories and histories as classroom content. Critical thinking permeates this kind of pedagogy from its inception to its implementation. Teachers and students engaged in critical thinking by questioning their practice and role, context and reality.

After reading about different pedagogical practices that promote critical thinking, I hope that you will be encouraged and motivated to develop your own research project and to study your own educational environment in order to promote change. In the afterword, Kathryn Herr guides the readers in the process of developing and using a genre of inquiry known as practitioner action research. Many teachers have reported that practitioner research has been transformative to their own practices as educators and a growing number of school districts have incorporated this approach into teachers' professional development plans. The chapter both outlines the possibilities of practitioner action research and offers initial steps in instigating a practice of inquiry in classrooms and schools.

Drawing on the author's own experience in researching her own classroom and larger school context as well as examples from others' practitioner action research, the chapter brings to life the possibilities of this approach in supporting teachers' growth and development. In addition, the basics of practitioner action research are offered for those interested in initiating their own inquiry process. The chapter argues that practitioner action research can deepen educators' understanding of the teaching task and help them to critically reflect upon and change their practices in support of their own growth and that of their students. It also locates the inquiry process within the larger context of school sites and the current educational climate.

The contributions in this book reflect different lessons, units, activities, projects, instruction, and strategies that have helped the teachers in each situation develop theirs and their students' critical thinking skills. I hope that through the examples described in this book, you too can develop lessons and teaching that are more geared toward critical thinking and that will transform the way you see and understand the role and the meaning of critical thinking in education.

Within a critical framework, knowledge is not seen as reproductive, but as productive and liberating. My aim is to inspire teachers to understand

and view their classrooms not just as spaces of knowledge reproduction, but production.Teachers need to start to view their classrooms and schools as spaces of interactional and dialogical action where teaching and learning are constantly being (re)negotiated and knowledge is constantly being questioned.

This book invites teachers to share our critical practices in order to renew their own. The key terms here are discuss, assess, and renew in order to redefine teachers' understanding of what knowledge is and what it represents. As you read the different chapters, you are invited to question what knowledge is, what knowledge is valued and why, and how knowledge can in fact be co-constructed within a critical framework.

As you consider the different approaches to critical thinking that the contributors of this book illustrate and analyze, I hope that you will also engage critically with the ideas, suggestions, and practices described here. Most of all, I hope these ideas will inspire you to rethink your own pedagogy and work toward developing more critically and meaningful classroom practices that can bring about changes in the lives of the students, schools, and communities where you work.

REFERENCES

Barzelon, E. (2013). *Sticks and stones: Defeating the culture of bullying and rediscovering the power of character and empathy.* New York: Random House.

Bradshaw, C. P., Sawyer, A. L., & O'Brennan, L. M. (2007). Bullying and peer victimization at school: Perceptual differences between students and school staff. *School Psychology Review, 36*(3), 361–382.

Brown, T. (2009). *Change by design: How design thinking transforms organizations and inspires innovation.* New York: HarperCollins.

Conn, K. (2004). *Bullying and harassment: A legal guide for educators.* Alexandria, VA: Association for Supervision & Curriculum.

Moll, L. C., Amanti, C., Neff, D., & Gonzalez, N. (1992). Funds of knowledge for teaching: Using a qualitative approach to connect homes and classrooms. *Theory into Practice, 31*(2), 132–141.

Shulman, L. (1987). Knowledge and teaching: Foundations of the new reform. *Harvard Educational Review, 57*(1), 1–22

Swearer, S. M. Espelage, D. L., & Napolitano, S. A. (2009). *Bullying prevention and intervention: Realistic strategies for schools.* New York: The Guilford Press.

Chapter 1

Understanding Critical Thinking

What Is It? Can We Teach It? How Do We Learn It?

Fernando Naiditch

A group of chemistry students was getting ready to take its final exam at the end of the academic year. During the semester they had studied the chemical properties of food components and the chemical interactions and reactions in different types of food. The test consisted of one essay question: What did you have for lunch today? Is this recommended for eating before taking a test?

The students were taking the test right after lunch and many of them wished they could be taking a nap instead of a final exam. The professor thought this was great: "If you feel lazy, tired, or sleepy, this is most likely an effect of what you had for lunch. Write about that."

If students were actually going to write about the meal they really had before coming to class or if they would come up with some kind of ideal meal or "power lunch," that was fine. The professor did not really worry about the meal being invented or real. Describing and analyzing their meals based on chemical components and interactions, and potential side effects of different food properties, was what the teacher was hoping the students would be able to do.

The idea of using their own meals was a pedagogical trick to make the test more interesting, realistic, and meaningful, as it was related to something that had just happened to the students before entering the classroom—and indeed the students engaged in the task with an enormous amount of motivation: "So, I just have to write about what I ate and defend my choices?"

"Exactly," said the professor.

In order to pass the test, students could have chosen any of the infinite menu possibilities they could have come up with as long as they were successful in arguing for their food choices. Their justification had to be appropriate, that is, the exam question required students to analyze their food choices by using what they had learned about chemistry during the semester.

Some of them may have chosen to write about the many cups of coffee they had before coming to class because of the caffeine and its ability to maintain one's alertness, but they could also have written about the potential side effects of having too much coffee, which include body jitters, increased heartbeats, and even a constant need to go to the restroom—not a good thing during an exam.

Some students may have focused on their dessert choices and the so-called sugar-high effect. However, these same students would need to remember that a sugar high can lead to a brain low, as too little and too much glucose are both problematic.

Students who are into natural food alternatives could have written about their light snacks filled with almonds, walnuts, fruit, and energy bars to keep their energy levels going during the exam. They could also have talked about the benefits of eating omega-3 fatty acids and their need for fish before the final test.

Answers could also include the consumption of proteins, such as beans or eggs, and the role of amino acids in maintaining focus and keeping attention. Of course, students' answers were much more academic than the examples given here and included deeper analysis of food properties and side effects. Part of the challenge consisted in finding a balanced meal that would not make them sleepy and that would keep them alert and focused while taking the test. Whether the student chose to eat a peanut butter sandwich or opted for a typical breakfast-for-lunch meal of bacon and eggs, the point here is that there is not only one possible answer.

The professor knew that each student would come up with a different answer, and that is exactly what he wanted. There was no need for any student to cheat on the exam. In fact, everyone had to have had a different meal before coming to class and even the students who happened to have eaten together may have had different types of drinks and may have opted for focusing on different aspects of the same meal. Each answer here was going to be unique and would reflect the knowledge each student had gained during the course applied to a simple but everyday situation.

This was a test of applied knowledge that required students to exercise their critical thinking skills. As students argued for their answers, they showed their knowledge of the properties and effects of eating different types of food and food groups, and also of the short- and long-term effects of digesting certain foods prior to engaging in a cognitively demanding task.

In order to develop their arguments, students would be using terms such as carbohydrates, enzymes, protein molecules, fibers, or syneresis, which require them to demonstrate their understanding of the semantic field and the technically specialized language they had studied during the semester. Academic language is very specialized and context-specific. Knowing how to use it properly reflects understanding of its meaning and demonstrates one's ability to engage in the appropriate discourse domain.

The test required students to apply the knowledge they had gained during the semester because they were using what they knew to justify a personal choice that has concrete and measurable effects on daily tasks such as studying, attending class, and being alert and attentive while taking a test. It required critical thinking skills because students had to demonstrate their ability to identify and collect information, analyze pros and cons, compare and contrast, and arrive at a conclusion that was informed and well supported. This was an original test for different reasons:

1. Students were asked to relate the knowledge gained during the semester to real-life applications. In other words, this was applied chemistry.
2. Students were talking about the use of chemistry in daily life. One of the big problems for many students studying chemistry (and many other content areas) in school is the inability to connect what is learned in the classroom to what happens outside school. Being able to relate classroom content to the outside world and bringing it to our own experiences makes it more meaningful and relevant, and chances are that you will retain the information and remember it for much longer than if you were just memorizing a number of facts, or in the case of their chemistry lesson, if you were memorizing the periodic table of elements, for example.
3. There was no one correct or expected answer. Students' answers varied tremendously, but as long as they were able to support their answers with appropriate justifications that demonstrated the application of their chemistry knowledge, the answer would have been accepted.
4. The professor was open and flexible to getting as many answers as students could come up with and to accepting them, as long as they made sense and were appropriately written using accurate information. In order to engage in an exam like this one, a teacher needs to be able to demonstrate flexibility and let go of control. Many teachers love to have one answer, only one option and possible way of looking at things.
5. When there is no one answer, students need to be able to demonstrate their knowledge of the content area and also to make their arguments strong and convincing. This means that they needed to elaborate on their answers with detailed information about the pros and cons of eating different foods and make a strong case for their meal choice.

This anecdote reflects the approach to critical thinking that you will find in the different contributions of this book. Throughout my career as an educator, I have seen teachers, students, administrators, and parents use the word "critical thinking" in different ways, with different meanings, and for different purposes. In fact, people use the term so often that sometimes it is difficult to understand what they mean.

In my classes, I have this recurring practice of having my students develop operational definitions of terms they will be using, that is, every time they are going to use a word or a term that is either jargon in education or that has become widely used or that is used differently depending on the context, I ask them to define their terms in the way they understand it and are using it. Developing operational definitions means that students are asked to say, "In this essay, I will use critical thinking to refer to the skills of X and Y," for example. An operational definition needs to be clear without leaving room for ambiguity and it also needs to be detailed and offer specific descriptors that determine the meanings you are attaching to a certain term.

What is the operational definition of critical thinking that this book uses? First of all, it is important to understand that *critical thinking is a skill*. As such, it needs to be practiced and developed. Students do not learn to think critically unless they are trained to do so. Students need to be exposed to and engage in pedagogical practices that require them to connect to what they know and do, to make meanings and consider possibilities, and to come up with creative and novel solutions to problems.

Willingham (2007) has argued that critical thinking is not the kind of skill that, once learned, can be applied to any situation, like riding a bicycle, for example. "The processes of thinking," he says, "are intertwined with the content of thought (that is, domain knowledge)" (p. 8). This means that looking at an issue from multiple perspectives requires students to actually have the knowledge about that issue so they can analyze it from different angles. What this means for the classroom teachers is that critical thinking needs to be taught along with content. Students need to learn about facts and they need to be able to relate them to their background knowledge before they can see the different sides or perspectives of an issue.

In many educational settings, teachers expect students to all arrive at the one correct answer—the only possibility that is accepted as correct. This may be true in a mathematical calculation (after all, seven times nine is always going to be sixty-three), but this is not always the case; not even in a math class. In many cases, an answer is reached at through having students engage in dialogue, reading different sources, connecting pieces of information, inferring meanings, considering possible alternatives, and presenting different solutions.

In the example of the chemistry final exam, students had to develop their answers using the information they had learned during the semester about the properties of the food and their chemical interactions to arrive at an answer—and there was more than one possible correct answer. Chemical elements are unique. However, the use we make of the information may be varied and creative.

Critical thinking is not about memorization of facts or the ability to regurgitate them. No one is a walking encyclopedia and you do not need to be. In fact, it is very easy to get any piece of information you need or want today with the click of a button. When I grew up, I remember having to spend hours memorizing names, places, and dates for history tests. Those days are long gone. Nowadays, information is everywhere and there is an overload of it.

Having access to information is extremely important, especially in a democratic society like ours, but what counts as critical is the ability to get to the information that you need, the ability to identify what counts as information, to select among the plethora of possible sources of information, to understand that some sources are more reliable than others, to identify, sort through, select, and finally apply information.

There are many people who believe in the value of knowing facts and numbers without any practical or specific application. If you ever watched the TV show *Jeopardy!* you know what I am talking about. People always get impressed by the candidates in the show who display an immense body of knowledge. This is a skill and in fact there is a place and a value for that kind of skill in society. The people we see on *Jeopardy* do in fact have the ability to store and retrieve information like a computer. But this is a show about just that—*presenting* information. Candidates are not asked to *use* that information in any way. They do not even need to explain, justify, or expand on their answers. The show even has a rule and participants need to answer the questions using "what is X?" This is a skill that also requires training, especially memory, and it is also thinking, but not critical. There is no assessment of the information used and no need to apply that information anywhere.

Critical thinking does require memory. Learning anything requires memory. People need to memorize passwords, phone numbers, personal information, locations, etc. We use memory all the time and we apply what we memorized to get money at the ATM, to call people up and, to go places. In order to think critically, we do need to be able to have access to information. But we need to know how to use it and for what purposes.

In schools that focus too much on training students to memorize and regurgitate information, students probably won't go very far. The world has changed dramatically and the ability to store information is only useful if you know when and how to apply what you have learned. Critical thinking is about applied knowledge and not about dormant knowledge. Dormant knowledge is stagnant and theoretical. Critical thinking is practical and applied.

WHAT IT MEANS TO THINK CRITICALLY

Critical thinking in schools has been associated with a large number of skills. People usually refer to it as teaching students to "think outside the box" or to learn to consider multiple perspectives of a problem or situation in order to make informed decisions.

Given the vast number of definitions and approaches to critical thinking, it is often understood as a major or primary skill under which we find a subset or subskills, such as assessing, reasoning, analyzing, interpreting, decision-making, and problem-solving, among others.

Indeed, in order to perform all these skills or subskills, one needs to learn to think creatively and critically about the situations at hand and the ways in which a problem or an issue can be approached, tackled, and/or solved.

The new set of standards laid out for schools through the Common Core State Standards also emphasizes this need to teach students to become critical thinkers and to learn to approach problems from different and varied perspectives, at the same time that they are expected to act creatively and respond innovatively to the tasks at hand.

The Common Core State Standards' emphasis on what is referred to as the "thinking curriculum" will require teachers and students not only to engage in critical thinking, but also to learn new ways of understanding classroom interactions, instruction, and the notions of what teaching and learning mean.

In an article describing a classroom project I developed with undergraduate students on the effects of the digital world and the Internet on our understanding and practice of diversity education, I used a definition of media literacy that is very much aligned with the idea of critical thinking: "Broadly defined, media literacy includes the ability to develop and use critical thinking skills (such as sorting through, analyzing and assessing information) to interpret media messages and to create meanings out of those messages" (Naiditch, 2013, p. 339). This definition highlights the idea of empowerment—by becoming media literate, people learn to use critical lenses both as consumers of media messages and as producers of their own messages.

Like my description of media literacy, critical thinking includes a series of general competencies, but also a set of subskills that are developed in particular contexts, depending on the tasks people engage in. For example, the ability to analyze is a general competency, but the abilities to problem-solve, examine, and scrutinize can be considered subskills of analyze, as they usually refer to specific aspects included in an analysis.

Critical thinking is also a meaning-making process. As students learn new information, and as they are confronted with new content, they need to learn to interpret and respond to what they are being presented. As students learn new things in school, they need to learn to react and respond to what they learn, and they can only do that if they can relate to the materials and content in a critical way, by displaying a series of general competencies and subskills which include, among others, an ability to inquire, to learn to ask questions and interpret answers contextually, to read between the lines and to express themselves in socially appropriate ways—all of which are needed to prepare citizens for a democratic society (Thoman and Jolls, 2005).

Being a critical thinker is also learning to be creative and conscientious. Students need to develop the ability to understand how meaning is produced and the impact the content of what they learn have in their lives. Undoubtedly, the abilities to understand text, to make meaningful comparisons and connections between ideas, to assess content, and to create new knowledge gives students the power to make informed decisions in their lives and to decide on courses of actions.

Critical thinking, therefore, leads to empowerment, as students become more independent thinkers and start developing informed opinions, they eventually understand that they have a voice and that their voice is relevant to the classroom and the larger society. Finding one's voice is also a transformative experience for learners, transforming their learning process by engaging them critically with the material.

The ultimate goal of critical thinking is to "enable people to live their lives as informed, critical and actively engaged citizens of their communities and society and to also develop a sense of responsibility towards themselves and others" (Naiditch, 2013, p. 340). Moreover, because we live in a message-saturated world (Potter, 2012), the need to be able to discern between messages, read between the lines, and understand cause and consequence become essential tools in forming educated citizens.

Critical thinking empowers learners and gives them independence. Critical thinkers are independent thinkers; they do not need a teacher or a textbook to tell them what to think, how to react or what the expected outcome should be. In education, we are always dealing with contradictions and paradoxes. Schools say that they want students to be independent thinkers, but they also expect them to give the right answer, to arrive at the same conclusion, to check the right box, to fill the right bubble, and to provide the one expected correct answer. Activities like filling the blanks or multiple choice do not usually require students to think critically, as these types of tasks do not require students to elaborate on their answers, provide justifications, or use higher-order thinking skills.

BEYOND THE CLASSROOM: CRITICAL THINKING AND DEMOCRACY

Many educators use Bloom's taxonomy (1956) in class as a way of making sure they are involving students in activities that will require the use of different types of skills and different levels of cognitive demands. Bloom's taxonomy has been widely used in education to help promote critical thinking skills, especially because it reminds teachers and students that there are different levels of difficulty and cognitive demands as they engage in different tasks.

Bloom's taxonomy includes six basic and fundamental skills that are the basis for developing critical thinking: knowledge, comprehension, application, analysis, synthesis, and evaluation. A revised version of Bloom's taxonomy includes the skills of remembering, understanding, applying, analyzing, evaluating, and creating as the main educational objectives (Anderson & Krathwohl, 2001). Each of these broader skills can be further developed into subskills. For example, synthesis is the product of learning in the sense that it includes the combination of ideas and the culmination of all the elements that have been presented to a student. In order to synthesize information, a student needs to take all different perspectives into account, reconstruct meanings, and elaborate conclusions, all of which are subskills of synthesis.

More than training students to be able to regurgitate facts or memorize figures, a classroom teacher that bases his instructional approach on critical thinking—from his educational philosophy to classroom practices and activities, is in fact preparing his students to become citizens of a larger democratic society and exercising their ability to understand and question content, to confront other people's values and their own, to learn to accept and reject in order to make conscious choices, and more importantly, learning to make educated and well-informed decisions.

What teachers do inside the classroom affects the lives of students beyond the school life and influences the person they will become and the citizenship they will exercise for the rest of their lives. By using critical thinking as the basis for a curriculum and as a pedagogical framework, teachers will instill in students the ability to make well-informed and educated decisions in their lives, taking into account different perspectives, weighing all different sides of an argument or an issue, exhausting all possibilities, searching for new answers and even thinking of solutions for problems they haven't yet been confronted with.

In teaching and learning democracy, teachers and students develop critical thinking, which includes understanding and accepting that the world is a conflicting place, that we all have our contradictions, our opinions, that we need to learn to accept those conflicts, contradictions, different values and beliefs in ourselves and in others, and that this is a process—and so is education. If education is a means of empowering students, critical thinking is the journey, the way we empower students to take ownership of their learning by engaging with the material in critical, meaningful, and varied ways.

The search for answers is always a relevant topic in any class that develops critical thinking. There isn't always a right or correct answer and teachers and learners need to learn to deal with multiple possibilities or ways of solving problems and getting an answer. Many times, the way to finding an answer teaches us more than the actual response. Being able to find solutions or to point to a direction can reveal a deeper understanding of the issue at hand.

Sharing and constructing together is another important component for developing critical thinking skills. Collaboration is a pedagogical tool that reflects a democratic practice: the ability to work cooperatively in order to share and negotiate meanings, understand points of view, and even learn how to reach a consensus.

Teachers who use discussion and interaction in their classrooms know that they promote learning not only by engaging students in sharing and negotiating meanings, but also because they instill in learners the practice of democracy: learning to listen, learning to speak in public, learning to accept and reject, learning to develop arguments—and learning to do all of that in an organized fashion and in a civilized manner. The reason people learn when they engage in discussion and debate is exactly because they need to learn to develop an argument, to present it logically to others, to explain it clearly, to answer questions about it, and to learn from others in order to revise, reformulate, and make it better and more convincing.

Teachers need to remind themselves that there is no one approach that will solve all of our pedagogical questions or instructional dilemmas in the classroom. Ready-made classroom formulas for teaching do sound appealing because they seem to be prepackaged with techniques that will work in every classroom, but they are based on a fictitiously created image of homogeneous classrooms with idealized students—and thus they mask the real face of the American classroom today.

Teachers are faced with diverse classroom environments that bring together students from various cultural and linguistic backgrounds. Moreover, there are socioeconomic issues that directly affect the work that we do in the classroom. In order to develop lessons that both challenge students and help them develop critical thinking skills, we need to consider every classroom on its own.

Part of the process of becoming a teacher involves learning how to understand teaching and learning within the context of a particular classroom in a particular school with specific students. Therefore, teachers who want to engage their students in critical thinking need to learn to identify the specific needs of their students and what is relevant to their context. Only then can they develop lessons that speak to their students and their learning context.

No matter where you teach, the setting or context, or even the different types of students that may come to your class, it is imperative that you teach students how and what to ask from the very beginning of their educational journey. Learning what to ask leads students to search for answers, consider alternatives, weigh possibilities, and arrive at informed conclusions.

Students need to be prepared to ask, to search for and provide answers, to compare facts and contrast information, to agree and disagree providing accurate and well-argued reasons for their choices. Critical thinking requires students to practice skepticism. Skepticism is a central aspect of critical thinking. Learning to question what is presented in the classroom, in textbooks, on TV, and in newspapers and magazines, and learning to question all sorts of information around us help students develop a positive attitude toward teaching and learning.

Writer Alvin Toffler (1970) is always quoted for saying that the illiterate of the twenty-first century will not be those who cannot read and write, but those who cannot learn, unlearn, and relearn. The quote has serious implications for educators committed to developing students' critical thinking skills; after all critical thinking is exactly about learning to learn, unlearn, and relearn.

As I have said repeatedly to my students, teaching and learning are also about creating an organized chaos: "disorganizing" and questioning what you seem to consider to be true in order to process new information, assess it, and reorganize it in order to create new knowledge, make it yours, and use it so it becomes ours.

REFERENCES

Anderson, L. W. & Krathwohl, D. (Eds.). (2001). *A taxonomy for learning, teaching, and assessing: A revision of Bloom's taxonomy of educational objectives.* New York: Longman.

Bloom, B., Englehart, M., Furst, E., Hill, W., & Krathwohl, D. (1956). *Taxonomy of educational objectives: The classification of educational goals. Handbook I: Cognitive domain.* New York, Toronto: Longmans, Green.

Freire, P. (1986). *Pedagogy of the oppressed.* New York: Continuum.

Naiditch, F. (2013). A media literate approach to diversity education. *Journal of Media Literacy Education, 5*(1), 337–348.

Potter, W. James. (2012). *Media Literacy.* Thousand Oaks, CA: SAGE Publications.

Thoman, E. & Jolls, T. (2005). *Literacy for the 21st century: An overview and orientation guide to media literacy education.* Santa Monica, CA: Center for Media Literacy.

Toffler, A. (1970). *Future shock.* New York: Bantam Books.

Willingham, D. T. (2007). Critical thinking: Why is it so hard to teach? *American Educator,* Summer Issue, 8–19.

Chapter 2

Philosophy for Children and Critical Thinking

Creating a Space for Children to Think in a Kindergarten Classroom

Olivier Michaud

Philosophy for Children (P4C) is an educational theory and method that brings philosophy into K–12 education. It has been the major approach to teach philosophy to precollege students in the United States and worldwide. Since its creation in the end of the 1960s, P4C has aimed to develop critical thinking of students (Gregory, 2008; Lipman, Sharp, & Oscanyan, 1980; Välitalo, Hannu, & Sutinen, 2015). There are two major elements in P4C that justify the claim that it is a pedagogical practice that promotes the development of critical thinking of the individuals who practice it (Fisherman, 2010).

First, P4C is based on the pedagogy of the community of inquiry, which is essentially a form of rational discussion, that is, a social environment in which individuals have to learn to reason together (Golding, 2011; Sasseville, 2000; Sharp, 1993). Second, in P4C, the community of inquiry takes place in the field of philosophy, a field fundamentally open to argumentation in the sense that there is no definite answer to philosophical questions (Castoriadis, 1991; Gregory, 2008; Hadot, 2002). Taken together, these two elements make P4C an educational practice that develops critical thinking in students.

This chapter presents a qualitative study of a kindergarten classroom where philosophy was integrated in order to create a space for students to engage in critical thinking. The teacher had a master's degree in P4C and had done philosophy with her students for many years at the time of the research. Through the description of her classroom practice, we will be able to see how P4C fosters critical thinking in a way that other forms of discussions in the classroom do not appear to be able to do.

CRITICAL THINKING

If critical thinking is universally valued as something that education should promote in the students and that educated human beings should have, it remains, like most of the fundamental concepts in education, open to discussion as to what it really means. It is therefore necessary to offer a minimal understanding of it.

First, critical thinking is the same as metacognition, as both concepts imply that the person who possesses them and exerts them is aware of his or her own thinking and of its quality, and has the ability to change it or to improve it if they find that it is incorrect or deficient. Promoting critical thinking in students would therefore be the same as promoting the development of their metacognition, which is the "the knowledge about our own thinking" (Woolfolk, 2014, p. 7).

Paul (1994) criticizes the idea that critical thinking is about the knowledge of a certain set of thinking skills and of their use. For him, and for others, critical thinking is more like a way of being: a person whose life is moved by reasons and the search for reasons: he looks and is curious for good reasons and tries to base their decisions on the best reasons available.

Matthew Lipman (2003), the founder of the P4C program, was also a critical thinker theorist. His definition of what critical thinking is offers an interesting and comprehensive perspective of what the concept means and of the complexities inherent in such notion:

> Critical thinking aims at reasonableness. This means that it is not just rational, in the sense of a thinking that is rule- and criterion- governed, but that it is also a thinking that accepts fallibility of its procedures, that engages in self-corrective practice, that takes the contextual differences into account, and that is equitable, in the sense that respects the rights of others as well as its own. Reasonableness thus entails the cultivation of multidimensional thinking. (2003, p. 238)

This definition is an example of the different factors that can be taken into account when defining what critical thinking is. It first states the classical view that critical thinking has to do with basing one's own thinking as well one's assertion on reasons, rules, and criteria. However, the definition goes further by adding that this knowledge is not enough; that the critical thinker must possess the habit or ability to change his or her mind and position when presented new evidence. Critical thinking, therefore, is about a way of being, a disposition to follow rational procedures and conclusions in one's life. Furthermore, a critical thinker does not only look at universal laws or concepts, but is also mindful of how they may apply or not in certain contexts. Lipman goes even further to add that critical thinking is related to the way we respectfully treat each other.

Critical thinking is ultimately a normative or philosophical concept, which is based not only on facts and knowledge of informal logic, but also on values that guide one's behavior, social life and, of course, education.

WHAT IS P4C?

P4C is constituted of certain fundamental ideas regarding the place of philosophy in education. First, in this approach, philosophy is not conceived as a corpus of knowledge that students should learn, but rather as an activity students should engage in. Philosophy is not about learning the systems of past philosophers, but instead it is about engaging in philosophical inquiry (Välitalo, et al., 2015; Vansieleghem & Kennedy, 2011), which means that philosophy should be seen as an action not as content. The definition of philosophy as more of an activity than a product is not new, but it has become in some way hidden in the contemporary teaching of philosophy (Hadot, 2002; Michaud, 2010).

The second fundamental idea of P4C revolves around who is allowed to do philosophy. Building on the previous point, philosophy has become an activity reserved to a group of persons who have been accredited inside the academic institution. There are recognized professors in philosophy who teach that subject to their college students. P4C blurs the distinction between those who know and those who do not know, those who are allowed to do philosophy and those who are not. Thus, inside a philosophical community of inquiry, everyone is entitled to think, to philosophize, and to be a philosopher (Gregory, 2014; Sharp, 1993). Children are also included in this group of people who can do philosophy and benefit from doing it.

Third, in P4C, the practice of philosophy should be done with others. There may be a form of philosophy that can be done alone—like there may be a form of philosophy specific to adults and that is better taught through transmission of knowledge. Yet for P4C, philosophy is a collaborative activity and is particularly fruitful when it is done with others. However, philosophical discussions are not unstructured, they required a certain process to be beneficial (Bleazby, 2006; Gregory, 2004; Lipman, 2003).

Based on these three ideas, P4C has developed into a pedagogical practice, which comprises more specifically of a curriculum and a pedagogy, the community of inquiry. The curriculum is made of philosophical novels written for children of different ages. These novels raise philosophical issues and the characters in them, children and adults, have philosophical interrogations and discussions. They give an example of individuals that can engage in communal inquiry on philosophical problems or questions they face. The novels are also accompanied by manuals for teachers in which philosophical ideas are developed, exercises proposed, and plans of discussion laid out (Gregory, 2008).

In addition to this curriculum, P4C also has a specific methodology, which is the community of inquiry: a form of social organization that aims to answer or to offer hypotheses to questions through dialogue, and through collectively reasoning on a problem. The philosophical community of inquiry is composed of certain steps that can be summarized in the following. First, students are presented a stimulus, which is most likely to be one of the philosophical novels of the P4C curriculum and that aims to trigger students' philosophical questioning. Second, they are asked to make questions alone or in small groups. Third, there is a vote on the question that will be discussed. The fourth step is the most central and longest step of the process, which is the discussion of the question that was voted. The final step is the evaluation of the discussion at the end (Gregory, 2008; Sasseville, 2000).

The role of the teacher in the discussion (or the facilitator, as it is called in P4C) is to ensure that the appropriate procedure is applied to construct and advance the inquiry. The facilitator is, in sum, the guardian of the format/procedure of the discussion and not the advocate of a specific position regarding its content. For example, he or she may ask students to give reasons for their claims, to evaluate the different reasons regarding an issue, to look for different points of views, to be respectful of each other, to uncover the consequences or the assumptions of a particular position, and to offer examples and counterexamples for an argument, and so on (Gregory, 2008; Sasseville, 2000).

The facilitator is there to be sure that these skills and others are practiced by inviting the students to use them or by modeling. His role is not to give an answer to the question being discussed. His or her function is usually summarized as procedurally strong and substantively weak: to focus the interventions on the form of the discussion rather than on its content.

The community of inquiry is a methodology that is used in different fields of knowledge, such as science, biology, mathematics, politics, etc. The uniqueness of P4C is that the subject of inquiry is philosophical, which includes the ethical, aesthetic, metaphysical, and epistemological dimensions of the human experience as they appear in children's lives. A philosophical concept is usually a concept that is central, controversial, and common to different individuals (Lipman & Sharp, 1980).

P4C AND CRITICAL THINKING

P4C was created as a program that aimed to develop critical thinking in children. This emphasis on critical thinking has been balanced with other forms of thinking: creative thinking regarding the importance of imagination in thinking in front of issues, and caring thinking as the capacity to pay attention to the well-being of the other individuals engaged in a discussion. However, critical thinking remains a strong and central component of the program (Biesta, 2011; Vansieleghem, 2005; Vansieleghem & Kennedy, 2011). There are two reasons why P4C is a good environment for developing critical thinking in children: It is constructed within a pedagogy of the community of inquiry, and it is situated in the field of philosophy (Fisherman, 2010).

The community of inquiry is founded and permeated by critical thinking; it is the central feature of that process, as well as its goal, of what it aims to create in the individuals who practice it. Hence, in the community of inquiry individuals have to pause and become aware of their own thinking. They have to do metacognition, to pay attention to their own thought processes. Claims are advanced in the process, but they have to be at least tentatively sustained with arguments, which in turn should be evaluated in the discussion. That can happen naturally as the person presenting an idea on a subject or a question explains why she believed it or it can also be prompted by questions from another student or from the teacher.

Furthermore, as the community of inquiry is a dialogical and communal process, it naturally creates cognitive conflicts within the students. Different claims will be made during a discussion and will be supported by one or various reasons, which the participants will have to evaluate. In other words, as different claims and reasons are presented on a particular topic, participants are lead to evaluate them and encouraged to sustain their judgment with an argument. By the same token, it creates the possibility for them to change their minds about a subject and, therefore, it promotes self-correction (Morissette & Voynaud, 2002; Vienneau, 2011).

In this process, the role of the teacher is not to defend a particular view on a subject, but rather to help the students in the process of assessing and evaluating claims. The teacher may for instance ask the student to give a reason to support a claim, to evaluate its assumptions or its consequences, to rephrase what another student has said, to give an example to support or exemplify an idea, to give a definition, to judge if a criterion is appropriate and sufficient to sustain a claim, to offer a hypothesis to a question, to make a distinction, to make a deduction or an induction, and so on (Gregory, 2008; Lipman, 2003; Sharp, 1993).

All these can be identified as thinking skills that a critical thinker should use and, consequently, that should be learned and practiced. They are critical thinking skills as they all serve to evaluate claims and the criterion on which they based their validity. The role of the teacher is then to invite students to use these different thinking skills and sometimes to model them. As students learn to use them, the teacher should have less and less to prompt them in discussions.

The idea that critical thinking should also be sensitive to context is seen in the community of inquiry in the use of examples and counter examples, lived by the students or invented, during discussions. Through these examples participants are brought to evaluate how claims or criteria change depending on contexts, which may also push a given discussion in new directions.

The specificity of P4C, in comparison to other domains that use the community of inquiry is that it situates such pedagogy in the particular field of philosophy. Hence, philosophy is a domain with special characteristics that creates an environment appropriate for students to practice critical thinking. The philosophical questions are usually, if not always, open to debate and argument, which is not or rarely the case in other fields of knowledge in which certain answers are expected. Therefore, when a philosophical discussion is started, it does not necessarily have a clear ending or expected outcome. In certain fields of knowledge, a discussion may have a specific answer, and, consequently, the argumentation on that topic will be limited to finding the correct answer and it will stop when it is found. In philosophy, there is no such definite answer to the questions tackled. Answers may be proposed, assessed, argued upon, or contradicted. It is, therefore, a field permeated by the possibility to reason.

By combining a specific pedagogical method, the community of inquiry, and a philosophical approach, P4C offers the students an environment favorable for them to practice their thinking abilities, which other school subjects are most likely unable to offer.

METHODOLOGY

The data analyzed in this chapter come from a larger study on the practice of philosophy, democratic education, and power relationships in a kindergarten classroom (Michaud, 2013). The classroom was chosen because the teacher, Annie—a pseudonym—has a master's degree in P4C and is committed to give to her students a democratic education. For Annie, democratic education is a perspective that permeates her pedagogy and her role as a teacher.

At the core of this idea was that children should experience democratic education in school, not only democratic education as a preparation for a future and distant life as full citizens. Her premise, in many ways, structured the life of the classroom. For example, Annie started the school year by asking her students what they would like to learn, and from their requests she structured the entire curriculum. For her, education had to start with children's interest and by giving them a voice in the educational decisions. Another example, of course, was the implementation of philosophy, which created a space inside the classroom where students could talk about issues that affected them and the teacher showed that she trusted them as being able to discuss important matters.

The classroom was part of a magnet public school situated in a mainly upper middle class and white neighborhood in the suburbs of a major city in the northeast of the United States. There were twenty-six children in the classroom and two aides (one of them was assigned to a special needs student).

As the goal of the research was to study how the practice of philosophy interplays with the general culture of a democratic classroom, a qualitative design was selected. Immersing the researcher in a particular site is the most appropriate way to study and document how a complex issue unfolds over time in its natural setting. The goal of such design is not to test a theory or to generalize results to other populations, but rather to inform theory through the deep study of how an issue unfolds in a particular context.

Data were collected through observations as well as through informal and formal discussions and interviews with the teacher. To understand the place of philosophy and how it influences the classroom culture, observations were made not only of the official philosophy sessions, but also of different moments in and outside of the classroom. These observations were done one and a half to two days a week. Notes of observations were transcribed and expanded into narratives (Michaud, 2013). Drawing on my data collection and analyses, we'll explore how the practice of philosophy in that classroom created a space for them to develop their critical thinking skills, which was one aspect documented during the study.

P4C AND CRITICAL THINKING IN ANNIE'S CLASSROOM

Philosophy was a central component in Annie's classroom. Its importance could be seen in the fact that philosophy was part of the weekly curriculum, which is rare in K–12 schools. If there were at some point a strong program of P4C at her school, it was no longer the case at the time of this study, and Annie was the only teacher who was doing it.

The newsletters that Annie was sending home every week to report on the classroom activities were always reporting on the philosophy discussions that were held that week and, by the same token, included philosophy in what counted as learning. Philosophy was therefore becoming an educational subject, just as mathematics, literacy, or science. Annie's commitment to P4C could be seen in the fact that she obtained a degree in it, integrated it in her pedagogy, and had the perseverance to keep doing it amidst the adversities. In sum, philosophy was an important element of the educational culture that Annie created in her classroom.

If philosophy permeated all Annie's teaching—at least that was her own perspective on it—there was, however, a specific time dedicated to it: the Thursday morning philosophy sessions. Although the researcher was able to notice at least one philosophical discussion that happened outside of the Thursday morning sessions, it was much harder to document these moments and the best moment to observe philosophy was in the official time reserved to it.

First, students were invited to sit in a circle on the perimeter of the round rug that was in the middle of the classroom. Being in a circle is the recommended seating arrangement for a P4C session. In the traditional format of the classroom, the teacher faces the students from the front, which is the best position if a teacher wants to impart knowledge to a group of students. The circle breaks this format and the pedagogy attached to it: students are now facing each other, which is impossible in the other classroom organization, and they are expected to create knowledge together in the discussion. Furthermore, the teacher in P4C moves in the circle with the students and does not stand in front of the classroom, which symbolically indicates that she changes her main function as the one having to transmit knowledge.

Annie would then take out a box in which there was a pair of puppets, which she only used in the philosophy class. She would make a few comments on the puppets, such as where they were for spring break. As she was doing that, there was a certain excitement in the group; students clearly enjoyed this moment. With one doll in each hand, one named Philo and the other named Sophie, Annie would enact a short piece of theater consisting of a dialogue between the dolls. Annie wrote the stories herself in the morning before the sessions, but sometimes she also improvised them. The stories were inspired by recent events in the life of the classroom.

The little dolls bowed at the end of the short play. As Annie was about to tell the story a second time, some students would ask her to make it longer, which she would sometimes do, following her inspiration at the moment. Before telling the story a second time, Annie would make the comment "One time for listening, one time for thinking," and then asked the students to put on their "thinking caps," which was done by some students with play-acting and sounds, as if they were putting on a cap like superheroes in a comic book.

After the story was told a second time, Annie asked the students what questions they had about the story. However, most of the time students started to discuss the story without raising a question. A question would at some point be asked by a student or through Annie's clarification and reformulation, and the classroom would informally agree to respond to this question, as rarely another question was proposed. The discussion would proceed for fifteen to twenty minutes before it ended in a certain kind of chaos coming from the behavior of students who became more and more restless as the discussion advanced.

The dialogue would progress through questions and answers between the teacher and the students. It was not uncommon to hear some students say: "I agree or disagree with that person or point." The word "because" could also often be heard from the teacher as well as from the students. At the time that data were collected, which was from April to June, it was already the last third of the school year. It was, therefore, clear for the researcher that the students had integrated the two essential skills to the community of inquiry.

First, the use of "I agree" or "I disagree with such and such" indicated that the children had integrated the skill of connecting their ideas with the ones of the other students and were, therefore, engaging in co-construction with others in that setting. Second, the use of "because" is related to the skill of sustaining one's opinion or assertion with a reason and not only enunciating it. It does not say if the reasons presented were good or not, but it does point toward students' developing ability to justify their statements.

Annie's questions and comments were of different kinds. For example, Annie asked the students to give a reason for their position and to develop it; she reframed or redirected the discussion by asking the students to see a new aspect of the issue discussed; or she restated the comment of a student and asked the other students what they thought about it. She also made comments about students' behavior during the discussion.

AN EXAMPLE: WHAT IS REAL AND NOT REAL IN A STORY

The following P4C session can be seen as a general example of the content and format of P4C sessions in Annie's classroom.

That day, the two dolls discussed the case of a woman who came to tell a story and argued about what was real and not real in that story. That dialogue referred to the actual visit in the classroom two days prior of a woman who gave a performance that combined poetry and dance. After the performance, there was a question period that was almost all used by students to ask questions to the actress about what was real and not real in her story: Was the alarm clock real? Was she really asleep? Did it really happen? And so on.

Annie noticed this interest, which was not taken up after the artist's latest performance and used it to launch the P4C session two days later. The philosophical problem was then the puzzlement regarding the relationship between an artistic creation and reality. The philosophical nature of that problem appeared in the fact that there is not a definitive answer to it, but that it has an importance for all human beings, as all may be intrigued regarding the peculiar relationship between art and reality.

The discussion advanced in several phases. The first one was about the relationship between a fictional story and a lie: Does telling a story that didn't happen count as lying? Is a story that was invented a *real* story? After the class argued about this problem, students concluded that lies should be distinguished from stories, that they were two different things. It was also proposed that real stories could be differentiated from fake stories. After these distinctions were proposed, the discussion moved to two TV shows, *Dolphin Tales* and *Ninjago*, and their relationship with reality. The discussion ended on how we can know which kind of TV shows are real and which ones are not.

If the discussion did not resolve the issue, in the sense that it did not offer a clear and definite answer to what is the relationship between art and reality, it certainly advanced and opened the space for that issue. For instance, the concept of lying gave a new dimension to the problem by tackling the ethical dimension of a fiction. In addition to differentiating between a lie and fiction, students understood that this last category could be divided between real fiction and invented fiction.

The discussion finished with the examples of the above mentioned TV shows and, therefore, on children and our relationship to a particular medium—more specifically, on how we can understand how real are the stories told to us on TV. This example helped situate, develop, and make the discussion on an abstract concept more meaningful and concrete for the students. The philosophical discussion here was a short, difficult, and intense exploration of a new and undetermined territory.

ANNIE'S AGENCY

Annie gave us an example of how a teacher may integrate P4C in her classroom and how it created a special space for her students to practice their critical thinking. However, before looking more closely at this space, it is important to understand how it was rooted in Annie's own agency.

A particularity in her practice was that she did not rely on philosophical stories that were already written by others, from the official curriculum or from other authors, to start the discussions. Rather, she looked at what were the philosophical subjects or issues that appeared in the classroom life and saw them as not only a trigger for philosophical discussions, but as something worthwhile for students to inquire about, as curriculum. Philosophy was, therefore, not a disconnected subject matter from the classroom or the students' lives, but was rather rooted in them.

Annie's agency in the way she used P4C in her classroom was seen both in how she chose the topics for philosophical discussions and in how she brought these topics to the students; she wrote stories and enacted them with two puppets. This technique added another element to create an interest in students in philosophy and philosophical discussions.

These were elements that she found and developed by herself, they were not transmitted to her by the P4C program. Annie adapted the program to her own needs, practice, and beliefs. She did not only aim to transmit critical thinking skills to her students or the philosophy, rather such transmission was taken related to her own engagement in thinking and to her sensitivity about philosophical issues.

WHAT PHILOSOPHY BROUGHT TO THE
CRITICAL THINKING OF THE STUDENTS

Annie gave a lot of opportunities for her students to discuss in class. There was always a buzz coming out of the classroom. There were daily multiple spaces for students to discuss with each other. Annie also saw philosophy as a state of mind that influenced all her teaching. In sum, her pedagogy and philosophy of education created multiple occasions for philosophical discussions. Yet, the philosophical discussions of Thursday morning, the official moment of philosophy in the weekly activities, were strikingly different from all other forms of discussions happening in the classroom, which were concomitant in the creation of a special opportunity for students to exert their critical thinking.

In comparison to other kinds of discussions in the classroom, the P4C sessions of Thursday morning had particular characteristics: they were about communal subjects without a definite answer, they were structured by the principles that govern communities of inquiry and they extended over time. The combination of these three points differentiated the P4C sessions of any other kinds of classroom conversations. There was therefore a clear time during the week for the social engagement of everyone with a communal problem.

The discussion on reality and art contained all these characteristics. Hence, it is an issue that potentially touched all individuals, as we may all encounter it in our lives—one of the reasons that art, which permeates human experience, puzzles us is that it seems to be real and unreal at the same time. Annie's students were also touched by this subject, to the point that they questioned the artist the day of her performance on that specific problem, but it was the P4C session that allowed them to engage directly with it.

The role of the teacher during the process was to accompany the students in that undetermined space, particularly by pointing new problems that appeared in the discussion. For instance, as a student explained that there was a difference between *Ninjago* and the *Dolphin Tale*, she asked how he could know that. He followed up by saying that it was written at the beginning of *Dolphin Tale* that it was real, to which she asked if it was necessary that it would be written at the beginning of a TV show that it was real to know if it was indeed real. The answer to a problem just opened new problems to be resolved.

Overall, Annie did not appear to be looking to find the most reasonable answer to the problem being discussed. The dialogue did not move toward a definitive theory or idea of the relationship between art and reality backed by a set of reasons. Instead of being a discussion aiming to a definite end, that discussion progressed toward more problems to be resolved. Annie's interventions in not foreclosing this space of questioning and puzzles were also creating a space for students to practice critical thinking. Hence, students were invited to support their claims with reasons, to make distinctions between concepts and situations and to connect their points with examples. As the space of thinking was not directed to be foreclosed, it just created more opportunities for students to think and argue.

However, these thinking or reasoning moves were related to another kind of moves, to which they appeared inseparable. The actions of giving reasons, for example, were at the same time notably social endeavors, as they were situated in a dialogue, in an open relationship with others. Students were indeed not only advancing in reasons, they were also listening to others' ideas and judging their reasons to support their claims. The reasons were being given within a cultural, social, and contextual setting. In other words, critical thinking in the P4C was fundamentally a collective process, a process of co-construction.

The peculiarity of the philosophical space and the environment to which it was related could only be effective because they were extended over time. Annie indeed kept the students in the philosophical and critical thinking space for a certain amount of time. To remain in such space is not something naturally done, as it is not easy to keep 26 kindergarten students talking and arguing about complex issues, especially problems that often do not have obvious, clear, and fixed answers. This separated P4C discussions from any other kinds of discussion during the week, because they lasted a certain amount of time. Students had to face an issue, or a number of issues, and to not abandon them after a few minutes: they had to stay with them and use the critical thinking skills required by such space.

As shown previously, Annie used different techniques to make the philosophy sessions appealing and accessible to her students, particularly through her skillful use of puppets and by connecting the philosophical stories to the life of the classroom. Yet, these techniques were not in themselves sufficient to bring the students to do philosophy and stay engaged with the problems discussed, because the philosophical questions are by nature big questions that are not easily answered and maybe not even be answered at all.

There are other things much easier and more fun to do, for students as well for adults, than to sit and contemplate philosophical issues. Therefore, the engagement of Annie's students into philosophy was not made possible only by making it attractive to them, but by requesting them to do it, to practice certain skills in it, and to stay with the philosophical problem for a certain time.

However, such demands had a specific limit, as the P4C sessions would usually last from fifteen to twenty minutes and as students' disruptions increased and forced the teacher to move to a new activity.

CONCLUSION

The data analyzed in this chapter confirmed the claim that there is indeed a relationship between P4C and critical thinking; that integrating P4C in a classroom will create a favorable and special space for students to exert their critical thinking skills. Annie presents us an example of how a teacher may adapt the P4C curriculum and pedagogy in his or her own context. This was particularly obvious in the sensitivity she showed toward philosophical issues that appeared in the classroom life and how she used puppets to introduce philosophical questions to her students. This may give an example for teachers interested in P4C in how to adapt that pedagogy to their particular context.

However, a teacher interested in P4C should indeed take into account the different characteristics of this pedagogy before integrating it in his or her own classroom. Philosophical discussions are not something easy to lead and are even more challenging in a large classroom with young students, even when strategies are used to make it more appealing to students, like the ones that Annie used with her students. The teachers interested in P4C must, therefore, be clear about their reason for integrating it in their classroom. It is not something that students initially want to do; it is something that the teacher asked them to do. Communities of inquiry do not just emerge by themselves. They are developed and implemented by the teacher who also keeps the students in that special space.

Teachers interested in P4C should also take into account the particular kind of critical thinking that P4C is more likely to develop in the classroom. In the P4C discussions, like the one presented in this chapter, critical thinking is not about finding which reasons are the most appropriate to answer a specific problem or a question. The discussion on reality and art appeared to be moving exponentially toward new problems and questions rather than in closing them. Consequently, critical thinking in P4C is more about how to explore a territory of an issue and the kinds of reasons that map that territory, rather than aiming to resolve it through a definite argument sustained by incontestable premises.

Therefore, a teacher should ask him or herself if they feel comfortable about opening such a space of questioning for the students, as it requires a certain ease in inhabiting ambiguities and doubts. The discussion we looked at was about the relationship between art and reality, which may not appear to be a question with important consequences, but there may be other discussions that may touch more sensitive subjects.

However, if the teacher is at ease in creating that space in his or her classroom, they can rely on P4C to offer students unique opportunities to engage in critical thinking. As pointed out, P4C sessions tends to create new conceptual problems as it progresses and, consequently, it also tends to constantly offer students new issues on which to argue and to exert their critical thinking skills. P4C will also give the chance for students to argue together, which is not a possibility naturally created in a classroom. In P4C, students are not only reasoning by themselves, they are reasoning with others. Therefore, children are not only learning to be critical thinkers in P4C, they are learning to be critical thinkers with others and learning the skills and habits necessary for collaborative learning, and also for our democratic forms of social life.

In sum, if a teacher is comfortable in inhabiting the space that creates P4C in a classroom, which includes, among other things, being able to sustain ambiguity regarding certain issues, integrating P4C in the classroom will create a valuable and special space for students to exert their critical thinking skills. However, this study does not allow us to know if students who practice P4C would be able to transfer the critical thinking skills learned in that space to other subject matters or other domains of their life. More studies are required to make that claim.

REFERENCES

Biesta, G. (2011). Philosophy, exposure, and children: How to resist the instrumentalisation of philosophy of education. *Journal of Philosophy of Education, 45*(2), 305–319.

Bleazby, J. (2006). Autonomy, democratic community, and citizenship in philosophy for children: Dewey and philosophy for children's rejection of the individual/community dualism. *Analytic Teaching, 26*(1), 30–52.

Castoriadis, C. (1991). *Philosophy, politics, autonomy: Essays in political philosophy.* New York: Oxford University Press.

Fisherman, D. (2010). Philosophy, critical thinking and community of inquiry. *Childhood and Philosophy, 6*(12), 211.

Golding, C. (2011). The many faces of constructivist discussion. *Educational Philosophy and Theory, 43*(5), 467–483.

Gregory, M. (2004). Practicing democracy: Social intelligence and philosophical practice. *International Journal of Applied Philosophy, 18*(2), 161–174.

Gregory, M. (2008). *Philosophy for children: Practitioner handbook.* Upper Montclair: Institute for the Advancement of Philosophy for Children.

Gregory, M. (2014). Ethics education as philosophical practice: The case from socratic, critical and contemplative pedagogies. *Teaching Ethics, 15*(1), 19–34.

Hadot, P. (2002). *What is ancient philosophy?* Cambridge, MA: Harvard University Press.

Lipman, M. (2003). *Thinking in education.* New York: Cambridge University Press.

Lipman, M. & Sharp, A. M. (1980). *Social inquiry: Instructional manual to accompany mark.* Montclair: IAPC.

Lipman, M., Sharp, A. M., & Oscanyan, F. S. (1980). *Philosophy in the classroom* (2nd edition). Philadelphia: Temple University Press.

Michaud, O. (2010). Monastic Meditations on Philosophy and Education. *Thinking, 19*(4), 40–42.

Michaud, O. (2013). *A qualitative study on educational authority, shared authority and the practice of philosophy in a kindergarten classroom: A study of the multiple dimensions and complexities of a democratic classroom.* Doctor of Education, Montclair State University, Upper Montclair, NJ.

Morissette, R. & Voynaud, M. (2002). *Accompagner la construction des savoirs.* Montréal: Chenelière/McGraw-Hill.

Paul, R. W. (1994). Teaching critical thinking in the strong sense: A focus on self-deception, world views and a dialectical mode of analysis. In K. S. Walters (Ed.), *Re-thinking reason: New perspectives in critical thinking* (pp. 181–198). Albany.

Sasseville, M. (2000). *La pratique de la philosophie avec les enfants* (2nd edition). Sainte-Foy, Québec: Presses de l'Université Laval: Distribution de livres UNIVERS.

Sharp, A. M. (1993). The community of inquiry: Education for democracy. In M. Lipman (Ed.), *Thinking, Children and Education* (pp. 337–343). Dubuque: Kendall/Hunt Publishing Company.

Välitalo, R., Hannu, J., & Sutinen, A. (2015). Philosophy for Children as an educational practice. *Studies in Philosophy and Education.* doi: 10.1007/s11217-015-9471-6

Vansieleghem, N. (2005). Philosophy for Children as the wind of thinking. *Journal of Philosophy of Education, 39*(1), 19–35.

Vansieleghem, N. & Kennedy, D. (2011). What is Philosophy *for* children, what is Philosophy *with* children—after Matthew Lipman. *Journal of Philosophy of Education, 45* (171–182).

Vienneau, R. (2011). *Apprentissage et enseignement : Théories et pratiques* (2nd edition). Montréal: Gaëtan Morin.

Woolfolk, A. (2014). *Educational psychology* (12th edition). Boston: Pearson.

Chapter 3

Critical Thinking in Action

A Collaborative Early Childhood Approach to Curriculum Design

Elizabeth Quintero

What is a collaborative approach to creating early childhood curriculum? Collaboration is often discussed as being between colleagues. In this chapter, the focus is on collaborative curriculum design and implementation among teachers, children, and families when possible. It can be complicated, but it is so much more enjoyable and more critically meaningful than staying on page 33 of a "curriculum guide" of a mandated curriculum. And, in cases where packaged curricula have been mandated, this approach can be used alongside the mandated guide.

Collaborative curriculum design begins with the children's interests, strengths, and needs. It includes the families' histories, and the histories and passions of the teachers. It is messy, and it is dynamic—always changing within the structure of the approach, which will be described in depth later.

Just to give a glimpse of the possibilities with this method, we peek into a set of experiences of a student teacher and her self-appointed helper in a preschool classroom in a low-income neighborhood in southern California. Knowing that one of the most important initial assignments in the university class is for the student teachers to observe and document the interests and strengths of the children before curriculum planning is to begin, Ana, this student teacher, noted:

I noticed that some of the children in the class really took an interest in butterflies after I read the book *Waiting for Wings* by Lois Ehlert (2001). While I was reading the book, Ed really showed interest in the metamorphosis process. Ed was really paying attention to the process that happens when caterpillars turn into butterflies. He was so interested that he stopped me during the book to ask, "Wait, what do you mean—glue?" He was referring to the "glue" that

made the eggs stick to the leaves. Later, during recess, Ed and Rene came to me
to show me that there was a butterfly flying around. When I asked them where
they thought it was going, Ed replied, "to look for some flowers." I asked him
why he thought they were going to look for flowers, and he replied, "to eat
some nectar."

The recurring conversation among Ed, Rene, and Ana, the student teacher,
became the starting point for her collaborating with these children on a
lesson. Ana reported that the lesson she was working on with them would
encourage the children to explore the butterfly life cycle in a variety of different ways. They will be able to see it in pictures and books, enact it with
props, and make a representation of it with a bracelet.

And as another part of the university class's assignment of identifying
learning outcomes for the children as established by the California Preschool
Learning Foundations, she explained the following:

> The goal for this lesson will be to give the children with a variety of ways to
> explore and learn about the butterfly life cycle. They will demonstrate knowl-
> edge of the sequence of events that take place during the butterfly life cycle by
> using props to retell a story or making a representation of the life cycle. They
> will also observe, and identify characteristics of caterpillars and butterflies. This
> experience will benefit the children by allowing them to engage and see the life
> cycle in different formats.

Furthermore, she elaborated upon her planning of small-group opportunities,
maintaining the focus of the life-cycle theme and honoring child choice in
selection of activities:

> There will be four centers already set up for the children, and one free table for
> an activity of the children's choice. The first center will be the art table in which
> children will be invited to make a painting of a butterfly. In this center, the
> children will be able to observe symmetry and patterns in their butterfly. In the
> second center, the children will be able to look at different books and pictures
> of the butterfly eggs, caterpillars, cocoons, and butterflies. In the third center,
> the children will be able to use props to reenact, or retell the story of *The Very
> Hungry Caterpillar* (Carle, 2002), or another book of their choice. In the fourth
> center, the children will be able to make a bracelet that represents the butterfly
> life cycle in an abstract and personal way. The last table will be left for a free
> choice activity.

This approach to curriculum design will be explained in more detail later in
this chapter, but to show how one child flourished with this experience we
look at an excerpt from a learning story about Ana's self-appointed helper,
Jessica:

Jessica was one of the first students to come over to the Butterfly bracelet activity table. She was so excited to make a bracelet, that she opened the zip lock bag, and in her excitement, turned it over and dropped all the beads on the table and on the floor. She got out of her chair quickly to pick them all up. As soon as she had picked them all up, she said "There Teacher, can you help me now?"

I said, "Sure Jessica, so let's think about what happened first in the butterfly life cycle?"

Jessica responded, "I don't know."

I directed her towards to the poster we had made during circle time. Jessica looked at the poster, and then said, "He turned into a butterfly." So I reminded her about the book *The Very Hungry Caterpillar,* and asked, "Do you remember where the caterpillar came from at the beginning at the book?" Jennifer thought about it for a minute, she looked at the poster, and then said, "an egg."

I said to her, "You're right, the egg was the first thing we saw in the book, so what color bead would you like for your egg to be to start your bracelet?" "White," she said. I asked if she had a white bead in her baggie. Jessica quickly looked for the white bead, and then said, "I found it Teacher! Do I put it in?" I said, "Sure." So she put it in quickly. As soon as she was done, she said, "Now what Teacher?" I asked, "Well what happened next in the butterfly life cycle?" Jennifer said, "The egg hatched." I then asked her, "Who came out of the egg?" Jennifer answered, "The caterpillar . . . he was hungry and he ate a lot of food". "That's exactly what happened Jessica! I can tell you were paying attention, because you remember what happened in the book".

In this excerpt, Jessica demonstrates her knowledge of the content by recreating the life cycle of the butterfly, as expressed in the learning outcomes of the California Preschool Learning Foundations. Her ability is further observed through her engagement in working with her peers and in helping them develop the same line of thinking:

Jessica finished her bracelet, but didn't want to go to another activity. I asked her if she wanted to make a butterfly, or if she wanted to do some story retelling, but she didn't want to do either. She said, "I'm going to be your helper, okay?" So she stayed a while longer at the table. She started handing out the zip lock bags to the students as they came in. Then she started helping me and the other students by pointing at the different parts of the poster as I asked them some of the same questions I had asked her about the butterfly life cycle.

Later, as I helped another student, I heard Jessica ask David, "What happened after he got fat?" David wasn't sure. Jessica then pointed at the cocoon asked, "What do you call this?" David then said, "A cocoon". Jessica responded, "Yeah, he turned into a cocoon—no, for butterflies it is a chrysalis thing [sic]".

Ana reported that Jessica enjoyed making the butterfly bracelet, and took on the role of being her helper during the activity. She said that it was interesting to see the child take on a helper role, and be so patient with her classmates. She really tried to help them by pointing at the pictures, and asking them questions. It was also interesting to see the child imitate the teacher's role, and ask them the same questions that Ana had asked of her.

In terms of learning outcomes, Ana reported that Jessica demonstrated enjoyment of literacy-related activities. She also showed that she understood the story by answering questions related to the story, and by showing she understood the order of events in the life cycle. She also showed understanding of the story, and the butterfly life cycle order by putting her bracelet in order. She went even further by showing, and helping others do the same.

WHAT IS EARLY CHILDHOOD CURRICULUM AND A COLLABORATIVE, INTEGRATIVE APPROACH?

Critical thinking in action is the basis of our work with children, families, student teachers, and teachers. I work with teacher education students in urban and rural schools in both pre-K/primary settings and in infant/toddler programs. We support children and students' multiple languages and recognize ways that multiple knowledge sources, identities, and language forms can contribute to the formation of new meaning in all aspects of learning.

We use an integrated approach to curriculum that combines multiple content areas with critical literacies (English and home language) to keep the student-centered integrity and provide the scaffolding needed for younger learners. This methodology, with its strong theoretical and philosophical underpinnings, encourages teachers not to limit their teaching to units and lesson plans. It encourages teachers to use as a point of departure the background 'funds of knowledge' (Moll, Gonzalez & Amanti, 2005) approach in which the children bring in to the learning arena concrete examples from their lived experience with their families and friends. The method encourages integration of the community knowledge, language, and culture with the standard school curricula.

This approach is framed by the multidisciplinary knowledge base of critical theory. It affirms the role of criticism and rejects the radical differentiation between theory and practice as two separate poles of a dualism. Critical theory encourages the production and application of theory as a part of the overall search for transformative knowledge. Paulo Freire (1985) illustrated critical theory by emphasizing participation through personal histories, the sharing of multiple ways of knowing, and creating transformative action. A critical theory framework supports working with children and families from a variety of historical contexts, language groups, and life experiences. This perspective is supported by data that show that effective learning is a dynamic continuum, always in flux.

The early childhood teacher education students collaboratively study, design, implement, and assess curricula based on critical theory. The participation and data collection methods involve participant observation, interviews with families, teacher journals, student teacher research journals, and collections of learners' work samples during their interactions with curricula. The data are analyzed by the categories that emerge, particularly as they relate to the theoretical perspective of critical theory.

But what is curriculum, where does it come from, and who decides what will be learned? Since times of prehistory this has been an important question (Campbell, 2008; Eisler, 1988). Several recent studies connect experiences with people and environments to learning and potential. In terms of young children, curriculum is everything. Curriculum can be watching a colony of ants working together; it can be the negotiation that happens among friends who want to use the same toys or materials when there is a limited supply; or it can be learning a song in a new language in order to communicate with a new peer or beloved teacher.

Bloch (2014) reflects on curriculum by asking: whose voices and knowledge count? Whose values are embedded in what we think is appropriate curriculum and for whom? Integrated curriculum (integrating different content areas of study in meaningful ways), based on critical frameworks, emphasizing family and cultural story and meaning made by children through play enhances multidirectional, participatory learning.

Early Childhood Studies university students begin thinking about integrated curriculum by thinking of their own family histories. What was meaningful in their interactions with loved ones and other people? What were examples of the beginnings of understanding story and communication? What was happening around them at the time? The information from these memories clearly influences the learners' choices for both process learning preferences and content learning passions. The reflections of our own learnings, often raw and dramatic, give us perspective about our approaches to designing and implementing curriculum.

One teacher education student, examining her personal stories related to her integrated learning as a young child, remembered her mother singing and dancing while doing chores around the house. She recalled her dancing around with a broom and whistling. The student explained also that her mother did not read or write, but she would always sit down with the children at the kitchen table while they did their homework. Her mother paid attention to the topics of the children's homework. She always had questions and comments that related the topics of study to the family's day-to-day life. She would also buy the newspaper and read it. The children didn't realize that all she did was look at pictures and cut the coupons.

The student talked about learning the music and the history from the songs. She said that looking back, she and her siblings learned the importance of sitting down every night to work on school assignments; and she learned the literacy behavior associated with "reading" a newspaper for gleaning information and cutting coupons to buy food (Quintero, 2009).

This same student teacher shared in class that now that her mother has grandchildren she nurtured a family tradition that involves imagination and pretend story with a "magic book." She gave her first grandson this magic book when he was a few weeks old. It is a wordless storybook and his mother (our student's sister) made it a habit to read to him this "magic book" every night. As he got older he would carry his book around and ask different family members to read this wordless book to him. The family had explained to him that anyone could use imagination and make up a new story every time. This magic book became the babies' curriculum.

Over the years, it became the evolving curriculum inclusive of literacy, family history, new interests and new ideas, which the boy, now six years old negotiates. Children often tend to memorize a story and when someone else reads the story a different way, not as they remember it, the child corrects the adult. The grandmother was wise to designate the book as "magic" so that the story can be changed to suit the reader and the audience and create new meaning in the process.

The boy continues the tradition with his younger cousins and his one-year-old sister. The rest of the family also participates in the tradition, but now the boy likes to read *them* the "magic book" himself. The student teacher, the boy's aunt, says, "It's amazing that he never repeats the story. It is interesting that he individualizes the story according to whomever he reads the story to. Our family members have different types and levels of education and life experiences and he seems to understand this perfectly" (Quintero, 2009, p. 111).

PERSONAL STORY, DUAL LANGUAGE LEARNERS, AND COLLABORATING ON CURRICULUM DESIGN

Personal story cannot be overrated for children and adults. A finding that has come up over and over again through our work is the dynamic way children use personal story in their pretend play, as they pretend to be the veterinarian, or the ballet dancer, or the superhero. This personal story through play is another important, dynamic aspect of curriculum for young children. When young children dramatize their personal stories through pretend play, topics become layered with the complex issues regarding development and learning that must be discussed and addressed in education.

Vivian Paley, during her decades of working with children in Chicago, documented the stories that children tell as part of their play and made the stories part of her daily curriculum. The stories consistently deal with issues of family and community and questions about fairness, justice, and about what it means to be in school (Paley, 2000, 1986). Pretend play is an important facet of young children's lives in terms of cognition, conceptual, and emotional experiences.

Research in many multilingual, multicultural neighborhoods shows that throughout the play and engagement of "pretend" and symbolic story, children have opportunities for language use in the home language, the target language, and other different forms of language. This language use that evolves naturally and holistically is an integral part of personal and communal story. Family knowledge and literacy are interwoven fabric of cultural practices. In addition, this multilingual communication that often occurs during play is the very crux of what Katherine Nelson (2009) designates as the crucial characteristic that distinguishes humans from other species: We make meaning and then we are compelled to share the meaning with others.

Integrated curriculum, based on critical frameworks, emphasizing family and cultural story, and multicultural children's literature encourages collaboration and enhances the support of home-language use while supporting target language development. We are now certain that teachers and family members must support both the home language and English, or dual language learners can lose the ability to speak and understand their home language, or lose the balance between the two languages (Castro, Ayankoya, & Kasprzak, 2011).

Research findings emphasize the importance of integrated curriculum, based on the children's interests, strengths, and needs and making multilingual opportunities available. The brain's increasing specialization for processing the first language during early childhood does not necessarily limit its ability to learn another language. "Because the brain is not a limited capacity system, it can accommodate the learning of new information. . . . Native language processing in early development was not adversely affected by exposure to another language" (Conboy, 2012, p. 32).

During play children use their home language and often negotiate a new language if another child is a speaker of the new language in order to further their communication during the interaction. The most effective advice educators can give families is to let the natural genius of children to communicate take over. They can understand each other long before, and in a variety of ways, than we adults can. What is most important is that young children are exposed to an effective language-learning environment, in an early childhood setting and at home.

A basis for integrated curriculum and critical approaches to our work in early care and education is the emphasis on participation through personal histories, sharing of multiple ways of knowing, and transformative action.

For example, the student teacher previously mentioned, as she described her family experiences with her mother in the past when the student was a child, and now more recently with the new generation of grandchildren, exhibits all these aspects of participatory learning. The student's mother when caring for her own children, taught important history and cultural content through her music, she showed complex intellectual guidance by asking the children the topics of study of their homework and then relating each topic to some events in the family's past or present life.

The mother, now a grandmother, showed the awareness of multiple sources of knowledge in her creation of the "magic book" so that each family member could contribute knowledge from a unique point of view. And finally, she showed transformative action with her own children and later her grandchildren by being involved in ongoing meaningful learning. The examples from this family illustrate the definition of critical literacy as a process of constructing and critically using language (oral and written) as a means of expression, interpretation, and/or transformation of our lives and the lives of those around us.

WHAT THE WORK LOOKS LIKE IN HIGHER EDUCATION

In the university classes, early childhood studies student teachers are pushed to connect early childhood theoretical information, family and community information, and pedagogical issues in the context of critical thinking. They participate in activities in which they use multicultural children's literature, interviews of community members, and educational research to give them background information to approach participant observation in schools and early childhood programs. Then, they begin collaboratively planning and implementing participatory curriculum in their teaching contexts—with two-year-olds to adult learners.

In curriculum class, beginning the senior year of early childhood studies undergraduate work, the university students reflect on their own family histories and stories of learning (as explained earlier), and practice qualitative narrative assignments about learning to observe and listen to children. They participate in:

a. writing a narrative description (from journals) of children's participation, strengths, and needs and the context of the classroom,
b. writing a brief account of children in school using their home language (other than English), and addressing the following questions:
   "What do the children say?"
   "When do they use their home language?"

"What supports their doing this? (The adults, the children, the materials, the personality of the child?)," and

c. noticing details about children's literacy and mathematics knowledge (at the placement), answering the following questions:
"What do you see as the children's strengths?"
"What do they know?" "How do you know they know this?"

This is the moment where students engage in strong discussion about the absolute necessity for all curriculum development to stem from children's interests, histories (including languages), strengths, and needs. Students discuss what that means, what it might look like, and ways through which we may all become more effective listeners and ethnographers.

The university class studies research that documents teaching with critical literacy using problem-posing that focuses on children's lived experiences and children's literature (Quintero, 2004, 2009). This method nourishes an integrated curriculum that supports young children's meaningful learning. Simply defined, the problem-posing method comprises three main components. These are: *listening, dialogue,* and *action.* In this method, participants:

- listen to their own histories through reflective writing and sharing of participants' stories, and gather new information in the form of mini-lectures, expert presentations, or scholarly research and academic information;
- dialogue about information that was shared and presented during the listening activities; discuss issues of power that have shaped their identities and current families, schools, and communities contexts; and make connections to the situations of the children and families they work with using personal and historical information; and
- collaborate on various curricular activities that encourage and support action or transformation on the part of children, families, and educators.

The adult student teachers practice in the university class and brainstorm with peers and instructors about ways problem-posing might be used with young children.

A brief example from a university class session illustrates this process and our strong commitment to dual language learners (shows the integrated format used somewhat differently.) As explained above, in the Opening Activities in the first class meetings, students are asked to review their personal field notes for information about children's use of their home language (other than English) in school and to answer the following questions: "What do they say?" "When do they use their home language?" and "What supports their doing this (the adults, the children, the materials, the personality of the child)?"

Next, in the Dialogue section, students are asked to discuss what they had noted about children's use of their home language and explain that in detail to their small groups. Then, for the Action section, they are asked to analyze the following questions about their observations of their journals: "Is this critical thinking?" and "In what ways does this relate to your research frameworks?"

Then the class continues with another Listening section. The instructor reads the storybook *I Love Saturdays y Domingos* by Alma Flor Ada (2002), which tells the story of a girl's life with both her English-speaking and her Spanish-speaking grandparents. For the Dialogue section, students are asked to relate the story to issues discussed that night in class. They then go back to another Listening section, listening to *Friends from the Other Side: Amigos Del Otro Lado* by Gloria Anzaldúa (1997), which is a story about a young girl befriending a boy who had recently moved to an American neighborhood from Mexico with his mother but without documentation. The story includes issues of friendship, coping with bullying, experiences related to how political situations in communities affect children, and cultural traditions including sharing food and natural healing.

For the Dialogue section, the students participate in a large group discussion that addresses the topics surrounding appropriate ways to address controversial issues and teachers' responsibilities to do so. For the Action section, students read and share some teacher research articles addressing controversial issues from the magazine *Rethinking Schools*. Then, in groups, they are asked to plan centers that could be set up to go along with the themes addressed in story.

INTEGRATED CURRICULUM DEVELOPMENT IN COMPLICATED CONTEXTS: PATTERNS OF FINDINGS

As explained earlier, we have found three areas that illustrated the importance of personal and community story. We see story as a way for young learners to experience many integrated content learning opportunities and social/emotional learning opportunities in meaningful ways. We see integrated curriculum as it reflects the social, emotional, and cognitive domains of young children in the context of their communities and historical richness. Nelson (2009) maintains, "The challenge is finding out how the mind-culture symbiosis comes about in the normally developing child" (p. x). She believes that "the major breakthrough in human development, the one that made us different from all other animals was, the ability to share subjective meanings" (p. 10).

Patterns of findings under the foci of critical, responsive curriculum for all children have illustrated new questions, provoked new trajectories of informants and connections to dynamic happenings in early childhood internationally. The issues involved in curriculum and assessment point to international discussions about what is "quality" in early care and education and who has the power to decide. These international dynamics highlight the inevitable connections among programs for young children, policies, and politics. Further connections regarding multiple histories, strengths, and needs of young children also illustrate little-discussed refugees and migrating people around the world—and their children who are growing and experiencing life wherever they are living in a variety of situations with or without support.

In a nationwide study, Yoshikawa, Weiland, Brooks-Gunn, Burchinal, Espinosa, Gormley, Ludwig, Magnuson, Phillips, and Zaslow (2013) compiled current research relating to the evidence base for quality early childhood programs for all children and concluded thus:

> Early experiences in the home, in other care settings, and in communities interact with genes to shape the developing nature and quality of the brain's architecture. The growth and then environmentally based pruning of neuronal systems in the first years support a range of early skills, including cognitive (early language, literacy, math), social (theory of mind, empathy, prosocial), persistence, attention, and self-regulation and executive function skills (the voluntary control of attention and behavior). Later skills—in schooling and employment—build cumulatively upon these early skills. (Yoshikawa, et al. 2013, p. 3)

Scholars in the field are seriously questioning the cavalier way claims such as these are being used in our discussions and policy rationales (Brown & Lan, 2014; Dahlberg, Moss, & Pence, 2013; and Penn, 2014). Furthermore, these skills and dispositions in their complexities, in the culturally layered and politically influenced societies, raise even more questions about which knowledge is valued in which context. Every day in our work with young children and families, the issues of strengths and needs of children and their families, and the diversity of contexts demand that we continually question our definitions of what counts as "evidence" as we attempt to improve services.

Consequently, in the discussion about curriculum, we also must revisit work compiled by Brown and Lan (2014) that analyzes the cultural clashes between developmentally appropriate practice (Bredekamp & Copple, 1997), and cultural, family, and historical values in programs for young children and families around the world.

All teacher education students document their journey as they experience the method in their teacher education classes and as they use the method with young children. They practice using this critical framework for focusing on story, multicultural children's literature, and creating writing and other literacy opportunities that extend beyond the classroom to use the words of their families and communities for literacy education. Over the course of several consecutive qualitative studies, sample findings illustrate some of the potential in the approach (Quintero, 2015).

INTEGRATED CURRICULUM AND CHILDREN'S LITERATURE

Children's literature, especially authentic and multicultural literature, provides opportunities for multilayered learning and sharing of histories. Bishop (1997) sees a two-faceted role for multicultural children's literature, serving as a mirror or a window. Children may see their own lives reflected in a story or may have an opportunity to see into others' lives. Multicultural literature incorporates the use of literary narrative and storytelling to challenge complex issues of race, historical authenticity, gender roles, and human responsibility.

Children's literature author, Lunge-Larsen (1999), reminds us of the importance of literature and folk tales in children's lives in the introduction to one of her children's literature books:

> Children, like the heroes and heroines in these stories perceive their lives to be constantly threatened. Will I lose a tooth? Will I be invited to play? Will I learn to read? By living a life immersed in great stories and themes, children will see that they have the resources needed to solve life's struggles. And, while listening to these stories, children can rest for a while in a world that mirrors their own, full of magic and the possibility of greatness that lies within the human heart. (p. 11)

Alma Flor Ada (2003) emphasizes that children's literature can be a window into the family, culture, and experience of children. Writer and poet Gloria Anzaldúa makes an even stronger statement about children's literature:

> I also want Chicano kids to hear stuff about la Llorona, about the border, et cetera, as early as possible. I don't want them to wait until they are eighteen or nineteen to get that information. I think it is very important that they get to know their culture already as children. Here in California I met a lot of young Chicanos and Chicanas who didn't have a clue about their own Chicano culture . . . later on, when they were already twenty, twenty-five or even thirty years old, they took classes in Chicano studies to learn more about their ancestors, their history and culture. But I want the kids to already have access to this kind of information. That is why I started writing children's books. (Hérnandez-Ávila & Anzaldúa 2000, p. 177)

A case study illustrates participatory integrated curriculum through a lesson in a first grade classroom in an urban school in a large city and shows the importance of home-language use and multicultural literature. The teacher and student teacher both believed in the importance of history, family, and community, and the importance of young children connecting their histories with stories in literature.

She was a twenty-year veteran teacher with the school district, a woman of Irish American decent. The student teacher with her was a Hmong male who is from the local community where the school is situated. The students in the class consisted of sixteen Hmong children, three African American children, and one child from South America. For this lesson, the teacher used the storybook *Whispering Cloth: A Refugee's Story* by Pegi Deitz Shea (1995).

The teacher began by gathering the children around her in the classroom center area, where she unfolded several quilts. She reminded them of previous discussions and stories they had shared about quilts. She wanted them to see the connection of past learning to this new learning. So, then she showed a weaving from Ireland and explained that it was from the country her family came from. Then, she held up a large, colorful "storycloth" that had been made by one of the school staff's relatives who is Hmong. To help the children to visualize the fact that while they were talking about important learning artifacts from both their cultures, Hmong and Irish, they represent two very distant geographical regions, she showed them the globe reinforcing the location of Vietnam and Ireland.

The teacher then asked, "Do you think a quilt could tell a story? Do you think you can hear a story from a cloth?" After the children discussed briefly what they thought about the question, the teacher passed the folded cloth around the circle, so that each student could "listen" to the cloth. Then, she showed the class the book, *The Whispering Cloth*, and told them just a little about the book. "It is a story about a Hmong girl and her grandmother who live in a refugee camp in Thailand. Grandmother is teaching Mai how to make story cloths and Mai creates one that tells her story."

Then the teacher showed the bilingual glossary in the book with Hmong words and English translations, and explained that she would read the story in English in a few minutes, but first, the student teacher would read it in Hmong. Again, the teacher wants the children to grasp that this important story is valuable as it is told via Hmong and via English—both languages.

The story was read in Hmong. The students who did not understand Hmong appeared to be fascinated by the words in spite of not comprehending. The teacher then asked questions: Can you guess what the story was about based upon Mr. Z's intonations, the pictures, and so forth?

Then the teacher read the story in English. The children were animated and shared understanding was seen through facial expressions, gestures, and questions and comments to the teacher.

During choice time, the children went to centers where they could begin drawing a storycloth and documenting the history it told. The geography center had maps and storybooks showing Laos and other Southeast Asian countries. There was a language center with a tape of a story being read in Hmong and a writing center where children could write questions to ask family and community members about their migration history.

At the close of the day the student teacher explained to the students that he had written a letter to their families explaining what they were learning about. The letter was written in English, Hmong, and Spanish. In the letter, the teachers ask the parents whether their child could share a storycloth, quilt, or an artifact that tells a family story. When the items were brought to school, extension activities were implemented. The students made a class storycloth with a contribution from each student's drawing and writing (native language or English or both) during the following days (Quintero, 2009). The home connection activity here is a direct example of the "Funds of Knowledge" of children's families being brought in to the classroom as a part of curriculum.

CHILDREN'S WRITING

Many scholars believe that the "texts" students "decode" should contain images of their own concrete, situated experiences with their friends, their families, and communities. This is a way to radically redefine conventional notions of print-based literacy and conventional school curriculum. This does not mean throwing out, or ignoring, or not providing access to, accepted bodies of information and canon in learning events. It means sharing the space, the time, and especially the importance of the old and the new. Even very young children are experts at writing about their worlds.

It has been found that children, with encouragement and acceptance, do gain self-confidence to do their own reading and writing. They will voice their own reality in terms of culture, social issues, and cognitive development when it is valued as a sharing of knowledge. Teachers can create classroom contexts in which all students can use their voices to affirm their social contexts and to create new situations for themselves through writing.

The work of Donald Graves (1994) and his colleagues suggests that three conditions are necessary for children to make progress as writers. First, they must be allowed and encouraged to write on topics they really care about, with the expectation that their work will be read seriously for its content. After all, why should they sustain the effort of writing and revising if they are not personally involved with their topics or do not expect to be read? Second, there is a fluid aspect to writing growth.

Children need time and frequent practice to get better at writing. Third, children need sensitive guidance from adults to become good writers. Twenty years of further research based on Graves's initial findings continues to validate these aspects of children writing (Calkins, Ehrenworth, & Lehman, 2012; Calkins, 1994; Fletcher, 2001; Strickland, 2010). An important question is, why are these ideas and findings about young children's writing considered to be so radical in some educational circles?

The following example, a case study of critical, integrated curriculum in a kindergarten class illustrates this point. The student teacher brought to the classroom a print that she had bought from the Vincent Van Gogh Museum in Amsterdam: Van Gogh's *The Bedroom in Arles* (or *Vincent's Bedroom in Arles* or *the Bedroom at Arles*). The children were immediately interested because they knew she had been on a trip over the school holiday and they saw a large case with something in it.

The student teacher sat in a rocking chair on the rug with the print rolled up in the cardboard case as the children gathered. Some of the children were able to notice the word "museum" on the case and predicted that is was a painting. She took out the painting and showed the class *The Bedroom in Arles* (or *Vincent's Bedroom in Arles* or *the Bedroom at Arles*). She then shared with the children a letter Van Gogh had written to his brother at the time he'd made this painting. She explained that she had found on the museum's website. The letter said,

> My eyes are still tired by then I had a new idea in my head and here is the sketch of it. Another size 20 canvas. This time it's just simply my bedroom, only here colour is to do everything, and giving by its simplification a grander style to things, is to be suggestive here of rest or of sleep in general. In a word, looking at the picture ought to rest the brain, or rather the imagination. (Harrison, 2001, p. 1).

She put the print of the painting on an easel and asked the children to look at it for a few minutes. She asked them to think about how they would draw or write a personal response to the painting. Before they began their creations, the student teacher shared her response, which was a poem she had written titled "My Bed."

Then she gave out pencils and blank pieces of paper to go wherever they wanted to go in the classroom with their writing tool and create a response and asked them to create a response to the painting. Most of the children drew pictures of their own bedrooms and wrote about the things that are in them or what they do there. Many children wrote a question that they had about the painting: "whose room is this?" Some of the comments they wrote were:

"BEDS R SAOFT AND RWOM" (Beds are soft and warm.)

"MY LAME IS CIDE. I SLIP WITH HR AVR NIT" (my lamb/lammie is cuddly. I sleep with her every night.)

"I LOVE MY BED I SLEEP WITH MY DOLL SARAH. MY MOMSINGS SONGS. I LOVE MY BED."
One child drew a picture of himself in his room and explained the items in it. He showed the blanket all around him, his apple, reading lamp, and ladder.
One child was compelled to write a heartfelt song filled with well wishes. "I WISH, I MAY, I WISH, I MIT (might), HAVE THE WISH TONIT (tonight), I WISH, YOU SEEP (sleep) WEL AND HOPE I DO TO (too)."
This activity shows how writing that is personal, addressed to a specific audience and supported by adult guidance can lead children to develop critical thinking skills by engaging them in dialogical action with the content through the written expression. After the activity, the student teacher reflected on how "seeing and hearing the children discuss and critically think and write about art promoted meaningful connections between language, content and thought through story, and write their thoughts culminated the activity for me" (Quintero, 2009, pp. 149–150).

SUPPORTING WRITING IN MULTIPLE LANGUAGES

This brings us to student writing and the creation of texts and opportunities for the growing number of dual language learners in schools around the country. Many researchers and practitioners maintain that learners develop their knowledge of second language writing and speaking conventions by using what they understand about writing in their home language. Many researchers and classroom teachers have shown that language interaction in the form of student-centered discussions and demonstrations, language experience story writing and reading, and holistic literacy development allow for home-language literacy to enhance English language literacy development.

Research shows that dual language learners benefit from instruction that focuses on decoding and comprehension in English (Genesee, 2010; Castro, Ayankoya, & Kasprzak, 2011). Research also shows that a strong home-language base makes it easier to learn English, and that young children can learn two languages as naturally as learning one (Bialystok, 2009; Kuhl, 2014). While early childhood educators understand that oral language development is a critical component of later reading success, the strategies for supporting this link between oral language/s and written language/s are often left out of teacher development. Integrated curriculum helps to bridge the strategy gaps for all children, and especially for dual language learners.

An integrated approach to support young learners and dual language learners has been proven effective (Maguder, Hayslip, Espinoza, & Matera, 2013) and adapted for use in the current study. This integrated approach includes: Print-rich labeling in English and all children's home languages, books, materials, displays, and artifacts that reflect all languages, cultures, families, and communities of children, anchor texts, vocabulary imprinting (use of photographs, images, and word walls to introduce new concepts and vocabulary and deepen comprehension), visual cues/gestures, and center extensions.

There is not enough discussion and exploration in teacher education circles regarding ways in which home-language writing can be used to enhance multiliteracy instruction (Matera, Armas, & Lavandenz, 2013). Some of the most convincing evidence of alternative theoretical propositions regarding bilingual writing comes from research of dual language or two-way bilingual immersion programs (Cummins, 2000). The contextual reality of many English Literacy classrooms in the United States and all over the world is that a large variety of native languages are present. It is almost always impossible for each teacher to be knowledgeable of every language represented in the classroom.

Reyes (2011, 1992) documents that rarely is it crucial for the classroom teacher to be proficient in all languages represented by students in the classroom. We have known for decades the importance of a work force with multilingual and diverse cultural and historical experiences. We know this is important for children who have recently settled in a new country, and more and more, data show that these multilingual educators offer monolingual children positive experiences, new perspectives, and important knowledge and dispositions.

In a collection of autobiographical experiences and family stories of educators (Reyes, 2011), Luis Moll introduces the book with an acknowledgment of the positive impact of the educators' knowledge and dispositions on all students, saying that "what is also clear in every chapter is the powerful role of emotions in language learning. These two related themes, resilience and emotions—constants in the book and of great theoretical importance in understanding language learning—are easy to miss by those who study only English monolingual development." (Moll, 2011, p. x)

Throughout the autobiographical stories there are a variety of literacy-related ways the families and communities supported the children's biliteracy. Moll (2011) recollects,

I do recall that my early biliteracy was supported almost invisibly . . . by my father's willingness to buy me comic books in English. He did not care what I was reading, or in which language, as long as I was reading. His intention was, then, not to teach me English, but to get me reading. (Moll, 2011, pp. ix)

Reyes (2011) shares her own story and the variety of meaningful literacy experiences in her home when she was a child:

Spanish was my mother's only language. Although she never attended school in Mexico, she had been provided a tutor for a few months to teach her to read and write so she was literate in Spanish. . . . She worked cleaning houses all day and doing laundry for priests at the Cathedral parish. After dinner and a long, hard day, *Mamá* made time to tell us stories, riddles, and rhymes, and to teach us some songs and games. Her conversations were often peppered with *dichos* or *refranes* (sayings or refrains) to teach us important lessons, or confirm values and attitudes we should inculcate in our behavior (p. 62).

CONCLUSION

By using integrated curriculum, any classroom teacher can orchestrate meaningful lessons that include writing in the students' home language.

This complexity of responsibility of responding to and respecting complexity in children's worlds is daunting and exciting. By focusing on integrating content in the curriculum and children's engagement with story as its framework, we see curriculum reflecting the social, emotional, and cognitive domains of young children in the context of their communities and historical richness.

Clearly, all the issues in our discussion about early childhood curriculum relate to all children. By nature of specific aspects of the issues and the urgent conditions under which many migrant families live, it is important to show how these issues affect migrant families and their young children. Throughout the discussions of the overlapping and intersecting issues, the findings show that context is of supreme importance in terms of children's experience, safety, relationships, and learning. Thus, context—demographic, social emotional, cultural, cognitive, and needs-based perceptions—must underlie all curriculum initiatives, assessment practices, policy and access. These realities are highlighted by the complexities of many children in the United States and across the world whose families have had to migrate away from the family's historical homeland.

We learn from each other's experiences. We learn from children and their families. We learn from colleagues we have yet to meet. When we can collaborate, be open, respectful, and inclusive, we have more possibilities in our thinking about curriculum for young children. We can follow the lead of the children's interests and histories—often revealed through their play. We can take risks to structure learning in ways that leaves open the door for including new, creative additions that we collectively—the children, families, and teachers—include in curriculum along with mandated curricular guidelines.

REFERENCES

Ada, A. F. (2002). *I love Saturdays y domingos.* New York: Simon & Schuster.
Ada, A. F. & Campoy, I. (2003). *Authors in the classroom: A transformative education process.* New York: Pearson

Anzaldúa, G. (1997). *Friends from the other side/Amigos del otro lado.* San Francisco: Children's Book Press.

Bishop, R. S. (1997). Selecting literature for a multicultural curriculum. In V. Harris (Ed.), *Using multiethnic literature in the K–8 classroom* (pp. 1–19). Norwood, MA: Christopher-Gordon Publishers.

Bialystok, E. (2009). Bilingualism: The good, the bad, and the indifferent. *Bilingualism: Language and Cognition, 12*(1), 3–11.

Bloch, M. N. (2014). Interrogating Reconceptualizing Early Care and Education (RECE)—20 years along. In M. N. Bloch, B. B. Swadener, & G. S. Cannella (Eds.), *Reconceptualizing early care and education: A reader* (pp. 19–31). New York: Peter Lang.

Bredekamp, S. & Copple, C. (Eds.). (1997). *Developmentally appropriate practice in early childhood programs* (rev. ed.). Washington, DC: National Association for the Education of Young Children.

Brown, C. & Lan, Y. C. (August 2014). A qualitative metasynthesis of how early educators in international contexts address cultural matters that contrast with developmentally appropriate practice. *Early Education and Development.* Routledge.

Calkins, L. (1994). *The art of teaching writing.* Portsmouth, NH: Heinemann.

Calkins, L., Ehrenworth, M., & Lehman, C. (2012). *Pathways to the common core.* Portsmouth, NH: Heinemann.

Campbell, J. (2008). *The hero with a thousand faces (the collected works of Joseph Campbell)* (3rd edition). New York: New World Library.

Carle, E. (2002). *The very hungry caterpillar.* New York: Longman

Castro, D. C., Ayankoya, B., & Kasprzak, C. (2011). *New voices/Nuevas voces: Guide to cultural and linguistic diversity in early childhood.* Baltimore, MD: Brookes.

Conboy, B. (2012). Research techniques and the bilingual brain. In C. A. Chappelle (Ed.), *The encyclopedia of applied linguistics* [online]. New York: John Wiley & Sons. Retrieved from http://onlinelibrary.wiley.com/doi/10.1002/9781405198431. wbeal1010/pdf

Cummins, J. (2000). *Language, power, and pedagogy: Bilingual children in the crossfire.* Clevedon, UK: Multilingual Matters

Dahlberg, G., Moss, P. M., & Pence, A. (2013). *Beyond quality in early childhood education and care: Languages of evaluation.* New York: Routledge.

Ehlert, L. (2001). *Waiting for wings.* New York: HMH Books for Young Readers.

Eisler, R. (1988). *The chalice and the blade: Our history, our future.* New York: HarperOne.

Fletcher, R. (2001). *Writing workshop: The essential guide.* Portsmouth, NH: Heinemann.

Freire, P. (1985). *The politics of education.* Granby, MA: Bergin & Garvey.

Genesee, F. (2010). Dual language development in preschool children. In E. E. Garcia & E. Frede (Eds.), *Young English language learners: Current research and emerging directions for practice and policy* (pp. 59–79). New York: Teachers College Press.

Graves, D. (1994). *A fresh look at writing.* Portsmouth, NH: Heinemann.

Harrison, R. G. (2001). Letter 554. Arles, 16 October 1888. The Bedroom in Arles. http://www.vggallery.com/letters/683_V-T_554.pdf

Hérnandez-Ávila, A. & Anzaldúa, G. (2000). Interview. In A. C. Elenes (Ed.), *Transforming borders: Chicana/o popular culture and pedagogy* (p. 177). Lanham, MD: Rowman & Littlefield.

Kuhl, P. (2014, January). How babies learn language: Q&A with Patricia Kuhl. *Cognitive Neuroscience Blog Archive.* Retrieved from https://www.cogneurosociety. org/cns-2014-blog-coverage/

Lunge-Larsen, L. (1999). *The troll with no heart in his body and other tales of trolls from Norway.* Boston: Houghton Mifflin.

Magruder, E., Hayslip, W., Espinoza, L., & Matera, C. (2013). Many languages, one teacher: Supporting language and literacy development for preschool dual language learners. *Young Children, 68*(1), 8–15.

Matera, C., Armas, E., & Lavandent, M. (2013, Spring). Dialogic reading and the development of transitional kindergarten teachers' expertise with dual language learners. The Multilingual Educator, 37-40, Retrieved from http://www.bilingual-education.org/ME/ME2013.pdf

Moll, L. C. (2011). Foreword. In M. de la luz Reyes (Ed.), *Words were all we had: Becoming biliterate against the odds* (pp. ix–xi). New York: Teachers College Press.

Moll, L. C., Gonzalez, N., & Amanti, C. (2005). *Funds of knowledge: Theorizing practices in households, communities, and classrooms.* Mahwah, NJ: Lawrence Erlbaum Associates.

Nelson, K. (2009). *Young minds in social worlds: Experience, meaning, and memory.* Cambridge, MA: Harvard University Press.

Paley, V. G. (1986). *Boys and girls: Superheroes in the doll corner.* Chicago: University of Chicago Press.

Paley, V. G. (2000). *White teacher.* Cambridge, MA: Harvard University Press.

Penn, H. (2014). *Understanding early childhood: Issues and controversies,* (3rd edition). Berkshire, England: Open University Press.

Quintero, E. P. (2015). *Storying learning in early childhood: When children lead participatory curriculum design, implementation, and assessment.* New York: Peter Lang.

Quintero, E. P. (2009). *Critical literacy in early childhood education: Artful story and the integrated curriculum.* New York: Peter Lang.

Quintero, E. P. (2004). *Problem-posing with multicultural children's literature: Developing critical, early childhood curricula.* New York: Peter Lang.

Reyes, M. de la Luz. (1992). Questioning venerable assumptions: Literacy instruction for linguistically different students. *Harvard Education Review, 2*(4), 427–444

Reyes, M. de la luz (Ed.). (2011). *Words were all we had: Becoming biliterate against the odds.* New York: Teachers College Press.

Shea, P. D. (1995). *Whispering cloth: A Refugee's story.* New York: Boyds Mills Press.

Strickland, D. (2010). *Essential readings on early literacy.* Newark, DE: International Reading Association.

Yoshikawa, H., Weiland, C., Brooks-Gunn, J., Burchinal, M. R., Espinosa, L. M., Gormley, W. T., & Zaslow, M. J. (2013). *Investing in our future: The evidence base on preschool education.* Ann Arbor, MI: Society for Research in Child Development. Retrieved from http://www.srcd.org/policy-media/policy-updates/ meetings-briefings/investing-our-future -evidence-base-preschool

Chapter 4

Promoting Respect through Collaboration

A School Responds to Bullying by Engaging the Community

Jean Ann B. Slusarczyk and Lucia Villaluz

It all began with Peter Yarrow singing the powerful and haunting lyrics, "Don't laugh at me, don't call me names, don't get your pleasure from my pain" (Shamblin & Seskin, 1998). The lyrics to Yarrow's rendition of the song *Don't Laugh at Me* evoked a deeply emotional response in the attendees of the Montclair State University Network for Educational Renewal (MSUNER) Summer Conference. The song, as well as his description of Operation Respect and the Don't Laugh At Me (DLAM) curriculum (Roerden, 2000) that Yarrow's team developed, inspired a small group of teachers from the Bloomfield, New Jersey Public School System to delve further into the area of anti-bullying.

As a result, four Bloomfield educators spent a week being formally trained in the DLAM curriculum, during which time they reflected upon their individual beliefs, prejudices, thoughts, and ideas. As the week progressed, the participants of the training became a community as a variety of team building exercises that were designed to encourage thought provoking discussion, personal connections, and reflection were conducted. Walls were broken down as each person began to share more deeply. From this profoundly personal experience, an idea was born. The Bloomfield teachers from Franklin Elementary School decided to apply for a grant to address bullying in a proactive manner by uniting and strengthening the school community through the collaboration of all stakeholders.

The idea of addressing the bullying issue in a positive manner was extremely enticing to the team especially since New Jersey has one of the strongest bullying laws in the nation. The Harassment, Intimidation and Bullying (HIB) policy that came into effect in 2011 has changed the way educators do business. School personnel are now held accountable for following strict procedures involving bullying incidents both in and outside of school hours.

All teachers, administrators, and staff are required to be trained "on how to spot and address bullying" (HIB, 2011). It is emphasized that "school employees are also required to report all incidents they learn of, whether they took place in or outside of school" (HIB, 2011). A school safety team—overseen and graded by the State Department of Education—must be created to review bullying complaints (HIB, 2011). Administrators are required to investigate reported incidents; those who fail to do so face disciplinary action (HIB, 2011). Similarly, "students who bully could be suspended or expelled" (HIB, 2011).

Franklin School teachers found that on a weekly basis countless hours were spent by the guidance counselor filing HIB reports. The word "bullying" had become a catch phrase that many parents and students used for any and all misdeeds. The team wanted to positively impact the school climate, and they knew it would only be successful if students and teachers devoted ample time to think critically about this topic.

The grant was awarded by the MSUNER and titled: Promoting Respect through Collaboration (PRTC). Its goal was to focus on creating a school-based, anti-bullying project aimed at fostering collaboration of all stakeholders, including: students, faculty, parents, community members, and higher education partners in order to advance conversations about bullying in an effort to create a positive school climate through proactive means. Other teachers in the school became interested and the team—consisting of three classroom teachers, a literacy coach, guidance counselor, and a Montclair State University (MSU) professor—was formed.

The team began with three foundational tenants: emotions drive attention, each brain is unique, and threat throws the brain into survival mode at the expense of developing higher order thinking skills (Jensen, 1998). Since the grant idea originated with music, it was decided that music and role play would be incorporated in the process, especially since cognitive skills develop better with music and movement (Jensen, 1998). School-wide guidance lessons were to include the DLAM curriculum.

In addition, literacy lessons designed for all grade levels would address the need to incorporate Common Core Standards while using literature to serve as a springboard for character education themed work. Furthermore, a special program for young children—Beginning Alcohol and Addiction Basic Education Studies (BABES)—that addresses drug and alcohol prevention, would be offered, and the MSU grant team professor would conduct diversity lessons for older students. Moreover, parent activity nights and community outreach programs would be developed.

Whole school initiatives would include a "One School, One Book" event, student created pledge and mission statement as well as a school-wide assembly. Developing lessons and activities that remained highly focused on trust and minimized an emphasis on threat would be crucial to the success of fostering a safe environment for all students. By shifting the paradigm of these lessons, life skills such as problem-solving, decision-making, collaboration, communication, conflict resolution, and creativity would be the heart of the grant initiative. Comprehensively, critical thinking would drive this project.

Before delving into the specifics of this curriculum, it is important to first understand what bullying means in this context. According to the Anti-bullying Bill of Rights Act of the New Jersey Department of Education, "bullying" is defined as "harassment, intimidation and bullying." In Chapter 122, part 6 section 10, the law recalls that

> Any pupil who is guilty of continued and willful disobedience, or of open defiance of the authority of any teacher or person having authority over him, or of the habitual use of profanity or of obscene language, or who shall cut, deface or otherwise injure any school property, shall be liable to punishment and to suspension or expulsion from school.

It is clear that the law exhibits strict guidelines against bullying, which furthers the importance of implementing a school-wide curriculum to teach students the effects bullying can have not only on others but themselves. Bullying is an act of "defiance" and therefore punishable by law. Bullying can stem within the "psycho-social context," which includes personal history, the relationship level closest to the individual including family and peer relationships, the community level, or the setting in which the individual lives and the societal level of cultural values and beliefs. The bioecological model of human development (Bronfenbrenner & Morris, 2006) emphasizes the transactional nature of gene-environment interactions that shape the individual's development. It also provides a useful paradigm that can be used to lay the theoretical foundation of effective bullying programs.

When a student or teacher witnesses bullying, he or she can act in two ways; either as a bystander or an upstander. A bystander is "associated with (a) self-preservation, (b) perceived inability, (c) situation ambiguity, (d) diffusion of responsibility, and (e) pluralistic ignorance. In essence, a bystander will not act in defense of a bully victim but rather ignore the defiant act. It is argued that a bystander is not necessarily a bad person or takes on the same role as the bully. The role of the bystander can initiate and perpetuate the bullying and can add to or fuel the authority that the bully feels. On the other hand, an upstander invokes a conscientious and immediate protective response and confidently and intentionally tries to diffuse the situation" (Salmivalli, Poskiparta & Haataja, 2013).

An upstander is someone who tries to reduce or end bullying behaviors. Focusing on and supporting upstanders has been shown to be an effective means of preventing bullying, and this is largely due to the critical role of peers in initiating and sustaining bullying behaviors (Salmivalli et al., 2013). This type of confident behavior shows a clear indication of right versus wrong; it is the kind of indication that is the desired outcome with this program.

ACTIVITIES FOR STUDENTS

The common thread that ran through the project was provided by the Project Respect: DLAM lessons (Roerden, 2000) administered by the school's guidance counselor. These DLAM curricular lessons were taught to all children in the school from kindergarten to grade 6, thus providing the cornerstone of the work. One especially powerful lesson required that students rip a paper heart as unkind words were spoken. The class then tried to repair the torn heart with tape. Once the heart had been reassembled, pupils discussed the results.

The visual of the patched and tattered heart led to amazing insights and deep exchanges among classmates about the ability to repair a heart despite the long-standing scars. The empathy participants felt was palpable as they shared personal stories of put downs that they have heard or experienced with peers who provided support through verbal and physical affirmations such as hugs and pats on the back. Students learned a common language including "put downs" and "stand ups" and began to implement these terms in their discussions.

This activity built an awareness of the impact of personal actions including words that hurt and words that heal. Allowing learners to actively participate, evaluate, and draw their own conclusions strengthened their critical thinking skills, modeling metacognitive practices. Torn hearts were posted throughout the building as a visual reminder of the lesson and the power of one's words.

To further develop students' thinking skills, Operation Respect's term "upstander" was introduced to the school population. An "upstander" was defined as a person who stands up for a victim rather than standing by and watching. Children role played a variety of bullying scenarios (see Appendix A) and brainstormed how an observer of these behaviors could stand up for the victim. These role play activities empowered learners by providing them with salient tools to communicate, collaborate, and resolve conflicts, all of which are life skills that require higher level thinking.

All staff and students now had a common language that became an integral part of the school culture. School personnel recognized learners for "upstanding" behaviors, and these children were acknowledged weekly by the principal both in a school-wide announcement and through the inclusion of their pictures on a bulletin board in the main office. The foundation had been laid for promoting respect and expecting accountability. It was now the norm for pupils who saw unkind behavior to respond in one of the appropriate ways defined through talks during guidance lessons.

The expectation students had for themselves evolved from "not my problem," to "see something, say or do something." Positive actions were recognized and acknowledged publically during morning announcements and the results proved to be powerful. Many children who had exhibited bullying behaviors were caught being kind. Recognizing these individuals for positive actions was a breath of fresh air.

In an effort to promote empathy, the guidance counselor also led a community outreach program. Students became actively involved in a variety of projects to assist the community. These included raising money for those who are less fortunate, providing cheer at holiday time to nursing home residents by performing songs and distributing small gifts and cards, participating in a coat drive, and collecting food for the needy in the community. Additionally, pupils seemed particularly involved in providing aide for the Hurricane Sandy victims, as this was a disaster that directly impacted their state and many of their own families. The children felt intensely connected to all of the projects since the outreach programs were co-created with students themselves, thus providing them with a sense of pride and ownership. Perhaps most importantly, personally connecting to the community encouraged a reciprocal respect.

LITERACY LESSONS

Literacy lessons, aligned with the Common Core Standards, went hand-in-hand with the DLAM curriculum, as they extended the learning by incorporating both literature and the anti-bullying theme in all classes. In every grade, learners created writing artifacts based on open-ended questions after being exposed to the literature (see Appendix B). As stated in *Psychology Today* "our brains still respond to content by looking for the story to make sense out of the experience" (Rutledge, 2011). Additionally, research proves that "stories allow us to understand ourselves better and to find our commonality with others" (Rutledge, 2011). Hence, using literature as a springboard for conversations about bullying was a natural progression.

In first grade classrooms, conflict resolution was addressed after reading *Matthew and Tilly* (Jones, 1991). In this story, two young children have a disagreement over a broken crayon. After responding to one another in a negative manner the youngsters learn to resolve their conflict and resume their friendship. Students discussed feeling frustrated and angry then spoke about how to deal with those normal emotions. Following the reading, a conversation about kind behaviors was conducted. The classes then reflected about their own actions, and finally created stories about personal acts of kindness. Exploring their individual abilities to make good decisions empowered learners and encouraged them to continue making socially conscious choices.

The focus for grade two was identifying unkind behavior as well as recognizing one's own uniqueness and the beauty of diversity. After reading *Giraffes Can't Dance* (Andreae, 1999), classes deliberated about isolation, embarrassment, teasing, loneliness, and self-esteem. Student insights expressed remarkably profound feelings of empathy for Gerald the Giraffe, the character in Andreae's story who is teased by peers for his inability to dance until one small creature gives Gerald the courage to embrace his uniqueness, persevere, and overcome ridicule ultimately leading Gerald to dance in his own way.

Letters were composed to Gerald describing personal experiences about the topics previously mentioned. Additionally, student writers described what actions they would have taken on Gerald's behalf. Many of the letters revealed heart-wrenching sentiments and provided instructors with a window into the personal lives and feeling of their students. By allowing the children to have a voice, many insights were gleaned by all involved.

Second graders also wrote stories about their own uniqueness; exploring their cultures and diversities instilled a sense of pride. As students described their personal and cultural customs, their peers became interested, asking follow-up questions and making connections to their own lives. Following these discussions, the children concluded that personal uniqueness is a gift, which was evident through their appreciation of the wide range of experiences and their articulations of commonalities among these experiences. Another insight gained from this activity was not to judge one another based on differences. Once students understood their classmates' customs and cultures better, they appeared more accepting of each other's differences giving one another verbal affirmations regarding these cultural experiences.

Christopher Myers' book *Wings* (2000) had a profound impact on third grade learners. This literature selection generated sincere discussions about inequity, diversity, isolation, and even suicide. In *Wings,* Myers's main character, Ikarus Jackson, is taunted by peers as well as authority figures due to his differences, which are actually quite spectacular. One child looks on sympathetically but silently due to her own fears of isolation and intimidation until she can no longer remain quiet. She takes a stand and by so doing, Ikarus is saved from despair. Pupils were given various bullying scenarios and formulated in writing what their personal responses would be to such situations.

The DLAM curriculum was vividly present in their writings as they described their thoughts for "upstanding" actions. Justifications were given as to why students chose the responses they had. The maturity and insights exposed by these lessons reflected a genuine understanding of the topic.

Fourth and fifth grade classes read a true short story written by an eighth grade girl (see appendix C) describing her isolation in school and its impact. The young author of this story was the literacy coach's daughter. Sharing her story made this lesson personal and provided a real connection for students. When viewing her smiling picture and outward demeanor, no one could see the negative effect her peers had had on the author. This knowledge opened up thoughtful conversations about the "iceberg effect," where each of us shows the world what we decide to portray, while the greatest portion of our authentic selves lies hidden beneath the surface.

Following these discussions, a teambuilding activity was conducted where each person had two minutes to tell the group what they would see if they really knew them. The candor and pain of many children was profound. However, the fact that they were willing to share proved that the culture had changed and feelings of safety had become prevalent. The personal connection aspect transformed this into one of the most responsive lessons of the project. Many individuals were emotionally impacted to the point of tears, and this led to poignant exchanges about how each citizen, regardless of age, needs to evaluate their behaviors and decide what proactive actions they can take to make their home, school, and community a safer, kinder place. Such conversations provided evidence that learners were becoming sensitized to the effects of ridicule and other unkind behaviors. Many children seemed eager to share their own personal experiences and did so through narrative writings.

The literacy coach was especially moved by the iceberg activity since she had known these children since kindergarten and yet had no idea what sadness and pain many were carrying with them. This experience gave her a new lens and insight into who they were and the reason for some observable behaviors they had exhibited throughout their elementary experience. This caused the instructors to once again reflect critically upon their own practice and reevaluate preconceived ideas.

The MSU faculty grant partner conducted lively and engaging lessons with sixth graders regarding diversity and similarity. After having students brainstorm multiple layers of diversity he showed them the similarities as well. Students began to see how alike we all are in spite of our differences. Each pupil was encouraged to complete a graphic organizer describing such things as their hopes, dreams, fears, and worries. Students then took their work and evaluated which had the strongest impact on them.

After they decided the importance of each feeling, they created word cloud posters where each experience was expressed in varying sizes that coordinated with its importance. The creativity of this visual representation of each thought was impressive. Many learners, who do not excel in the traditional aspects of school such as language arts, could now shine. Viewing the posters enabled the youngsters to see how closely their deepest feelings and wishes aligned to peers who had once seemed so different.

EARLY GRADES: K–2

The Franklin School Grant Team wanted to reach all grade levels with their grant project, and they remained particularly interested in starting at the bottom, with the youngest children. After some research, they were able to bring in the BABES (Beginning Alcohol and Addiction Basic Education Studies, 1979) program. BABES is a unique program, as it focuses on early elementary school-age children from four to eight years old. It is tailored to young minds, facilitating dialogues about feelings and emotions. The seven-week program was funded by the Bloomfield Alliance, thus providing another example of various stakeholders working hand-in-hand.

The program introduced first graders to seven puppet characters. Five of the characters were the same age as the first graders while two older, wiser ones were used to model appropriate behavior. Using BABES puppets helped children receive accurate, nonjudgmental information by using a format designed to enable students to grasp the importance of positive life skills and good decision-making techniques. By exploring these concepts, the program helped children deal with their feelings and self-esteem. Students were encouraged to believe that they are special, and they learned ways to help themselves experience more positive emotions during difficult situations.

The BABES program also helped individuals deal with peer pressure; through the puppets in the program they were taught not to listen to peer pressure. They developed the cognitive and emotional skills necessary to cope with challenging situations, promote self-esteem, define peer pressure and bullying, and were provided the tools necessary to make good choices. Puppets, as well as high-quality literature, were used to engage the young learners. Each lesson was taught in a comprehensive sequence, building upon previous tenants during each subsequent week. Students engaged in real-life scenarios with the puppets, challenging them to evaluate options and develop problem-solving skills. Through active engagement, they were able to arrive at solutions to complex issues.

Furthermore, they were given the opportunity to practice and generate alternate solutions to issues. Students were active and reflective learners when they were asked to explain how they solved their problems. At a first grade level, verbalizing feelings is often difficult for students; this program gave children an emotional vocabulary, opening an avenue for students to feel comfortable. Pupils participating in the BABES program were developing critical thinking skills by acting out real-life scenarios.

During these lessons, children absorbed the importance of communicating feelings. The concept of self-image and individual uniqueness introduced through the use of puppets and storytelling served as an influential strategy for the young learners. Students were encouraged to summarize, reflect, and retell during discussions following the lessons. BABES lessons also utilized songs and chants, in an effort to emotionally hook and engage youngsters.

PARENTS AND COMMUNITY: EXTENDING THE PROJECT

To further involve all members of the school community, the grant team recognized the importance of the parent-school connection. Therefore, they organized a parent activity night, inviting all kindergarten through grade two parents for an evening of fun and games with their children. Babysitting was provided for younger siblings, and bilingual teachers were easily accessible to assist and welcome all families.

One of the cornerstone motivations was to include reluctant parents in order to strengthen the connection between school and all homes. Notices were sent home in both English and Spanish. An abridged notice was also included on the school website. Finally, students were encouraged to share information about the events with their parents. The team hoped that creating a positive dialogue between parents and the school community would assist in promoting a safe environment for students, as well as preventing polarization between parents and school when issues arose.

The evening started with a variety of families gathered at different tables; there was an entertaining, learning-based board game situated at each group. By playing the games with other families, all present were exposed to the thought processes of others. This encouraged students and their families to see that there are multiple ways of approaching problems, not just one correct way. This lesson was especially eye opening for parents, many of whom realized they had more static tendencies in the way that they view answers. Conversely, parents gained insight into student thought. Through these problem-solving activities, parents became aware that all children learn and think differently.

The grant team's goal for the evening was to give parents a tool kit to take home and use with their youngsters, thus extending these critical talks and activities beyond the school walls. These kits comprised several make-and-take projects from the night: a game to review math facts and sight words, a chore chart, and reading windmills with comprehension questions to spark discussion before, during, and after reading. These kits provided families with strategies that they could use on a daily basis to foster independent, critical thinking, as often parents revert to giving children answers if they do not know them. As families left, they were equipped with a cadre of ideas to support their learning.

Furthermore, using learning to benefit the home environment, parents were encouraged to create a chore list, teaching children to prioritize obligations. These chore charts were visual as well as interactive, requiring children to move their clothes pins as a way to engage them in the process. Parents customized these chore charts. One used it to give her child visual cues as the steps necessary to get ready for school, while another used it as ways for her youngsters to budget their time wisely.

Teachers also gave the families simple solutions to help their youngsters become problem solvers. For example, parents were encouraged to play fun, educational games during down times such as a car ride or waiting in a restaurant. Some examples included identifying the geometric shapes of signs on the roadway, doing origami with a napkin in a restaurant, and playing "I Spy" while waiting for an appointment. By reinforcing critical thinking and modeling this type of thought process for parents, those who attended left that evening full of ideas about simple, accessible ways to spark their child's creative thinking on a daily basis, encouraging these thought patterns in all settings, and creating a more continuous learning experience.

After creating a connection between the home and school, team members felt the need to strengthen the professional community within the school. Franklin Elementary School implemented a cohort initiative, targeted at student teachers and novice teachers. Often, student teachers and first year teachers do not immediately feel as if they are part of the school community (Ingersoll, 2012). This, of course, is not done intentionally; however, veteran teachers and school leaders often become so engrossed in the school day that they do not take the time to make new staff members feel welcomed.

To address this issue and model a collaborative work community, the Bloomfield teachers from Franklin Elementary School made a concerted effort to make each new staff member and student teacher feel comfortable, accepted, and part of a cohesive team. Student teacher interns were welcomed into the professional community through a "Get to Know the Staff" luncheon. All staff were invited for a chance to meet and welcome new junior faculty. Introducing the student teacher interns to the staff encouraged a collaborative school atmosphere, creating a place where all could feel valued.

The cohort of six continued to meet periodically at lunchtime throughout the school year for interactive mini-sessions, covering a wide range of topics. Sessions addressed salient topics: teaching strategies for higher-level thinking, specific techniques and strategies used in the classroom, training on the use of assessment materials, advanced uses of the SMART board, implementation of 6+1 Trait Writing (Culham & Coutu, 2009), and using guided reading centers. Interns and novice teachers were able to ask questions and learn about initiatives that the Bloomfield School District, specifically, was implementing in a comfortable setting. Since these sessions were a safe place for learning, no questions were considered too rudimentary, and everyone gained from the experience—including the seasoned teachers. The continuous sessions were an opportunity for all to develop synchronously and professionally in a comfortable setting.

Such meetings provided an opportunity for teachers to share ideas they were using in the classroom. Several grades were able to collaborate, compiling a shared professional resource of educational websites that enhance learning. Teachers were engaged and excited as they discovered new apps, websites, and games available to them on their SMART boards and iPads.

Additionally, discovering the nuances of administering a Diagnostic Reading Assessment, also known as a DRA (Beavers, 2006), was helpful. Resources such as this that are easily accessible to teachers are often underutilized due to the fact that teachers have not been properly trained to administer such assessments. To meet this need, the grant team gave each interested staff member and all novice and student teachers training on administering a DRA, highlighting each of the various components. Instructors were given the opportunity to apply these concepts by administering the assessment; using these genuine examples, teachers were taught how to score the assessment and find each student's reading level. This practical, experiential meeting was extremely beneficial in aiding educators to meet district requirements and standards.

Guided Reading Centers were also discussed allowing attendees to delve into differentiated instruction for individual pupils and to create centers that promote hands-on opportunities for learning. During this cohort meeting time, instructors shared centers that were being used, and created universal centers for the variety of learners in the classroom.

The grant team found that having specific time set aside monthly allowed educators to share things that were working in their classrooms. It also gave them an opportunity to offer constructive suggestions to any teacher struggling in a particular area, whether it be classroom management or a reading assessment. The entire staff was eager to meet during their lunch hour, highlighting their true commitment to lifelong learning and professional growth. These sessions were not mandatory nor were they monitored by administration. They were meant to be a professional space for the co-construction of knowledge curated by teachers of all ages collaborating and learning from each other. This cohort strengthened the school community and made it a place where all staff members felt valued and respected—collaboration at its finest.

This collaborative environment seeped into the culture of the school; students saw their teachers meet regularly, along with school staff, parents, community members, and higher education partners. Most members were modeling what was being echoed on the loud speaker every morning: respect. The vast majority of the school community was working together, helping members develop in a way that was powerful and reverent.

ASSESSING AND IMPROVING

Midway through the year the grant team continued to strategize about how to further involve the entire school community in the PRTC project. Two initiatives were decided upon. First was a school-wide contest to create an anti-bullying pledge to further strengthen the school-wide commitment to this topic. The response to this was tremendous. Students from all grades submitted entries. The winning pledge—"I promise to be respectful and polite to everyone at Franklin School. I'll use kind actions and words. I promise to report unkind behavior. Be a friend, not a bully"— was written by a first grade student. A second grade student's entry became the school's mission statement: "Attention to all students! Children all over the world are getting bullied. Let's start off small and make Franklin School a BULLY FREE ZONE! We can avoid bullies by simply walking away. If that doesn't work, tell a trusted adult. A way we can stop bullying before it starts is to treat others the way we want to be treated. So you can see, altogether we can make bullying vanish!"

Second, all students would read *Pedro's Whale* (Kluth, 2010) during class in order to develop empathy and increase awareness for of autism in an effort to promote tolerance of differences. Each student would complete a response to the literature by creating posters which were displayed throughout the school building.

Following the pledge contest, a school assembly was held. Students who received honorable mention shared their pledges. "Upstanders" were recognized, and then the piece de resistance—the school mission statement—was shared followed by a school-wide adoption of the anti-bullying pledge. Listening to five hundred children recite the pledge left a resounding impact on each person in the room.

As a culminating activity, the pledge was inscribed on the school building's main bulletin board and each student signed it agreeing to its tenants. Upon signing, the pupils were given an anti-bullying wrist band. The pledge had now officially become part of the school culture, and the standard had been set for a community that valued tolerance, acceptance, and empathy.

At the conclusion of the first year, students in grades three to six were given a survey to document the impact of the PRTC project. Students also rated their feelings of physical and emotional safety before and after the project. Overwhelmingly, they reported greater understanding of what bullying was and how to address the problem. Out of 101 students polled, 100 percent understood the definition of an "Upstander," 93 percent of students felt confident that they could stand up to a bully, and 84 percent felt bullying was uncool.

The common language established through the team's efforts was evident. When asked in the survey what they had learned, students stated: I learned how to be an "Upstander," how to prevent bullying, everyone is equal, how to treat others kindly, what it feels like to be bullied. In addition to the exit survey students were also interviewed by team members. Their responses indicated that they both comprehended and enjoyed the program.

CONTINUING THE WORK

After a very successful year of Promoting Respect through Collaboration (PRTC) at Franklin Elementary School, the grant team decided to continue their work for a second year. For the second year of the program, the lens shifted to highlight pedagogy, diverse learners, technology, and reading content. As the school community was strengthened the previous year, building an emotional foundation in order to prevent bullying, in the second year, the school community would work together to advance individual literacy while helping others.

Franklin Elementary School created a One Book, One Community Initiative. This program was designed to provide a singular reading experience for all members of the school community, including all parents, students, teachers, and support staff. The program essentially fostered a school-community book club.

The Bloomfield Education Foundation (a community organization), along with the Franklin Home and School Association (a parent organization) collaborated to provide funds for the purchase of the same book, *The Lemonade War* (Davies, 2007), which was donated to every student and staff member. Prior to the kickoff celebration of *The Lemonade War* a school-wide contest to design a bookmark for the One Book, One Community Initiative was conducted. Children in all grade levels were asked to design a bookmark that represented a community of readers. The winning bookmark was announced during the school-wide assembly. Every child was also asked to wear yellow—for lemonade—to the kickoff, at which time they each received the winning bookmark along with a copy of their brand new book.

A reading calendar was created to help families set aside fifteen minutes per night to read one chapter of the book aloud together, engaging the family unit in the initiative and modeling key ways for guardians to assist literacy development. Each day in school, text-based trivia was read over the intercom, and the school participated in enriched vocabulary experiences. Digitally extending the initiative, each night a question was posted on *The Lemonade War* school blog.

All students, at every grade level, were encouraged to respond to the blog, and time was allotted in the classroom for youngsters who did not have access to the Internet at home. Teachers and other faculty members also participated in reading and responding to posts. Students were excited to be communicating with their teachers in the evening. Each day the principal would announce a "Blogger of the Day," selecting one blogger that had responded to a question in an insightful way or participated by responding to other children on the blog. There was always great excitement to see who would win this prestigious title each morning.

In the classroom, instructors employed critical thinking questioning, engaging the higher levels of Bloom's taxonomy (Bloom, 1956) to provide close alignment with the Common Core Standards. To supplement this component, teachers attended mini workshops, providing them with an opportunity to develop higher order thinking questions appropriate for their grade levels. Although the book was written on a third grade level, educators in the lower grades were able to reread the chapter in class and dissect it to make learning meaningful. They responded to the blog as a class and were able to read posts from all the other grades. Instructors in the upper grades challenged students to conduct close readings of the text and respond to the literature in a more complex way. Teacher-questioning was essential in making this a meaningful experience across all grade levels.

Children responded daily to the literature in their *Lemonade War* response journals, a practice also conducted across all grade levels—kindergarten through sixth grade. Math teachers used *The Lemonade War* to create lessons regarding money and investment. In addition to staff support, parental involvement in the project was also crucial in helping make this reading initiative a success. Their enthusiasm for family reading time, their participation in the blog, and their excitement for the project made learning a family event on a daily basis.

In order to solidify learning and reinforce the empathy built during year one, the grant team developed the Franklin Lemonade War, a fundraiser to benefit the Alex's Lemonade Stand Foundation, an organization that raises money for childhood cancer research. The "War" officially started on National Lemonade Day, June 6. While the story *The Lemonade War* centers on two siblings that are in competition to see who could earn the most money with a lemonade stand, the school wanted to see which class could raise the most money to help support childhood cancer research. The friendly competition in the school heated up following daily reports of which grades were leading in contributions.

Some competitive first graders even started their own lemonade stand on the weekend, bringing in their earnings on Mondays to help boost their class average. When the competition was over, the school had raised over $2,000 dollars, which was donated to Alex's Lemonade Stand. The fundraiser was featured in the local newspaper; the superintendent and the school board president also visited the school to recognize the empathy, commitment, and perseverance of its students.

The community involvement and student participation surpassed expectations. The Franklin Lemonade War fostered a true community of learners and a community of advocates. Participation in a real world project-based learning experience fostered teaching for social justice as students' social awareness was increased. As young citizens in a democracy, the children of Franklin school were exposed to the positive impact they are capable of making.

The PRTC project was able to incorporate critical reading skills through the efforts of this ambitious project. Children across all grade levels became excited about literacy, sharing their thoughts at school, at home, and online. The support exhibited by the community represented collaboration with all stakeholders involved.

LESSONS LEARNED: CHALLENGES

Although this project positively impacted student understanding of bullying and its effects as evidenced in the exit survey data, not all teachers were as enthusiastic as the team. Since there was administrative support, all staff participated; however, some teachers felt the initiatives were too time-consuming. They were concerned that the One School, One Book initiative, collecting donations for the community outreach projects, and school-wide assemblies would take too much time from their required curriculum. The team had welcomed all staff to join in the PRTC efforts and meetings, knowing that inclusion in the project would increase ownership. However, the team was also aware that pressing for participation would breed resentment. This became a dilemma that needs to be worked on moving forward.

The attempt to develop a greater connection with parents was the greatest disappointment. The parents who are typically involved were enthusiastic and participated in all aspects of the project; however, the reluctant parents that the team was striving to include remained distant in spite of the strategies put forth to include them. The team's future goals include home visits to bridge home and school, strengthening the connection as well as employing phone banks in both English and Spanish to remind and encourage parents of upcoming events. Furthermore, the team would like to train parents in reading comprehension strategies in order to assist them in helping their children improve literacy skills. The challenge will continue to be finding a way to entice reluctant parents to become more involved.

CONCLUSION

It is clear that educators must address social issues if they expect to have students attain the desired academic results, and this is possible to do while still meeting state standards. In addition, character education lessons such as the ones described in this chapter can provide teachers with invaluable insights into the lives of the young people sitting before them. Moreover, educators must model a cooperative spirit with peers, parents, and children in order to promote respect. Respect must be explicitly taught and become part of the everyday school culture if it is to be a successful common goal. It is worth the time invested, not just for social aspects but for the academic rewards as well.

PRTC shone a light on the fact that students, even as young as five, have a tremendous capacity for reflection, compassion, empathy, and critical thinking. By employing brain-based strategies such as using emotional hooks, encouraging active participation, and designing lessons to engage Multiple Intelligences, students were engaged in the dialogue. It became clear that many who act out as bullies are wounded individuals themselves.

The grant team began with the premise that respect cannot be expected if not given. This two-year project strengthened that belief. Furthermore, teachers, administrators, parents, and students alike must all work together to successfully create a cooperative environment where everyone feels safe and accepted.

APPENDIX A

Bullying Scenarios:

1. Students refuse to allow a peer to sit with them during lunch in the cafeteria
2. Students call a peer names based on appearance
3. One student pushes a peer out of line
4. Students isolate a peer during recess, refusing to allow him/her to play with the group
5. One student grabs a peer's backpack and runs away with it
6. Students tease a peer because of the way he or she speaks

7. Students make fun of a student who has a physical handicap
8. Students want a peer to join them as they make fun of someone else
9. Students gossip about a peer
10. One student posts a mean comment about a peer online

APPENDIX B

Table 4.1 Literature Selections

Grade	Text	Writing Prompt	CCCS
1	Matthew and Tilly (Jones, 1991)	Brainstorm: Acts of Kindness Organize your ideas and write about your own gifts of kindness.	R.L.1.1, 1.2, 1.3, 1.7 W1.2, 1.5
2	Giraffes Can't Dance (Andreae, 1999)	Write a letter to Gerald the Giraffe discussing his experience with unkind behavior.	R.L.2.1, 2.2, 2.3, 2.7 W.2.1, 2.3
3	Wings (Myers, 2000)	Answer the following question: If you saw someone being bullied, what would you do?	R.L. 3.1, 3.2, 3.3, 3.7 W. 3.1a, 3.1b, 3.1c, 3.1d, 3.3
4, 5	The Worst of Eighth Grade (Slusarczyk, 2002)	Write about your own experiences or observations of the struggles of your peers with the issue of exclusion.	R.L. 4.1, 4.2, 4.3, W.4.3a, 4.3b, 4.3c, 4.3d, 4.3e R.L. 5.2, W.5.3a, 5.3, 5.3c, 5.3d, 5.3e

Source: New Jersey Core Curriculum Content Standards

APPENDIX C

The Worst of Eight Grade

By Brittany Slusarczyk

In the eighth grade, I have had a lot of great times, but somehow the bad always overshadows the good. I've had a couple of bad experiences in eighth grade, but I'm going to tell you about the one that hurt the most and was the worst.

When I was little everyone was friends. Then, as I grew up "clicks" started to form. I wasn't in the "popular group" because my mom wouldn't let me do what they did. I just didn't get along with some people. I had a "best friend," but eventually we grew apart. She started hanging out with some people who weren't too fond of me. I really didn't get to know my two real friends until this year. My closest friend, Mary, and I became close around two years ago, but my friend Janine and I didn't really get to know each other until this year. They are the best, and they're always there for me.

I was on the phone with Mary, as we often are, and she asked me if I had got my invitation to Joey's party. I told her that I hadn't, and we figured it was coming, since I am friendlier with that group of people. On the day of the party, she didn't mention it until lunchtime. I had no idea that it was going to be that night. We had the next day off, and I wound up sleeping over Mary's. She asked me if I had RSVP'd (replied) yet. I told her I hadn't been invited. I questioned Joey, and he played dumb. Then, I asked some other people, and they thought that everyone had been invited. I thought that I was the only one. It hurt a lot. I couldn't believe it.

After school, I had to ask my teacher Mrs. O'Rourke about a grade. She asked what was wrong, and I told her. She made me feel a lot better. I later talked to other people who told me not to worry that there were five others that were in the same boat that I was in. I wouldn't even have gone, but that's not the point.

Almost seven months have gone by and in one more month I will never have to see his face. This experience in some ways made me think of people differently. It also has made me stronger. About two months after this experience, I wrote a poem that describes everything.

There was a girl named Lucy,
Who was never quite accepted.
Dougy threw a party,
And Lucy was rejected.
23 invitations sent,
6 left behind.
All invited but one went,
Lucy was left to cry.
She confided in her favorite teacher
Who said, "You're in a different class,
That really is horrible,
But one day it will pass."
Lucy looked at her teacher,
Who was so very kind.
And she started to think
And recall things in her mind . . .
. . . She began to think that Dougy,
Through the years,
Had never been quite accepted either,
And here came the tears.
Dougy knew rejection,
But he made sure to do his part.
Leaving someone out,

Is like breaking someone's heart.
Lucy felt terrible,
She felt like dirt.
There is no excuse
To cause such a hurt!
Now Lucy is famous,
High up on the scale.
And Dougy is a loser,
On every good opportunity he would bail.
So if you are thinking,
And it may be only thinking,
Of excluding just a few.
BEWARE!!!!!!!
For it will come back to you!
There is a God
And he knows all you do.
Anything bad,
May come back and haunt you!
So reach out to all.
And save someone from
A great internal fall.

If you've ever been left out, then you know how it feels, so NEVER do it to someone else.

REFERENCES

Andreae, G. (1999). *Giraffes Can't Dance*. New York, NY: Orchard Books.

BABES World. (1979). *Beginning Awareness Basic Education Studies World*. Retrieved from Babesworld.org

Beavers, K. (2006). *Developmental Reading Assessment 2*. New York, NY: Pearson.

Bloom, B. S. (ed.). (1956). *Taxonomy of Educational Objectives: The Classification of Educational Goals—Handbook I: Cognitive Domain*. New York: Longman.

Bronfenbrenner, U., & Morris, P. A. (2006) The bioecological model of human development. In R. M. Lerner & W. Damon (Eds.), *Handbook of child psychology: Vol. 1. Theoretical models of human development* (6th edition, pp. 793–828). Hoboken, NJ: Wiley.

Culham, R. & Coutu, R. (2009) *Getting Started With the Traits: Grades 3–5*. New York, NY: Scholastic.

Davies, J. (2007). *The Lemonade War*. New York, NY: Sandpiper.

Ingersoll, R. (2012). Beginning teacher induction: what the data tells us. Phi Delta Kappan, 93(8), 47–51.

Jensen, E. (1998). *Introduction to Brain-Compatible Learning*. San Diego, CA: The Brain Store.

Jones, R. C. (1991). *Matthew and Tilly.* New York, NY: Penguin Group.

Kluth, P. & Schwarz, P. (2010) *Pedro's Whale.* Baltimore, Md: Paul H. Brookes Publishing Company, Inc.

Myers, C. (2000). *Wings.* New York, NY: Scholastic.

Roerden, L. P. (2000). *Don't Laugh at Me: Teachers Guide: Grades 2–5: Creating a Ridicule-Free Classroom.* New York: Operation Respect.

Rutledge, P. (2011). The psychological power of storytelling. *Psychology Today.* Retrieved November 25, 2015 from https://www.psychologytoday.com/blog/positively-media/201101/the-psychological-power-storytelling

Shamblin, A. & Seskin, S. (1998). Don't laugh at me. On *Don't Laugh at Me.* [CD]. Singapore: Sony/ATV Tunes.

Salmivalli, C., Poskiparta, E., Ahtola, A., & Haataja, A. (2013). The Implementation and effectiveness of the KiVa Antibullying Program in Finland. *European Psychologist,* 18, 79–88. doi 10.1027/1016-9040/a0000140.

Chapter 5

Co-Construction as a Critical Approach to Mathematics Education

Mark Francis Russo

Many high school students in senior elective classes do not consider mathematics class to be useful for their lives, nor do they learn much while they are enrolled in these courses. Countless strategies have been attempted to try and engage these students, but it may be that the problem isn't so much the pedagogy as it is the content itself. How can students who performed poorly in previous algebra courses get excited about a course that is more of the same, especially when the content has little to no significance for their lives?

Would a vastly different approach be necessary to positively impact students' experiences in these courses? With these things in mind, the course described in this chapter was based entirely on mathematics that related to students' lives or future goals. Specifically, the focus of the course was on developing students' quantitative literacy (QL), or the skills and knowledge that are necessary "to engage effectively in quantitative situations arising in life and work" (International Life Skills Survey, 2000). These types of skills are essential for educated citizens, and situations that require these skills may be an impetus to involve students in critical thinking.

Math teachers often try to incorporate applicable mathematics into their teaching, but as Appleton and Lawrenz (2011) suggested, "Mathematics teachers' ideas of what is real world or practical are not the same as their students'" (p. 150). Since one does not always know the exact type of mathematics that will speak to students' lives or experiences, students were invited to co-construct the course along with the teacher. Unlike more traditional techniques where teachers incorporate students' feedback, co-construction is a process where students work alongside their teachers to plan units, lessons, and assessments. By giving students a real voice in determining the content and structure of the course, co-construction provides a unique opportunity to engage students in significant mathematics.

Co-construction is not widely discussed in the literature, and only a handful of studies (Ahn & Class, 2011; Maskiewicz & Winters, 2012) have investigated anything similar to what was attempted in this course. In fact, there were no known studies that investigated whole-class co-construction or attempted to use co-construction in a QL classroom. The primary way that co-construction began to be understood, then, was by actually trying it with students. As a result, a deeper understanding of co-construction evolved over the course of the year.

This chapter will consider the impact of co-construction and teaching for QL on the teaching and learning of mathematics by drawing on the literature to frame the study, describing the logistics of the co-construction process, and drawing on students' and the author's reflections for examples of when students engaged more deeply and thought more critically about mathematics. Finally, implications for teaching mathematics through a more critical lens will be discussed.

ON QUANTITATIVE LITERACY

Madison and Steen (2009) argued that quantitatively literate individuals confront problems by gathering useful information, performing the mathematics, and reflecting on whether solutions are reasonable, generalizable, and valuable. This ability to think critically and solve problems is an important feature of QL, which can also help to promote the twenty-first century competencies of decision-making, communication, information literacy, and media literacy (National Research Council, 2012).

In order to foster QL skills, teachers employ certain techniques that can develop students' critical thinking skills. Teaching for QL emphasizes everyday contexts, applications, and modeling (Alsina, 2002; Quantitative Literacy Design Team, 2001), and as a result, it is often interdisciplinary (Madison, 2004; Orrill, 2001; Steen, 2001a). The fact that QL relies on context is a strength (Madison & Steen, 2009; Steen, 2001b), as context not only lends itself to motivation and student learning (Steen, 2004), but it also adds a level of complexity and significance to problem-solving.

Authors have argued for the importance of QL in interdisciplinary settings such as social studies (Crowe, 2010), English (Lutsky, 2008; Miller, 2010), business (Albers, 2002; Taylor, 2008), economics (Schuhmann, McGoldrock, & Burrus, 2005), and sociology (Howery & Rodriguez, 2006; Lindner, 2012). In an increasingly quantitative world, QL becomes ever more important, because it can help students "make reasonable judgments of and inferences from information presented to them in the media, by the government, or by other citizens" (Crowe, 2010, p. 105).

Unfortunately, in many traditional mathematics classrooms, instruction focuses primarily on preparing students for calculus (Kennedy, 2001; Steen, 2001b). This "isolated trajectory of increasing difficulty and abstraction" is appropriate for some students (Carnevale & Desrochers, 2003, p. 21), but it does not address the unique needs and interests of all. In order to engage all students, teachers can incorporate some of the tenets of democratic mathematics education. Ellis and Malloy (2007) describe democratic mathematics education as a process where students and teachers work together to reconstruct curricula that are accessible to all students, predicated on the belief that all students can learn, and designed so that each student can develop the tools to be active and responsible citizens.

The more traditional approach to mathematics education does not work for everyone, because too many students are unable or unwilling to think deeply and creatively about mathematics that is abstract, difficult, and seemingly irrelevant. What is needed is an approach that will promote critical thinking for all students by utilizing the principles of a democratic mathematic classroom and focusing on QL. Since both of these strategies require students to provide input on the direction of the course, co-construction can serve as a mechanism to promote critical thinking for all students. Despite the lack of research on whole-class co-construction, the author decided to implement this practice in two of his high school mathematics classes (Russo, 2014).

METHODOLOGY

In order to determine how teaching for QL and co-construction impacted these two classes of students, practitioner action research was chosen, because "action research is best done in collaboration with others who have a stake in the problem under investigation" (Anderson, Herr & Nihlen, 2007, p. 3). In addition, action research calls for multiple cycles of planning, acting, observing, and reflecting, thus providing opportunities to adjust instruction and planning throughout the year.

The courses were two sections of an upper-level elective course that was traditionally designated for lower-performing students. Forty-five students were enrolled in these courses, out of which forty-three were seniors. Most of these students had gone through the school's lower mathematics track, and not surprisingly, many of them did not consider mathematics to be their favorite subject.

In practice, the course was highly collaborative, as students relied on one another, as well as technology and outside resources, to engage with appropriate and important mathematics. The course was heavily project-based, as units typically built toward the creation of an end product. The unique aspect of this course, though, was the fact that students participated in the process of co-construction. Co-construction can refer to any process where teachers and students collaborate on course planning, but for this particular course, students engaged in co-construction in the following ways:

1. Students participated in large- and small-group discussions. These discussions were the key mechanism for co-construction, because they provided opportunities for students to reflect on previous units and plan for subsequent ones. These semi-structured discussions were organized around themes from student questionnaires, but students were also allowed to brainstorm and move the course in new and unexpected directions.
2. Several times per unit, students completed written questionnaires that asked about their interests and opinions regarding the course.
3. Students had the option to speak with their teacher individually or in small groups, regarding their feelings on the course. They were encouraged to communicate if they ever felt that the current unit of study was not engaging them or developing their QL, and there were several occasions where students proposed and carried out alternate units of study.
4. Finally, students were able to provide input into the type of end product they wanted to create for each unit. These decisions were sometimes made during planning discussions, but more often they were made by individuals or small groups once students were engaged in the unit.

The five units that were eventually constructed focused on statistics, budgeting, cryptography, nutrition, and road trips. Each unit was designed so that students could complete a quantitative task that was important to their lives or their futures, such as a budget or a road trip itinerary (see Appendix for examples of these assignments). In order to help students successfully complete this task and tasks like it, lessons focused on related content and skills. Students regularly completed questionnaires that helped to monitor and adjust instruction, and toward the end of each unit, planning sessions were held for students to co-construct the next unit.

The data gathered include surveys, questionnaires, assessments, and transcriptions from large- and small-group discussions, as well as the author's reflections and observations in field notes and a research journal. The constant comparative method was utilized, which involves coding data, combining events and their properties, defining theory, and putting theory into writing (Glaser & Strauss, 1967), and (Anderson & Herr's, 1999) criteria of outcome validity, process validity, democratic validity, catalytic validity, and dialogic validity were employed to ensure validity and reliability. Additionally, as both teacher and researcher, the author constantly reflected on his positionality throughout the research process, and frequently considered how he impacted students and the study in multiple, complex, and sometimes unexpected ways.

CO-CONSTRUCTION, OWNERSHIP, AND STUDENT ENGAGEMENT

The study was based on the premise that students need to be engaged in order to consistently think deeply about mathematics. The hope was that co-construction would lead to higher levels of student engagement, and that QL content would give students opportunities to think critically and relate mathematics to their lives and their future aspirations. The first charge was to engage students, and the primary way to accomplish this was by giving them more ownership through co-construction.

QL classrooms should be "driven by issues that are important to people in their lives and work" (Quantitative Literacy Design Team, 2001, p. 18), but at the beginning of the year, students seemed unaware that mathematics could be germane to their lives. As a result, during early brainstorming sessions, students suggested traditional topics like volume and area, rather than things that were more pertinent to their lives or future aspirations.

Students may have responded in this way because they were trying to impress their teacher, or perhaps because they'd never really been asked to consider the relationship between mathematics and their own interests. This is one of the deep flaws of the traditional curriculum, and one of the primary reasons why so many students struggle with mathematics. If students can't see themselves in the curriculum, then how can they think critically about the content and its application to the world around them?

As the year went on, students became more willing to engage in co-construction, whether through small-group discussions, questionnaires, project proposals, or informal discussions. This change likely took place for two reasons. First, after many conversations and planning sessions, students began to believe that their teacher genuinely cared about their ideas. Second, as the year went on, more and more students' ideas were implemented into lessons, which reinforced the fact that their suggestions and contributions actually mattered.

This change in students' attitudes toward co-construction was particularly evident in a unit on nutrition, where one student exclaimed out loud how "pumped" he was for a cooking assignment, and others expressed surprise that their idea to hold class in the kitchen was really happening. One student summed up this sentiment when he said, "It was good to have a teacher who was willing to actually listen and take note of what we wanted to learn in the class." This process took a while to develop, because the author had to modify his own preconceived notions of how the course should run in favor of what students actually wanted. Once students realized they had a real say in the style and substance of the course, they were much more willing to participate in the co-construction process and engage in the day-to-day activities of the course.

This process of ceding more control to students was evident during the co-construction of the second unit, when students were encouraged to think about some of the more complex financial decisions they would have to face as adults. It did not take long to realize that students were not interested, nor were they necessarily ready to talk about these things.

At first the author thought he was operating within their zone of proximal development (ZPD; Vygotsky, 1978), because the mathematical tasks were designed to appeal to high school seniors and prepare them with the skills they would need in college and beyond. As the year went on, though, the focus began to shift from directing students where the author thought they should go to helping them get where *they* wanted to go. For example, in one instance of co-construction a student stated the following:

> Right now I have a [poor grade] in this class because I'm not doing all the work because [our unit on codes] doesn't interest me . . . like, do I want to [work on codes], when I think I have been very active at looking at [other] things that interest me, but that's not always in my best interest.

This student admitted that he was not completing the work because the unit on codes wasn't interesting to him, and he further suggested that there was a disconnect between active learning and success in class. This was a fundamental misunderstanding of how to operate within the student's zone of proximal development (ZPD), because he had no interest in going where his teacher wanted him to go. It became clear that true co-construction requires students to have a real say in determining the objectives, and not just the process by which they get to their teacher's objectives. In order for more students to think critically about mathematics, they need to see how mathematics can be valuable in their lives, and they need to solve problems that are useful and interesting to them.

In response to this student's legitimate concerns, a more individualized co-construction process was initiated, where he was invited to work alongside his teacher to set objectives that he believed would best develop his QL. Van Oers (1996) stated that the ZPD "is constructed in the cooperation between the child and the adult on the basis of what the child wants and the actions the child actually can carry out, as well as the help the child gets from the adult" (p. 97). Previously, the co-construction process considered the

ZPD mainly in terms of "actions the child can actually carry out," but now it shifted to take into account "what the child wants" as well.

A more individualized approach to co-construction was a critical shift toward increasing student engagement. While this lesson was learned primarily through the course planning process, it also proved effective with students' actual assignments as well. In particular, developmentally appropriate lessons and assignments that enabled students to demonstrate expertise proved to be more effective at promoting interest, engagement, and as a result, student achievement.

Hidi and Renninger's (2006) model of interest development suggests that situational interest, or "focused attention and the affective reaction that is triggered in the moment by environmental stimuli," can develop into individual interest, or "a person's relatively enduring predisposition to reengage particular content over time" (p. 113). The goal of this course was to trigger students' situational interest, but also to provide opportunities for students to develop the more lasting individual interest.

One example of an assignment that triggered students' situational interest was a budget simulation, because it was the first one to meet students at a pertinent place in their development. As opposed to other assignments before it, a critical mass of students bought into this project, as students who were not usually interested were discussing what house they would live in, what car they would drive, etc.

This particular assignment also operated within students' ZPD, not only because they were able to understand the basic premises of income and expenditures, but also because the assignment grew out of students' actual interests. Most students were in the midst of college applications at the time, so they were already thinking in earnest about their lives after high school. This higher level of interest transformed the atmosphere in the room, and it likely had a positive impact on student learning. One student's reflection illustrates this point:

When doing this assignment I learned a lot. I learned that it is very, very, very expensive to live each year, and even more expensive if I were to have children. That was definitely one reason why I was turned away from having children. I definitely did not know the reality of how much my parents spend each year on everything. One thing that shocked me was the price of gas a year. In this plan we only had one car but in real life my family has four cars in which my parents pay for gas, car insurance, and any leases and repairs. This project definitely made me realize how expensive it is to live in a nice community. This definitely opened my eyes about college. I got lucky to receive a scholarship and I was very proud knowing that the cost of college a year was going to be significantly less for my family. However, it shocked me to see that college is definitely a lot more than I thought and loans are definitely going to be needed.

It appears that the budget simulation stimulated this student's situational interest, both because it drew on her experiences and things that mattered to her and extended her knowledge in significant and tangible ways. This assignment was unique in its ability to engage the majority of the class for an extended period of time, and this was due to an opportune intersection between the assignment's objectives and students' concerns at the time. In some ways, the characteristics of this assignment were not dissimilar from another successful technique that stimulated students' situational interest by tapping into their areas of expertise.

Students' situational interest increased when assignments aligned with their individual fortes. Two examples demonstrate this point, as one student who was skillful with Excel helped his friends navigate a credit card project from the unit on budgeting, while another student who was deeply withdrawn demonstrated an impressive amount of knowledge regarding fitness in the nutrition unit. In both situations students were able to study an area of interest and share their expertise with a classmate, with their teacher, or with the class as a whole.

While situational interest was promoted with well-designed lessons or lessons that acknowledged students' unique expertise, it was much more difficult to foster the more lasting, often self-generated individual interest (Hidi & Renninger, 2006). The data were analyzed to see if any of the students exhibited signs of individual interest by reengaging with "tasks related to emerging individual interest," generating "'curiosity' questions about the content of an emerging individual interest," or exceeding "task demands in their work with an emerging individual interest" (p. 115).

These descriptors pointed to a handful of students in the class, and particularly to those that initiated an individualized co-construction process. These students chose topics of interest, crafted questions that related to these topics, and worked diligently to answer these questions so that they could satisfactorily explain each topic to their teacher or peers. Individualized co-construction was a key mechanism for students to express individual interest, and furthermore, it was the single most successful technique to engage students deeply in mathematics.

CO-CONSTRUCTION, QL, AND CRITICAL THINKING

In addition to increasing student engagement, co-construction and teaching for QL provided opportunities for students to engage in higher-order thinking. In particular, small-group discussions, alternate or modified assignments, and the authentic aspect of teaching for QL spurred students to think critically about mathematics and find useful applications to their lives.

Small-group discussions were a good way to engage students in higher-order thinking, because they provided opportunities to question students about their interests. For example, in one small-group discussion on finances, the author was able to help students develop a more nuanced understanding of cost of living. At the beginning of the discussion, one student wondered whether it might be beneficial to move across the country, because the "cost of living would be drastically different if you live in New Jersey than if you live in Wyoming."

After the group reflected on this, the author asked students to consider why more people don't pack up and move to Wyoming. It was not long before a classmate mentioned the impact of salary as well as expenditures, and based on the student's "aha" reaction, he clearly came to understand cost of living in a more nuanced and complete way.

Alternate assignments were another mechanism that helped students think more purposefully about educational goals and their relationship to mathematics. It was initially uncomfortable to allow students this opportunity, but this changed when the student mentioned earlier informed the author that despite his best efforts, he could not engage in an assignment that he considered inconsequential for his life. The first reaction a teacher may have in a situation like this is to lecture the student about the importance of hard work and perseverance, but in this alternate approach to math instruction, the aim is to always have students engaged in critical thinking both with the content and the pedagogy. Therefore, students were reminded that all recourse would be taken, including alternative assignments, to enable students to improve their QL.

The decision to provide an alternate assignment (an analysis of the US highway system instead of the cryptography assignment) was somewhat risky, because it hinged on this student's ability to complete the work and his classmates' willingness to accept the decision without begrudging him or his teacher. In the end, this student's level of engagement spiked. When he delivered a presentation to the class that demonstrated a sound understanding of the topic, his classmates were impressed with the work he had done and demonstrated interest in his contribution. This example illustrates how individualized assignments that are built on student's unique interests and strengths can provide more opportunities for critical thinking, while simultaneously avoiding a potential disciplinary issue and excessive time off task.

This experiment was a success in part because of the conscientious nature of this student, but also because this student had an opportunity to reflect on the relationship between mathematics and his interests and craft an assignment that would promote both of these ends. Despite its many advantages, not all students expressed an interest in alternate assignments, perhaps because it required a certain amount of creativity to create the assignment and maturity to then relay that information to the teacher. Nevertheless, these students were able to obtain similar benefits by reconstructing or reconsidering portions of existing assignments.

For example, in a unit on finances, students had to create a budget simulation that was appropriate to their unique life circumstances, and some students asked to loosen the rules to make the assignment work better for them. The original instructions prompted students to research an average starting salary for a career of their choice and give themselves 3 percent raises annually, but one student said that as a future firefighter, it would be more appropriate to consult the salary guide and apply his raises accordingly.

Despite some initial reluctance, the author realized that a course built on QL had to use mathematics as a tool to better understand real-life contexts, rather than the other way around. In many ways, the student was given an even better opportunity to think deeply about mathematics, since instead of mechanically applying 3% raises, he could now think deeply about the structure of the salary guide and compare it with other approaches to giving raises.

Similarly, students were given a handful of requirements for the road trip assignment in the fifth unit, but some students asked If they could rent a recreational vehicle (RV), as long as they could find a place to rent it, calculate the costs of the rental, and find gas stations along their route that sold diesel gasoline. The result of these modifications was an assignment that was more interesting to students, but the fact that they adjusted these assignments was equally important, because it required students to think about how their own situations related to the mathematics, or alternatively, how mathematics interacted with their understanding of each particular situation.

A third technique that fostered critical thinking in the math classroom was the implementation of authentic tasks. The data showed that many of the less successful lessons fell victim to Ainley, Pratt, and Hansen's (2006) planning paradox, either because tasks were unrewarding due to "tightly focused learning objectives" or "less focused [and] difficult to assess" when they focused on engaging activities (p. 24). Finding the right balance between authenticity and pedagogical structure was challenging, but a handful of assignments were able to achieve this balance.

For example, both the road trip assignment and the budget simulation could be completed effectively with nothing more than a computer. Authentic assignments that proved to be successful required that students had the proper tools and technology, and this was simply impossible in the classroom for topics like codes (special encryption and decryption machines) and nutrition (monitors that measure physical activity).

Technology was an integral component of the course, because on the one hand, it made certain assignments more relevant and realistic, but on the other hand, it supplanted some of the more traditional mathematical techniques.

For example, in the nutrition unit, a student mentioned an app that could do everything they were being asked to do in an assignment. If an app can do it, and do it much better, then why should students have to do it?

Technology cannot be censored if a teacher wants to develop students' QL, nor should it be. Technology does not make mathematics obsolete, and this point is absolutely essential. Procedural skill might not be as important as it was in previous generations, but mathematical reasoning has become even more important. Students have access to all of these technologies, but they are now charged with understanding, evaluating, and applying them in various situations. While technology may have limited the amount of traditional mathematics that was done in the classroom, it increased the amount of thinking. In addition, since the thinking related to real-life situations, its value surpassed much of what was done in previous courses.

IMPLICATIONS

This study has implications for practitioners, and especially mathematics practitioners, who want to promote student engagement and foster critical thinking. One of the primary vehicles that promoted engagement in this study was whole-class co-construction. For practitioners who are not comfortable with whole-class co-construction or who operate with curricula that do not allow for this freedom, well-designed assignments that allow for self-pacing can be a valuable alternative. These types of assignments (i.e., the road trip assignment and budget simulation) were effective for the following reasons:

1. These assignments acknowledged the deeper interests and goals of students. As opposed to assignments based on perceived catchier ideas, such as codes and fantasy football, these assignments appealed to students' developing interest in the freedoms and opportunities that were going to be available to them after graduating high school.
2. Self-paced assignments were most effective because they enabled the teacher to circulate the room and work closely with small groups of students. They mitigated tensions that could have arisen if the teacher was constantly demanding everyone's attention, and they reduced unnecessary anxiety, because the teacher could focus on asking important questions of individual students rather than correcting students who were off task.
3. These lessons used appropriate and readily available technology, which increased the authenticity and relevance of assignments, and demanded an additional set of critical thinking skills.
4. Each of these assignments allowed for differentiation and individualization, which encouraged student ownership and limited cheating.

These assignments increased the level of student engagement in these classes, but more importantly they created an atmosphere that valued quantitative reasoning and critical thinking over basic skill development. Since these assignments were authentic in nature, students thought critically about the nuances of each scenario, rather than applying mathematics in an oversimplified way.

Additionally, since students either helped to create these assignments or adapted them to meet their specific interests, they were able to cultivate skills that were uniquely appropriate for them and their lives. Whether through whole-class co-construction or the creation of well-designed assignments, student choice, the ability to individualize assignments, and the presentation of problems in context can be key ingredients to help increase student engagement and critical thinking in mathematics classrooms.

CONCLUSION

With the advent of the Common Core State Standards for Mathematics, mathematics teachers are faced with the challenge of not only reaching all students, but also helping them understand more rigorous and complex mathematics than ever before. To meet this challenge head on, teachers must engage students in critical thinking, but they also need to consider new ways of understanding classroom interactions, instruction, and notions of what teaching and learning really mean. Co-construction and teaching for QL are two approaches that do just that, because they engage students in aspects of the teaching and learning process that they may have never considered before.

For perhaps the first time in their educational careers, students were asked to brainstorm and determine topics of study, propose and follow through on suitable, useful assessments, modify and even replace assignments to best meet their needs, and reflect on and evaluate the importance of these topics for their everyday lives. So, while the quantitative reasoning that took place during this course was an important factor in students' critical thinking, so too was the opportunity for students to engage in co-construction and think deeply about the structure, content, and relevance of mathematics to their lives, their desired careers, and the world around them.

APPENDIX

Budget Simulation Assignment

For this assignment, you will create a budget simulation for yourself for your twenties (22–29). In particular, your budget should have the following components:

- Income
- Spouse's Income (if applicable)
- Taxes
- Mortgage/Rent
- Loans
- Insurance (car, health, life)
- Car payments (if applicable)
- Other expenses
- Charitable contributions
- Retirement savings
- College savings
- Savings

Along the way, we will have smaller assignments that will help to prepare you for your final project.

Day 1. Today, you will create an outline for your budget.

1. Create a spreadsheet with the following columns: age, income, spouse's income, and total salary. Enter ages 22 through 29 under the age column.
2. Perform some research on your dream job. Find out the average starting salary for this job, and plug that into your income column for age 22.
3. Let's assume that you get a 3% raise per year. How can you figure out what your salary will be when you turn 23? You can use a calculator to do this, but I would like you to plug in an equation and then drag it down. If you need some help, think of how you would do the math on the calculator, except instead of plugging in the salary on your calculator, just click on the correct cell. Then, drag this down so you have your salary for every year of your twenties.
4. I know this is projecting quite a bit, but this is just a simulation. Do you plan on getting married? If so, how old will you be? Now, to get even more creative, think through an ideal job for your spouse. Then, repeat steps 2 and 3 for your spouse, and enter his or her salary for age x–29 (where x indicates your age when you get married).
5. Now, type in an equation to determine your total salary. You may want to color code this column, but that is up to you.

Day 2. Today, you will look into taxes, loans, and your mortgage/rent.

1. Visit http://www.bankrate.com/finance/taxes/tax-brackets.aspx to find out the tax brackets for 2013 (we will use these, even though they may change before you turn 22). Create a column for taxes, and calculate your total taxes for each year in your twenties. This is slightly challenging to do,

so let me give you an example. Let's say that you and your spouse make 175,000 together. You will be charged 10% on your first 17,850, 15% up until 72,500, 25% up to 146,400, and then 28% beyond. The mathematics here will be as follows: .10 (17,850) + .15 (the difference between 72,500 and 17,850) + .25 (the difference between 146,400 and 72,500) + .28 (the difference between 175,000 and 146,400). If you need help, please ask me or consult http://www.moneycrashers.com/calculate-federal-income-tax-brackets-rate-tables/. Once again, please use Excel to do this, rather than an online or personal calculator (note: this is a drastically oversimplified version of your tax liability. In reality, children, loans, charitable contributions, and mortgage payments all reduce the taxes you have to pay. If you want to make your budget more realistic, please ask me for help, but this is optional).

2. Once again, visit amortizationtable.org and determine your monthly payment. Please add this to your budget (convert to yearly).

3. Let's assume, for the sake of argument, that you eventually want to buy a house. Most people cannot buy a house right away, because they need to save up some money for a down payment. Let's assume that you want to rent for the first five years (22–26), and then you want to buy when you're 27.

   a. Create a column entitled mortgage/rent.

   b. Do some research on apartments/condos/houses for rent in an area of your choosing (you can use craigslist for this, among other websites). Determine the type of apartment you want, and determine the monthly rent. Add this to your budget (convert).

   c. Do the same research for houses (you may have to use a different website—njmls.com works well for NJ). Find an area that you want to live, a type of house that you want, and then calculate your monthly mortgage payment. You can use http://www.zillow.com/mortgage-calculator/ to calculate your monthly payment. Note: many people get a 30-year mortgage, and for argument's sake, assume a 5% interest rate. Now, to figure out your mortgage amount, you will need to subtract the price of the house from whatever you think you can pay upfront (down payment). You can always go back and change this later, but make a prediction about how much money you will be able to save from your first five years of working. Then, the difference between the house price and your down payment will be your mortgage amount. Please calculate your monthly payments, and add this to your spreadsheet (convert) (note: the calculator on Zillow.com includes taxes and home insurance).

   d. In addition to your rent/mortgage, you will have to pay utilities and the cable bill. These vary so much from month to month and house to house, so just for argument's sake, assume $250 a month for all utilities and $125 a month for phone, cable, and Internet (if you want these things). Please add these to your spreadsheet (convert).

Day 3. Today, you will look at insurance, car payments, other expenses, and charitable contributions.

1. You will more than likely need a car. You can either buy new, buy used or lease a car.
   a. If you want to buy a car, do research on the price. It is possible that you might not have enough money when you are 22, so maybe you use your old car until you turn 24 or 25. If so, put a 0 in car payments for age 22, 23, etc., and then put the lump sum payment in car payments for whatever year you will buy the car. Then, you can put 0 in all years after that.
   b. Perhaps you want to lease. If so, do some research on the car you're interested in, and calculate your monthly payment (you can use http://www.edmunds.com/calculators/car-lease.html, for example). Make sure you convert. Cars are often leased for three years, so at the end of those three years you will have the option to lease a new car, or buy out the rest of the lease on your current car. If you choose to buy out your lease, you should include a lump sum (assume 50% is the residual value of your car) in that final year, and then 0 subsequently. Alternatively, you can continue leasing a new car.
2. Calculate your monthly car insurance. You will probably have to Google something to the effect of "What is average monthly car insurance payment for 22-year-old female in New Jersey?" Make sure you convert.
3. It would probably be good if you received health insurance from your job. If this is not the case, then you will have some challenging, potentially expensive work to do. For the sake of this project, let's assume that you have coverage from your employer.
4. Now, include additional expense columns (per year, remember), for things like cell phone, gas, groceries (if it helps, I spend about $125 a week for a family of five, and I spent around $100 for just me and my wife), charitable contributions, etc. If you plan on having a baby(ies), you may want a baby column as well. You might also want to consider an emergency expenses column, a gift column, an entertainment column, etc. These will all be estimates, but remember, you want yearly (not monthly) estimates.

Day 4. Today, you will look at savings for kids' college and your own retirement.

1. Do you plan on having kids? If so, how many? You might want to consider starting a college fund. Look at http://www.archimedes.com/vanguard/csp.phtml. I would just put the child's current age at 0, choose a price for the college you think you might want to send your child to, put $0 as your planned contribution, and finally, I would put the percentage of cost at

33%. The reason I say this is because you may want to split up your kid's college costs between your savings, the amount you can pay at the time, and then loans. This is just a suggestion. Find out the amount you must save per month, and then convert this to yearly. Do the same for all of your children, and combine these totals into a column for college savings.

2. Calculate your yearly retirement savings (http://finance.yahoo.com/ calculator/retirement/ret02/ is a good website). Play around with this website for a bit. Notice how much the numbers change if you are aged 35 as opposed to 25 (It is a really good idea to start saving as soon as you can). Also notice the number of years of post-retirement income. Basically, this is asking you to predict how long you will live after retirement. Please add this amount to your spreadsheet.
3. Now, you can create an expenses column. Please use an equation to calculate this (you may want to color code. This is up to you).
4. Finally, create a savings column (again, use an equation).

Day 5. Today is the day you have to finish your project. Now that you have your savings, you need to go back and see whether you have saved enough to get a down payment for your house, buy a car, etc. Once you have finalized and cleaned up your budget, find three cells underneath your budget and describe, in words, the following:

1. What do you plan on doing with your savings? Please be specific. Your discussion should relate to some of the other items in your budget, such as mortgage, car, etc.
2. Describe, in detail, something you learned from this assignment. Please be specific.
3. What questions did this project raise? What would you like to know more about? Please be specific.

Road Trip Assignment

For this assignment, we will explore some of the mathematics that you might encounter in a road trip. You are welcome to work with one other person, if you would like, but then you will have to factor in expenses for two people, and also split the bill.

This project will have multiple parts, and I will outline them below.

1. Before starting your road trip, I would like you to get a bit more comfortable with your car, and specifically, with all of the indicators on your dashboard. For each gauge, answer the following questions:

a. What does each gauge measure?
b. What are the unit(s)?
c. Is there an acceptable range with which you should be driving?
d. How does the gauge actually work?
Speedometer, Odometer, Tachometer, Fuel Gauge, Temperature
2. Now, you will plan a road trip. Your road trip must meet the following requirements:
   a. It must be a loop that returns home by a different route.
   b. It must include at least five stops, not including home (points of interest).
   c. Assume you cannot go more than four hours without a bathroom break.
   d. It must be at least twelve hours in each direction.
   e. You must stop for food at least three times every day.
   f. You must stop for gas, obviously (note: you should find out how much gas your car holds, and your car's average MPG).
   g. Your road trip must include at least two days.
   h. You must stay overnight somewhere.
3. Please describe, in detail, each leg of your journey (note: you may want to do steps 3 and 4 together).
   a. Starting Point—What time do you leave and why did you choose this time?
   b. Leg 1—How far do you drive? What is your speed? How long do you drive? At what time do you arrive at your first stop? Please explain, in detail, how you determined your speed. This description must include research on speed limits, and a reference to traffic congestion on that particular route during the specific times you will be driving.
   c. Stop 1—Give me an address, and tell me the purpose of your stop (i.e., gas and food, or bathroom, food and Tour of Jacobs Field).
      i. Is this a gas stop? What time do you arrive? How long do you stay? How much gas is left in your tank when you arrive (**show me the math**)? How much is gas at this gas station? How much will you pay, based on how empty your tank is?
      ii. Food stop? What time do you arrive? How long do you stay? Do you have to buy anything? If so, do research to determine how much you will pay.
      iii. Bathroom stop? What time do you arrive? How long do you stay?
      iv. Or point of interest? What time do you arrive? How long do you stay? Do you have to buy anything? If so, do research to determine how much you will pay.
      v. A sleeping stop? What time do you arrive? How long do you stay? Do they have a vacancy on the given date? What type of room will

you get? Do they provide breakfast? Wi-fi? Will you need to pay extra
for those things? Do research to determine how much you will pay.
  vi. Note: If there is an overlap (i.e., gas and food, bathroom and sleep-
      ing, food and bathroom and sleep), please answer questions for
      each category (no need to answer same question twice, such as
      how long will you stay).
  d. Leg 2—Repeat
  e. Stop 2—Repeat
  f. Continue repeating for the length of your trip.
4. Please print out a map, and in pen, draw your road trip on the map. Your
   annotations must include all stops, including food stops, gas stops, bathroom breaks. Please label the time and date at each one of your stops.
   In between each stop, please label the distance, time, and estimated speed
   you will be traveling on the road.
5. Calculate the total costs of the trip. Please include the following:
   a. Gas (include your first tank of gas)
   b. Food
   c. Hotel
   d. Points of Interest
   e. Depreciation of Car: Note, go to KBB Cost to Own Calculator.
      Go through the process to calculate your five-year cost to own. Once
      you finish, click on "See Yearly breakdown," and zone in specifically
      on the depreciation cost for your year (i.e., if it is a 2010, you are in
      year 5; if your car is older than five years, just choose 5). Write this
      number down. (Let's say it's $1,100, for argument's sake.) Then, go
      down to customize, and change the number of miles. The default is
      15,000. Change it to 17,500, and see how your number changes. For
      example, let's say that $1,100 is now $1,275. That means that an addi-
      tional 2,500 miles would depreciate your car by $175. Now, you prob-
      ably didn't drive 2,500 miles, but you can use this ratio to figure out
      how much your car depreciated in value.
   f. You can set up a proportion:

$$\frac{\text{depreciation \$ based on KBB}}{2500} = \frac{x}{\text{number of miles you drove}}$$

   Solve for x

6. By the time you are done, you must have answers to question 1, a detailed
   map, a detailed accounting of each leg and stop of your trip, and total costs.
   Your final project will be a PowerPoint (and handwritten map) or a poster.

REFERENCES

Ahn, R. & Class, M. (2011). Student-centered pedagogy: Co-construction of knowledge through student-generated midterm exams. *International Journal of Teaching and Learning in Higher Education, 23*(2), 269–281.

Ainley, J., Pratt, D., & Hansen, A. (2006). Connecting engagement and focus in pedagogic task design. *British Educational Research Journal, 32*(1), 23–38.

Albers, D. J. (2002). A genuine interdisciplinary partnership: MAA unveils mathematics for business decisions. *Focus, Mathematical Association of America, 15.*

Alsina, C. (2002). Too much is not enough: Teaching maths through useful applications with local and global perspectives. *Educational Studies in Mathematics, 50,* 239–250.

Anderson, G. L. & Herr, K. (1999). The new paradigm wars: Is there room for rigorous practitioner knowledge in schools and universities? *Educational Researcher, 28*(5), 12–21, 40.

Anderson, G. L., Herr, K., & Nihlen, A. S. (2007). *Studying your own school: An educator's guide to practitioner action research.* Thousand Oaks, CA: Corwin Press.

Appleton, J. J. & Lawrenz, F. (2011). Student and teacher perspectives across mathematics and science classrooms: the importance of engaging contexts. *School Science and Mathematics, 111*(4), 143–155.

Carnevale, A. P. & Desrochers, D. M. (2003). The democratization of mathematics. In L. A. Steen (Ed.), *Quantitative literacy: Why numeracy matters for schools and colleges* (pp. 21–31). Washington, DC: National Council on Education and the Disciplines.

Crowe, A. R. (2010). "What's math got to do with it?": Numeracy and social studies education. *The Social Studies, 101,* 105–110.

Ellis, M. & Malloy, C. (2007). Preparing teachers for democratic mathematics education. In D. Pugalee, A. Rogerson, & A. Schinck (Eds.), *Proceedings of the ninth international conference: Mathematics education in a global community* (pp. 160–164). Charlotte, NC.

Glaser, B. G. & Strauss, A. L. (1967). *The discovery of grounded theory: Strategies for qualitative research.* New Brunswick, NJ: Aldine Transaction.

Hidi, S. & Renninger, K. A. (2006). The four-phase model of interest development. *Educational Psychologist, 41*(2), 111–127.

Howery, C. B. & Rodriguez, H. (2006). Integrating data analysis (IDA): Working with sociology departments to address the quantitative literacy gap. *Teaching Sociology, 34*(1), 23–38.

International Life Skills Survey. 2000. *Policy Research Initiative.* Statistics Canada.

Kennedy, D. (2001). The emperor's vanishing clothes. In L. A. Steen (Ed.), *Mathematics and democracy: The case for quantitative literacy* (pp. 55–59). Washington, DC: National Council on Education and the Disciplines.

Lindner, A. M. (2012). Teaching quantitative literacy through a regression analysis of exam performance. *Teaching Sociology, 40*(1), 50–59.

Lutsky, N. (2008). Arguing with numbers: Teaching quantitative reasoning through argument and writing. In B. L. Madison & L. A. Steen (Eds.), *Calculation vs. context: Quantitative literacy and its implications for teacher education* (pp. 59–74). Washington, DC: Mathematical Association of America.

Madison, B. L. (2004). Two mathematics: Ever the twain shall meet. *Peer Review, 6*(4), 9–13.

Madison, B. L. & Steen, L. A. (2009). Confronting challenges, overcoming obstacles: A conversation about quantitative literacy. *Numeracy, 2*(1), 1–25.

Maskiewicz, A. C. & Winters, V. A. (2012). Understanding the co-construction of inquiry practices: A case study of a responsive teaching environment. *Journal of Research in Science Teaching, 49*(4), 429–464.

Miller, J. (2010). Quantitative literacy across the curriculum: Integrating skills from English composition, mathematics, and the substantive disciplines. *The Educational Forum, 74*(4), 334–346.

National Research Council. (2012). Education for life and work: Developing transferable knowledge and skills in the 21st century. *Report Brief*, July 2012.

Orrill, R. (2001). Preface: Mathematics, numeracy, and democracy. In L. A. Steen (Ed.), *Mathematics and democracy: The case for quantitative literacy* (pp. xiii–xx). Washington, DC: National Council on Education and the Disciplines.

Quantitative Literacy Design Team. (2001). The case for quantitative literacy. In L. A. Steen (Ed.), *Mathematics and democracy: The case for quantitative literacy* (pp. 1–22). Washington, DC: National Council on Education and the Disciplines.

Russo, M. F. (2014). *Quantitative literacy and high school mathematics: The evolution of a collaboratively constructed course and its impact on students' attitudes and numeracy.* Ed.D. dissertation, Montclair State University, 293 pp.

Schuhmann, P. W., McGoldrock, K., & Burrus, R. T. (2005). Student quantitative literacy: Importance, measurement, and correlation with economic literacy. *American Economist, 49*(1), 49–65.

Steen, L. A. (2001a). Embracing numeracy. In L. A. Steen (Ed.), *Mathematics and democracy: The case for quantitative literacy* (pp. 107–116). Washington, DC: National Council on Education and the Disciplines.

Steen, L. A. (2001b). Mathematics and numeracy: Two literacies, one language. *The Mathematics Educator, 6*(1), 10–16.

Steen, L. A. (2004). Everything I needed to know about averages . . . I learned in college. *Peer Review 6*(4), 4–8.

Taylor, C. (2008). Preparing students for the business of the real (and highly quantitative) world. In B. L. Madison and L. A. Steen (Eds.), *Calculation vs. context: Quantitative literacy and its implications for teacher education* (pp. 109–124). Washington, DC: Mathematical Association of America.

Van Oers, B. (1996). Learning mathematics as a meaningful activity. In L. P. Steffe, P. Nesher, P. Cobb, G. A. Goldin & B. Greer (Eds.), *Theories of mathematical learning* (pp. 91–113). Mahwah, NJ: Erlbaum.

Vygotsky, L. S. 1978. *Mind in society: The development of higher psychological processes.* Cambridge MA: Harvard University Press.

Chapter 6

Critical Pedagogy and the Teaching of Reading for Social Action

Fernando Naiditch

When the teacher asked the students "What did the author mean?" I blushed. Did she actually know what the author meant?—because I didn't. More often than not, teachers like the one I was observing that day ask students to read and find the right answer, the one and only meaning of a text, as if reading were about uncovering one particular truth that a writer had established. Teaching reading as deciphering or guessing what writers mean does not seem to be the appropriate route to developing reading skills.

In practice, one cannot know the author's intentions or messages unless the author is there to guide readers in the process. What we, as readers, can do is create our own meanings based on the ways we understand and interpret what we read or, at the very least, reconstruct meaning by using the clues that an author gives us.

Reading is not a guessing game, some kind of treasure hunt where teachers reward the student who can rescue the "original" meaning of a text. More-over, there is no such thing as original meaning that needs to be salvaged from incorrect or misguided interpretations. One cannot say that reading is not about getting meaning, though. People do read to get information and to expand their knowledge. However, much of the meaning of reading has to do with assigning meaning. Reading is an interactive process and mean-ing is constructed as a result of the dialogue between a text and a reader (Rosenblatt, 1996).

Reading teachers, novice or experienced, face the hard task of having to teach students how to read by moving beyond the mere "surface level" of reading (finding meanings in the text) into a more critical perspective (assign-ing meaning to what is being read). Many teachers struggle in trying to recon-cile these two perspectives as they teach learners how to read.

In addition, teachers also struggle with assessment, particularly as it relates to the expected outcomes of reading. Instead of being evaluated based on what the students consider relevant and meaningful (what the text means to the students), students are evaluated on what teachers expect them to take from a reading activity (what the teachers think the text should mean).

In this chapter, we will explore the contributions of critical pedagogy to the teaching of reading and discuss an approach that helps learners move beyond the level of comprehension and use what they have learned in reading toward engaging in some kind of social action. For reading to be effective and purposeful for both teachers and students, there needs to be a concrete connection between the text and the real world; and this connection can be achieved through encouraging social action.

CRITICAL PEDAGOGY AND THE TEACHING OF READING

Reading has been used in classrooms both as a tool for language development and as a way of supplementing and extending content area knowledge (Rudman, 1993; Smallwood, 2004). In order to develop the ability to read, learners need to be taught not only to understand what is presented in a text (comprehension), but to activate their previous knowledge, make comparisons and connections (analysis), and create new knowledge (synthesis).

A critical approach to the teaching of reading involves the search for multiple possible interpretations and requires that teachers stimulate differences in the way readers relate to a text. Equally important, learning to read a text critically requires developing an awareness of how the themes that students read can lead to individual and collective transformation.

Paulo Freire (1970) hit a nerve when he elaborated on the dichotomy of students as subjects as opposed to objects of their own learning process. In contrast to more traditional or conservative approaches to education that are based on rote learning and that do not encourage the development of critical thinking skills or creativity in the classroom, the idea that students should take a stance and express their own beliefs and views toward the material at hand must have sounded revolutionary. Approaches like this, which essentially constitute students as objects, deny learners the opportunity to become engaged in their own learning. Teachers silence any other voice but theirs, and reading becomes an activity of finding the meanings the teacher expects students to find—the right answers, the one accepted interpretation.

A critical approach to education, on the other hand, highlights the importance of having learners actively engaged in their leaning process and being able to find and develop their opinions and positions (Freire, 2005). Even for teachers who believe that to be true, however, there still seems to be a distance between this philosophical orientation and the actual classroom practice. Freire (1992) believed that for the learner to move from *object* to *subject*, he or she needed to be involved in dialogical action with the teacher and the materials being studied. Dialogical action has two basic dimensions, reflection and action. Freire's view is visually expressed through the following function: Action + Reflection = word = work = praxis.

In transposing this "formula" to the teaching of reading, teachers need to encourage learners to reflect on what they read, create, and discuss possible interpretations, and move toward some kind of action based on what is read. In the Freirean praxis, the word is the precursor to work and that is the ultimate purpose of becoming a reader. Engaging in critical reflection requires "moving beyond the acquisition of new knowledge and understanding, into questioning existing assumptions, values, and perspectives" (Cranton 1996, p. 76). Assisting learners in undertaking critical reflection is a frequently espoused aim of education (Bright, 1996; Brookfield, 1994) but it is a goal that is not easily achieved.

For Freire (2002), literacy is a political act. In a democratic society, schools serve as the place where students learn to become informed citizens. Schools empower learners toward participation and action by teaching them how to listen, how to identify alternatives, how to consider possibilities, and how to search for multiple possible answers. From this perspective, reading is a liberating activity. and not an action of conformity (Freire, 1992). In and outside the classroom, the political awareness that one gains through assigning meanings to the knowledge one brings into the school leads further to the dissemination of that knowledge and to the production of new knowledge.

Freire's political-pedagogical discourse reveals an interconnectedness between the social and the political being. In fact, his well-known problem-posing framework is a result of this concern of education being associated with people learning how to solve daily problems collectively and collaboratively. As established through the idea of dialogical action, critical pedagogy presupposes the teaching and learning of words and actions. This means that a sound critical pedagogical practice needs to focus on identifying and discussing problems that affect a certain community, and it will only result in transformation if accompanied by some kind of action (Freire, 2006).

The power of knowledge and the ability to question and reflect should be seen as an essential tool to intervene in the world (Gadotti, 2005). Through cooperation, dialogic subjects are able to "focus their attention on the reality which mediates them and which—posed as a problem—challenges them. The response to that challenge is the action of dialogical subjects upon reality in order to transform it" (Freire, 1970, p. 149).

The teaching of reading is an appropriate vehicle for teachers to help learners develop critical thinking skills (Krashen, 2004), a way to enable students to develop reasoning and argumentative skills, and a means to learn to express their opinions in socially acceptable ways (Naiditch, 2006). Reading approaches like the one described in the introduction of this article, where the teacher asks students to identify the author's intended meanings, personify Freire's criticism of "banking" education where learners are constituted as repositories to be filled with information by a teacher, who embodies both official knowledge and the established authority (Apple, 2000).

Many teachers would choose this *one-way-street approach* (Naiditch, 2003) to reading as a way of establishing authority and hierarchy in the classroom. This often results from a need to preserve control and maintain the teacher's sense of security. Established curricula often provide rigid scripts for content and teachers often feel pressured to "get through" the material. In addition, many teachers are not prepared to deal with diversity of opinions and pluralism in the classroom and prefer to have students search for the one "correct" answer. These kinds of teachers are the ones who usually choose a top-down approach to education (Senge, 1990) and do not see their classroom as an arena for learning and practicing democracy. Students who are taught to find the expected or the acceptable answer echo Freire's own observations as he developed his approach to the teaching of literacy under Brazil's military regime.

In fact, for learners who are taught under such circumstances, the idea of one only way of looking at the world goes beyond learning how to read; it is part of what is considered their official history: one only widely accepted possible interpretation of world events. In his well-known motto of reading the word as a metaphor for reading the world (Freire & Macedo, 2001), Freire argued for multiple voices to coexist in the classroom. These voices represent not only pluralism or diversity, but the actual existence and acknowledgment of multiple identities in the classroom that need to be affirmed, recognized, valued, and respected.

A critical approach to the teaching of reading, thus, looks at learners as *subjects* who need to be empowered to elaborate on and express their views. Reading becomes as much about getting information as it is about assigning meanings and creating interpretations based on what is presented. This does not mean that, in reading a text, anything goes. Interpretation needs to be based on facts presented in a text and students need to learn how to develop points of view based on reality. However, reality is a much broader concept than what some teachers would like to think and it encompasses each individual student and the personal and collective histories in a classroom.

The Freirean praxis presupposes a shared dialogue of experiences among educators and students in order to understand social, political, and economic context as well as creating new knowledge and possible solutions for the challenges one faces. From a critical perspective, the teaching of reading should reflect Freire's praxis of exercising dialogue as a way of potentially transforming social condition. Teaching students to read critically requires strengthening the dyad "comprehension-action" (Freire, 1992) in the Freirean approach and assessing its effectiveness in transforming the relationship between teacher, student, text, and knowledge.

The classroom, therefore, becomes a locus for the generation of knowledge and action. It is a participatory sphere, engaged and sometimes improvisational, that promotes liberation from established, official narratives and conventional action. The challenge is not limited to the students—it is also assumed by the teachers who must continually question and renew their own practice. In this space, learners develop a deeper understanding of their social environment, their histories, and themselves. They also learn to develop their social visions (Simon, 1992) and explore possible ways of acting upon and affecting the world around them.

Learning to Read Critically: Skills and Strategies

The problem-posing approach to education has been used as a way to help learners develop critical thinking skills. It has also been associated with a student-centered curriculum that promotes active, inquiry-based learning (Shor, 1992, Quintero & Rummel, 2003). Problem-posing also extends on Freire's idea of dialogical action by putting learners in a position of "critical co-investigators" who engage "in dialogue with the teacher" (Freire, 1970, p. 68) and with the material at hand (Naiditch, 2009).

The problem-posing approach to developing critical thinking skills starts with the identification of a problem that comes from students. It can be a personal, collective, or social conflict that needs to be addressed. A teacher must be able to listen carefully to students in order to establish trust and to elicit the issues that the students bring to class. This model of listening represents one of the foundations of critical thinking skills. The problem-posing approach develops this and other skills, including:

- Identifying (students identify issues)
- Understanding (students develop a broad understanding of the issue they identified)
- Making meaningful relationships (students relate their issue to other issues and to the larger socioeconomic and political contexts)
- Analyzing (students understand cause and effect, reasons and consequences, and make generalizations)
- Creating solutions (students come up with possible ways of addressing the issue at hand)

Auerbach (1992) has elaborated on five steps for learners to go through within the problem-posing approach. By following these steps, teachers will be guiding students toward the development of their critical thinking skills:

1. Describe the Content

The content comes from what is referred to as a code. Codes originate from learners' experiences and reflect the problem being posed (Wallerstein, 1983). They are presented through any kind of media (written, oral, visual). The code, for example, can be a reading passage, a newspaper article, a photograph, a brochure of some kind, etc.

2. Define the Problem

Defining the problem means uncovering the issue presented in the code, that is, what students have identified as a problem that needs to be addressed.

3. Personalize the Problem

It has been argued that unless students are able to personalize an issue and relate it to their lives, cultures, and experiences, the process will not make sense to them (Duckworth, 2006). An issue needs to be *theirs* to become meaningful and relevant.

4. Discuss the Problem

Once the problem has been identified and personalized, students need to engage in a contextualized discussion. This implies analyzing all the different aspects of an issue: its socioeconomic importance, political consequences, personal and collective values, how it affects the students individually and as a community.

5. Discuss Alternatives to the Problem

This step involves students' suggestions on how to deal with and resolve the problem being posed. Students need to create different ways of addressing the problem and weigh all the possible consequences of their various choices.

As can be seen from these steps, the development of critical thinking skills is associated to not only selecting a problem to be investigated but making it meaningful to one's context and larger community by relating to it on personal (the individual student) and collective (the classroom, the school, the community or the larger society) levels. Teachers act as facilitators of this process, and it is their job to guide the students through these steps with questions that engage students and make them consider an issue from different angles.

LEARNING TO READ CRITICALLY: CONSCIENTIZAÇÃO AND PROBLEMATIZAÇÃO

Freire's (2002) idea of *conscientização* (consciousness) embodies this educational tenet, which establishes that learners need to access and make use of their personal experiences so they become shared experiences and generate the content (generative themes) to be dealt with as part of the class. All of these are considered skills that need to be developed as part of a critical pedagogical approach to education. As far as reading is concerned, these skills are essential in forming critical readers. To do so, teachers need to observe the following three steps:

1. Understanding and defining reading

In order to establish new relationships between reader and text, teachers need to develop new understandings of reading. One can only do that by first uncovering what students understand by reading. Some of the responses I have received from students in class, for example, included: "We read to learn new things;" "Authors are people with a lot of knowledge and teachers want us to read to learn about things;" "Reading is very lonely;" "Reading is boring;" "We have to read because we need to learn about the world." How do we move from these ideas to the idea of reading as an active process, one that involves collaboration between text and reader? If the reader does not believe that he has an active role in the process, then reading classes are bound to become boring and meaningless, as some students describe them.

2. Problematizing the relationship between text and reader

Based on students' understanding of what reading is and what it entails, and how it can be used to develop critical thinking, teachers can move on to the problematization (problematização) of the relationship between text and reader. This process requires students to confront the views expressed in a text with their own views of the topic being presented. This is not an easy skill to develop, as any kind of problematization involves drawing critically upon one's experiences and asserting one's position.

Students need to understand that a text is not always "right." They need to be taught to argue with a text, to agree and disagree with an author, to confront what is being read. This requires the development of a skeptical attitude. In a critical reading class, it is essential that teachers encourage learners to question what they read by brainstorming possible ways of interpreting a text. The process of questioning an author's voice can help students to find their own voices.

Passive readers are taught to always relate to a text to get or extract information. They are taught to look for the author's meaning or the message that is being conveyed. Active readers, on the other hand, understand reading as a pluralistic activity; an activity which requires students to engage in an interaction with what they read with the purpose of generating meanings and ideas. Teachers also need to make sure they expose students to a variety of text genres, so students can get enough breadth and depth for their subsequent analysis.

In the end, students need to imagine themselves as "co-authors" of the texts they read and teachers need to develop classroom procedures that allow students to search for their voices in the texts they read. The classroom can only became a real place of knowledge production in the moment learners and teachers take ownership of the learning space and use it for reflection and research.

3. Becoming active readers by developing horizontal power relationships

Transforming students into active readers implies elevating them to the level of co-writers of a text by empowering them to dialogue with a text. What this means is that learners are encouraged to develop a conversation with a text by identifying its perspective and contrasting it with their own. This is not an easy task, especially for learners who have been taught to believe that their contribution or knowledge is not valued in the classroom or that they read to get information only. This kind of vertical power relationship that we see in more traditional classroom settings does not encourage pluralism. The teacher represents the knowledge that needs to be gained and the texts are the vehicle through which this knowledge is transmitted.

Developing a critical perspective requires teachers to create an atmosphere of *horizontal learning patterns* (Naiditch, 2009) where everyone's knowledge and backgrounds are recognized and learners' contributions and perspectives are encouraged and valued as much as that of the teacher or the authors of a text. Students can only begin to develop critical thinking skills when they perceive the classroom as a space of horizontal power relationships where there is no one-knowledge that is more important or more valued. In fact, when teachers position themselves as equal members of the classroom community as opposed to authority figures, students will feel more at ease when sharing their personal histories.

Critical thinking presupposes no asymmetrical power relationships between teachers and learners or between learners and text. Everyone is on equal status and everyone's experiences are valued and relevant. The teacher and the text are just two more voices that add to the multiplicity of perspectives in the classroom.

Developing horizontal power relationships for classroom instruction implies seeing everyone as both a teacher and a student, as both a reader and an author. It also implies understanding reading as a dialogue and classrooms as dialogic spaces for comprehension and action. This approach to education has the potential of helping maximize the classroom space and time by creating an emancipating perspective for developing teaching and learning.

Traditional approaches to the teaching of reading have focused on teaching learners the subskills involved in reading (Harmer, 2001). Those subskills were also used as reading strategies for learners to deconstruct a text into smaller parts, search for specific pieces of information, and, in doing so, reconstruct the larger meaning. Such subskills and strategies involved, for example, skimming and scanning. Students are taught how to skim through a text to find the main ideas (reading for gist) and how to scan it to find specific information, usually in the form of proper nouns, names, dates, and numbers (Matthews, Spratt & Dangerfield, 1990).

As reading strategies, skimming, and scanning are useful tools that help students achieve that first layer of meaning, which is reading for information—what the text is about and the arguments presented. Further strategies need to be used for readers to interact with the text on a deeper level to uncover other layers of meanings.

In developing a more critical approach to the teaching of reading, teachers need to think of strategies that help learners move beyond the mere identification and description of the elements of a text. Learners do need to be able to identify the topic of a reading passage and describe the elements that were mentioned by its author. However, the focus of a critical reading class should be on strategies that require learners to extrapolate the meanings of a text by exercising skills, such as the following:

Creating Meaningful Relationships

The first step in developing critical thinking skills through reading is to ask learners to relate what they read to what they know about the topic. Many teachers use this approach as a pre-reading activity, as a way of arousing students' interest in reading a certain text, and creating a reason for learners to read. This skill can also be developed as a post-reading activity to help learners examine and question "previous" and "new" knowledge: what they knew about something and what new information they have gathered.

Comparing Information

The process of comparison, by definition, requires that learners recognize at least two realities. By comparing two points of view, learners are challenged to confront "new" information with what they already knew (or thought) about a certain topic.

Interpreting the Meaning of a Text

When it comes to interpretation, it is extremely important for the teacher to recognize the value of different (but plausible) interpretations. Interpreting the meaning of a text requires that students contrast the reality described in the text to their own reality and context so they can make sense of what they read and create meaning. Interpretation also involves filtering what is read based on individual experiences and emotions. As part of a larger critical process of interpretation, it is essential for teachers to realize that students have different perspectives based on their own life experiences and their way of relating to the word and the world. Therefore, as long as learners are able to use the text to support their interpretation, teachers should allow for and expect open-ended possibilities.

Analyzing the Text

Analysis of a text is a result of the interpretation process. Students are required to look at the text in terms of what it means for them culturally and socially. An analysis of a text may also require students to direct their attention to specific parts of the text and focus on the nature of a particular element or feature of the text. Analyzing a text involves being able to look into its nature and production conditions aiming at understanding its constituent elements.

Synthesizing

The process of synthesis refers to students' ability to summarize what was read and to create possible generalizations. If interpretation and analysis require breaking up the larger text into small components to understand the whole picture, the process of synthesis represents the opposite. Students need to be able to elaborate their conclusions and this requires that they combine (or better, recombine) and (re)arrange the different elements of a text to get to a conclusion. In a way, synthesizing is a process of reconstructing mean-ing—personal (what the text means to individual students) and collective (what the text means to the group) meanings. The process of synthesis can also be understood as reconciliation, as students need to take all the perspectives presented in class into account and formulate their own perspective.

Assessing

The assessment of a text is perhaps one of the most difficult skills learners need to develop. This is because assessment requires the development of personal values and judgment. Assessment involves establishing both your personal set of values in relation to what was read and the criteria used to judge the esthetic and content value of a text. Critical assessment does not mean what some traditional approaches to reading suggest (*Did you like this text?*); it goes further into selecting appropriate criteria for the appreciation of the social value of a text. The concern with assessment within the framework of critical pedagogy should be on how the text contributes to our understanding of the human condition. A critical assessment also allows learners to develop an appreciation of the elements of nature and humankind present in a text.

Developing Social Action

From a critical perspective, assessment should also be translated into some kind of social action (Freire, 2006). Students need to develop their understanding of the human condition taking its socioeconomic elements into account. This involves developing a broad understanding of power and oppression in society and how students can act on the world around them by contemplating transformation—of society and of themselves. Within a critical pedagogical approach to reading, developing social action is a way of responding to the reading by making use of Freire's (2001) tenet of using the word to transform the world. In the Freirean praxis, reflection translates into action, and this is what happens in the process of developing critical literacy—you appropriate yourself of the word and the world.

Some of these steps are complementary and developed almost simultaneously. Many reading specialists, in fact, argue that creating relationships, comparing information interpreting meanings, and analyzing a text overlap, because in order to create relationships one needs to compare and contrast information and the interpretation of a text requires an ability to analyze it (Rosenblatt, 1994). Assessing and developing social actions are the steps that may require special attention from the teachers' point of view. From a critical perspective, assessing a text and students' reading comprehension needs to take into account what students take with them from the reading activity and how reading affects their lives. This is why assessment should be related to social action, a stage that gives students an opportunity to display not only the knowledge gained, but their ability to transform that knowledge into productive action for the betterment of society. Reading that results in social action leads to transformation, and this is the ultimate aim of learning to read the world.

Learning to Read Critically: An Example

In order for the reader to understand how all these skills and strategies actually translate into a critical pedagogical practice, in this section I provide an example of classroom procedures using the elements that were described in this chapter, that is, how to use critical pedagogy in the teaching of reading for social action.

The example that follows illustrates the steps taken in one of my classes. The identification of the theme came as a result of a school event. It all started when one of the high school students made it public that he was going to bring his boyfriend to the graduation prom and that he expected to be treated like anyone else—without being judged based on his sexual orientation and without being made fun of. He also expected the school to guarantee that he and his partner were going to be safe and respected like all the other students.

The students in my class decided that this was an issue they wanted to study and discuss further. For many of them, talking about sexual orientation was a new experience and having someone in the school come out and be so open about his relationship with another male student was a situation that needed to be processed and elaborated. Moreover, given the environment of homophobia and all the jokes and threats that followed the episode, students realized the need to learn more about a topic many of them condemned without being able to understand.

In their journals, students were able to write about their doubts, fears, questions, and share stories that involved other gay people they knew—family members, people in the community, celebrities, and even other students at school. Admitting to being gay or questioning your sexual orientation was not an easy task for high school students in a predominantly immigrant Spanish-speaking area, so when students expressed an interest in learning more about it, we decided to develop a whole unit on the topic, and the unit involved reading for social action.

After analyzing and selecting a number of resources that were age-appropriate and adequate for classroom use, we decided that we were all going to read a book called *Reflections of a Rock Lobster: A Story about Growing Up Gay* written by Aaron Fricke (2000). The description of the theme came not only from the book students read, but from a variety of resources, including their journals (for those students who wanted to share them), newspapers and magazines, television shows, their own experiences, and from different members of the school and the community. It was important to have students exposed to a variety of resources, as this promotes multiple views and presents different perspectives on the topic.

This is a useful aspect of classroom procedure that helps students to develop an informed opinion on the issue at hand, particularly in terms of a critical approach. In this case, students read about and studied the emotional, psychological, and social processes a teenager goes through in search of his or her sexual identity.

The stage of discrimination with this particular topic was extremely relevant for these students, as it involved sorting through and learning to discriminate fact and fiction, reality from opinion. Students developed a "fact and fiction checklist" based on all the pieces of information they had gathered. This checklist helped them to develop their points of view based on evidences from the texts they had read and from other sources they deemed reliable. Understanding the value of different sources of information and comparing them forces students to make decisions as to which sources they can trust and why. This process also included a discussion on objective and subjective perspectives with students learning how to distinguish concrete facts from opinions disguised as facts using linguistic devices and stylistic resources as clues used by a writer to develop his or her point of view.

After students had gathered, selected, compared, and contrasted information on sexuality and sexual orientation, it became much easier for them to develop an analysis of Aaron Fricke's book. The interpretation students developed was contextually based, as they transferred the context and situation described in the book to their own context of the classroom and school setting. As they discussed the issues raised by a gay teen who needs to confront himself and the school at the same time he deals with societal pressures, students realized how much of our personal feelings and perceptions are filtered through the act of reading and how much meaning we actually bring to what we read.

Without even noticing, the research students had done, their checklists, their search for facts and accurate information, interviews, and discussions had transformed them into active readers. While writing in their journals, many of them shared with me and their classmates, how much they had "talked back to the book and to Aaron"; how much they could "relate to the characters in the book"; and how the process had made them reconsider the situation they were experiencing at their own school where a teenage student was coming out and asking for school support and understanding.

The process of synthesizing what they had read did not come easy, as many students realized they had conflicting thoughts and feelings whereas some others needed more time to process all they had been exposed to. This is a natural reaction, particularly when the topic is both personal and still taboo for many of these teenagers who are still developing their identities. This is why the next steps, assessment and social action, are extremely important and necessary not only for practicing active reading, but for preparing informed students to become citizens for democracy and social justice.

A number of suggestions were given as possible courses of action for students to engage in. As a teacher, my role was to guide and encourage them to weigh all the pros and cons of their possible actions and help them develop their projects once a decision was made as to how to transform their findings into social action. Furthermore, it was also decided that we would pursue different courses of action, thus allowing students to engage in multiple activities at the same time and to assess the value and effect of each one. Below are some of the social actions in which students engaged:

* Students contacted the local chapter of GLSEN (Gay, Lesbian and Straight Education Network) to get information and materials in order to transform their school into a safe school.
* Students collected and distributed educational resources about sexual orientation around the school and the community.
* Students collected money and donations to buy more books about gay themes for the school library (which had no books on the topic before this project).
* Students contacted a number of people who could volunteer their time as guest speakers and come to the school to talk about their coming-out experiences and about the importance of tolerance and respect to sexual diversity.
* A group of students developed and acted out a play based on certain scenes from Fricke's book to perform at school.
* Some students created posters to hang around the school focusing on the idea of a safe school.
* Some students initiated the process to officially start a Gay-Straight Alliance (GSA) student club in the school. They believed that by having both gay and straight students together, it would be easier to recruit members.

As can be seen from these examples, social action means translating what you have read into some kind of work that will benefit the larger community and that will demonstrate your understanding of what you have read (which is part of the assessment process). The actions students engaged in as part of this project also reflected their talents and strengths. Each student contributed based on his skills and they were all equally valued and important: students who were more artistically oriented engaged in creating posters or acting; students who enjoyed communications contacted agencies and speakers, while others worked on creating text or visiting local places around the community.

This critical approach to translating reading into social action also makes students understand the importance of reading for their personal growth and for the development of their cognitive and social skills and maturity level. When students realize their role in promoting change, they feel empowered. They understand that their contribution and participation can in fact have an effect on the world around them and this motivates them to want to read even more.

From the teacher's point of view, reading for social action also promotes inquiry-based learning that is truly student-centered. Students need to learn to take responsibility for their learning and a critical approach to teaching encourages student-led activities that are based on students' needs and interests. At the same time, it also gives students a sense of purpose while building their self-esteem and independence.

CONCLUSION

Reading in the classroom should be a fun and motivating activity that engages students at the same time that it promotes the development of critical thinking skills. While reading, students learn to question and to search for answers. They also learn that there are different ways of interpreting a text and that these reflect the different ways of interpreting the world and to relate to life situations and circumstances.

When selecting texts for students, teachers should pay close attention to the problems students bring up in class and to the topics they express an interest in. This way, reading will be relevant to the classroom context and meaningful to the students' lives. Readings should reflect students' experiences, but it should also expose them to new experiences, broaden their horizons, and widen their perspectives.

One of the greatest concerns for teachers is what to do with the texts selected and how to go about developing classroom activities that will effectively result in learners' development of reading, social, and critical thinking skills. The approach described in this chapter aimed at addressing this issue and was developed based on critical pedagogical principles that establish that in order to develop critical thinking skills and become socially engaged citizens, students need to relate to the texts they read on a deep and personal level, and that this is only achieved when students take an active role in the reading process.

The first thing to bear in mind is that the learner of the twenty-first century is as much a reader as he is a *co-writer* who contributes meaning to what is read by bringing in his or her own experiences, previous readings, and views of the world. Reading is not a one-way street and readers contribute meaning as much as they get meaning from a written text. Teachers who ask students to find the moral of a story or the meaning behind an author's words express a misunderstanding of what reading entails. Reading should be an open door of possibilities and classroom activities should enable students to search for multiple interpretations. By encouraging students to dialogue with a text, teachers will be helping them to find their own voices and to develop a critical view of different topics and issues.

As a matter of fact, the reading skills and strategies described in this chapter can be readily transferred to any kind of learning. Additionally, this critical approach also encourages teachers to work collaboratively across disciplines. In developing the unit about *Reflections of a Rock Lobster,* for example, I worked closely with teachers from other content areas, such as health and physical education, biology, and social studies. This integration helps students create connections and analyze a topic from different disciplinary points of view.

Apart from that, this inter disciplinary approach helps students distinguish between fact and opinion and identify different text genres. This way, learners can activate specific knowledge every time they read a new text since they can predict the kind of language they will encounter and the kind of vocabulary and syntactic structures (e.g., an academic text uses more passive voice) they will find.

Over the years I have developed this approach, I have witnessed how students' perceptions about reading have changed. They learn that reading is a dynamic process that is always being reconstructed because we are never the same. As context and time change, so do our views and ways of interpreting and relating to the world. This is a result of the way we process and internalize our experiences. We are always constructing and reconstructing meaning every time we interact with a text. Above all, I have learned that texts need to speak to the students and that developing social action is a way for students to speak back to the texts.

REFERENCES

Apple, M. (2000). *Official knowledge: Democratic education in a conservative age.* London: Routledge.

Auerbach, E. (1992). *Making meaning, making change: A guide to participatory curriculum development for adult ESL and family literacy.* Boston: University of Massachusetts.

Bright, B. (1996). Reflecting on "Reflective Practice." *Studies in the Education of Adults* 28 (2), 162–184.

Brookfield, S. (1994). Tales from the dark side: A phenomenography of adult critical reflection. *International Journal of Lifelong Education* 13 (3), 203–216.

Cranton, P. (1996). *Professional development as transformative learning: New perspectives for teachers of adults.* San Francisco, CA: Jossey-Bass.

Duckworth, E. (2006). *The having of wonderful ideas and other essays on teaching and learning.* New York, NY: Teachers College Press.

Freire, A. M . A. (2006). *Paulo Freire: Uma história de vida.* Indaiatuba, SP: Villa das Letras Editora.

Freire, P. (2005). *Education for critical consciousness.* New York, NY: Continuum International Publishing Group.

Freire, P. (2002). *Pedagogia do oprimido.* São Paulo, SP: Editora Paz e Terra S/A.

Freire, P. & Macedo, D. (2001). *Literacy: Reading the word and the world.* London: Routledge.

Freire, P. (1992). *Pedagogia da esperança: Um reencontro com a pedagogia do oprimido.* São Paulo, SP: Editora Paz e Terra S/A.

Freire, P. (1970). *Pedagogy of the oppressed.* New York, NY: Continuum International Publishing Group.

Fricke, A. (2000). *Reflections of a rock lobster: A story about growing up gay.* New York, NY: Alyson Books.

Gadotti, M. (2005). O plantador do futuro. *Memória da Pedagogia 4: Paulo Freire.* São Paulo, SP: Segmento-Duetto.

Harmer, J. (2001). *The practice of English language teaching.* Harlow, UK: Pearson.

Krashen. S. (2004). *The power of reading: Insights from the research.* Westport, CT: Heinemann.

Matthews, A., Spratt, M., & Les Dangerfield, L. (Eds.) (1990). *At the chalkface: Practical techniques in language teaching.* London: Longman.

Naiditch, F. (2009). *Critical teaching for social justice in Brazilian favelas.* Paper Presented at the Annual Meeting of the American Educational Research Association. San Diego: CA.

Naiditch, F. (2006). *The pragmatics of permission: A study of Brazilian ESL learners.* Dissertation Abstracts International 67-05A.

Naiditch, F. (2003). *Bi-literacy development in the classroom: Examples from the South Bronx.* Paper presented at the NYS-TESOL Annual Conference. Rye: New York.

Quintero, E. & Rummel, M. K. (2003). *Becoming a teacher in the new society: Bringing communities and classrooms together.* New York, NY: Peter Lang Publishing.

Rosenblatt, L. M. (1996). *Literature as exploration.* New York, NY: Modern Language Association of America.

Rosenblatt, L. M. (1994). *The reader, the text, the poem: The transactional theory of the literary work.* Carbondale, IL: Southern Illinois University Press.

Rudman, M. K. (Ed.). (1993). *Children's literature: Resources for the classroom.* Norwood, MA: Christopher-Gordon.

Senge, P. (1990). *The fifth discipline.* New York, NY: Doubleday.

Shor, I. (1992). *Empowering education: Critical teaching for social change.* Chicago, IL: University of Chicago Press.

Simon, R. (1992). *Teaching against the grain: Texts for a pedagogy of possibility.* New York, NY: Bergin & Garvey.

Smallwood, B. A. (2004). *Children's literature for adult ESL literacy.* Washington, DC: National Clearinghouse for ESL Literacy Education.

Wallerstein, N. (1983). *Language and culture in conflict: Problem-posing in the ESL classroom.* Reading, MA: Jossey-Bass.

Chapter 7

Think Critically and Act Collaboratively

A Critical Framework for Teaching Students with Special Needs

Mark Alter and Joan Rosenberg

For the teacher educating students with disabilities, the development and implementation of instruction is a multi faceted process. Fundamentally, this process involves assessing student performance, determining goals and objectives based on that assessment, and evaluating the combined effects of what and how to teach. This process is not without tensions and obstacles. That is why collaboration and thoughtful intervention is essential. An emphasis on collaboration provides the teachers with the tools necessary to design and implement instruction. With shared decision-making, teachers have opportunity to optimize and re-design the management and content necessary for academic success.

The general education classroom should be the first placement option considered before a more restrictive environment is selected. The overriding rule in placement is that each student's classroom must be individually determined based on the individual student's abilities and needs, and it is the individualized program of instruction and related services reflected in each student's Individual Education Program (IEP) that forms the basis for the decision.

In determining if a placement is appropriate under the Individuals with Disabilities Education Act (IDEA), the following factors are relevant: (1) the educational benefit to the student from regular education in comparison to the benefits of special education; (2) the benefit to the student with a disability by interacting with students without disabilities; and (3) the degree of disruption of the education of other students resulting in the inability to meet the unique needs of the student with a disability.

Inclusive practice is an approach to teaching. It is an attitude about teaching that can have a positive impact on academic learning. Research does indicate positive results when settings are integrated, although studies that compare inclusive and segregated education indicate that there may be no significant difference in achievement (Peterson & Hittite, 2010). It is the opinion of these authors that inclusive practices and teaching strategies result in improved social and academic outcomes.

Based on the work of (Kurth & Gross, 2015) a key tool for successful inclusion is ongoing communication, relationships that support personnel and co-teaching in which adaptations promote the strengths of the students. Furthermore, instruction in the content areas along with strategies and accommodations provides the meaningful input required by all students. Placing a student with disabilities into a general education classroom may not be enough for a successful outcome although it may be considered inclusive. In order to determine success of an inclusive process, collaboration throughout the entire school faculty is necessary.

Few aspects of Public Law 94-142 The Education for All Handicapped Children Act (1975) and its reauthorization in 1990 and 1997 as the IDEA have received more attention, created more administrative concerns and litigation than the development and implementation of the individualized education program (IEP). In 2004, with the reauthorization of Individuals With Disabilities Education Improvement Act there is a continued commitment to children with disabilities with new initiatives to strengthen special education with a focused agenda based on No Child Left Behind ensuring greater educational opportunities to students with disabilities.

Since 1975 when IEPs were first introduced as a mandated component of instructional program planning, parents, teachers, administrators and related service providers have discussed, argued and even litigated about all aspects of the IEP including how inclusive or exclusive the content should be, what is the most appropriate environment in which to place the student in order to receive instruction, what type of related services are needed to complement the instructional program, how often and where should those services be delivered.

The IEP was not designed in 1975 to be a barrier to instruction. It was conceived as a best practice to engage professionals and parents in a process to plan instruction, utilize resources to ensure adequate delivery of instruction, and have some measure of instructional accountability (e.g., annual goals, short-term objectives, mastery levels for each short-term goal). What has emerged over the past thirty years is the IEP as a management plan and not an instructional plan.

What happened to the original conceptualization of an IEP? What is it about an IEP that causes such debate? What is it about the IEP that is so important that thirty years later the reauthorization strengthens and reinforces the involvement of the parent, special education teacher, general education teacher, related service providers, psychologist, and anyone else who may positively affect decisions regarding what is best for a student, including the inclusion of the student in the decision-making process? Why is the process of IEP development and the substance of the plan still the most critical, foundational and innovative process in both general and special education?

To begin to answer these questions requires a basic understanding of what is an IEP. There are many books, websites, and articles that were written for parents and teachers describing the IEP process. It is very important to know that the IEP process and the decisions made regarding the content of an IEP is made by a group of people, a team. The team can be called an IEP Team, a Child Study Team, a Committee on Special Education, or a Pupil Personnel Team. Regardless of the title of the team, IDEA identifies the members of the team.

Specifically, the team is made up of (1) the parents of a child with disability; (2) at least one regular education teacher; (3) at least one special education teacher, or if appropriate, at least one special education provider; (3) a representative of the local educational agency; (4) an individual who can interpret the instructional implications of evaluation results; (5) at the discretion of the parent or the agency, other individuals who have knowledge or special expertise regarding the child, including related services personnel as appropriate; and (6) whenever appropriate, the child with a disability.

All members have equal say in determining the content of an IEP; all members have the right to contribute information; all members have the right to voice an opinion, and most important; the IEP is a dynamic plan which can change at any time if members of the team feel it is not working or is working and believe that the plan needs to be changed to ensure the student receives an appropriate education in the least restrictive environment.

The law is very clear. Every opportunity must be explored to place a student with a disability with students without disabilities. Students with a disability must have access and placement in the least restrictive environment (LRE) that will give the student every opportunity to maximize learning. A team makes a decision based on the content of an IEP and decisions must not be based on predetermined criteria, such as all students with autism go into a specific class.

Our approach in this chapter is not the traditional approach to the topic of instruction in special education. In traditional models, the content is presented through facts and assessed by testing the memory of the students through multiple choice exams or exams that only require memorization. Friend and Bursuck (2009) point out this approach does not assure the understanding or possible generalization of content or concepts.

Our position is that, through collaboration, innovation, and individualization, all students and especially students with disabilities should have inclusive opportunities to acquire the skills, attitudes, and knowledge that will increase the probability of their functioning and participating in society.

The implementation of our position is too complex to implement without collaboration. It is insufficient for teachers alone to plan instruction; it is insufficient for teachers to limit learning to one or two annual goals; it is insufficient to prepare students to just take a test.

The question facing all teachers is not which program will work but which program will be most effective for a particular student. Until a definitive answer is provided, teachers working with related service providers, parents and other teachers must develop an instructional environment in which they feel the student can succeed.

SETTING THE INSTRUCTIONAL STAGE

It is clear that there is an instructional dilemma in special education. Historically, the instruction of students with disabilities has been driven by approaches that correlate with a specific diagnosis. To level the playing field and provide all students with access to a unified curriculum, the Common Core State Standards (CCSS) were drafted to prepare all students for college coursework and entry level careers with success after high school. However, this one-size-fits-all approach (suggested by the CCSS) cannot effectively measure the performance of all students with disabilities, nor can it always be the most appropriate education for all students with disabilities.

The use of the Common Core Standards is designed so that children nationwide can become competent and master the identified outcomes. Students with disabilities often fail to master the outcomes due to the lack of planning appropriate instruction. Children who are asked to reach goals beyond their abilities simply lower and reduce their achievement (Beals, 2014).

Instruction and decisions that meet the unique needs of students with challenges is a multi phased process. Each phase requires collaborative decisions answering a series of instructionally related questions:

1. Who should be referred for evaluation? when a child's skills or behavior shows a lack of improvement or a lack of progress or when the interventions implemented are not successful, collaboration is required between the special education and general education teachers, parents, related service providers.
2. What are appropriate instructional supports?
3. Where is the least restrictive environment? It is required that a child with disabilities must be educated with students without disabilities to the maximum extent possible.
4. What related services should be implemented?
5. How do all the decisions come together to provide an appropriate education for one student? Assuming the *right* decisions have been made, the

major instructional challenges for teachers is to measure student success and maintain individuality for diverse learners.

There are no easy solutions for achieving high-quality instructional programming for students with a disability. Teachers are challenged to define instructional approaches that will meet national, state, and local standards. Students with special needs require teachers who are skillful in developing effective learning strategies that help the student develop deeper and more sophisticated thinking skills. What does this actually mean in practice?

When a teacher leads a class discussion, the student who has difficulty processing and understanding information needs instructional strategies and techniques in order to relate to the content and to develop an effective understanding of the ideas. The student who has a problem finding patterns or showing evidence needs instructional strategies and interventions, such as scaffolding, rubrics, independent work, careful progress monitoring, small-group instruction, alternative explanations, and then can learn how to read for meaning and deepen his or, her understanding of the content.

HOW TO TEACH CRITICAL THINKING SKILLS OR THINKING CRITICALLY ABOUT CRITICAL THINKING

Starting as early as kindergarten, children can learn to organize ideas, defend arguments, draw inferences, and ask questions. For example, strategies for teachers to use when teaching how to think critically have been developed by McMillan (2007) and Ennis (1987). They include:

- Ask open-ended questions; for example, "Why is this fact important?" What are the most important reasons for eating green vegetables?
- Ask questions that have several possible answers; avoid questions that require yes or no answers.
- Play games that include and require classification and categorization.
- Ask students to make decisions—look at pros and cons.
- Make connections and patterns: "What makes this similar to another problem we discussed?" What are the patterns that you see?
- Compare and contrast everything.
- Focus on reading comprehension skills and understanding the text.
- Outline sequences: What comes first? Second?
- Provide word problems in mathematics.
- Teach the scientific method.
- Point out situations that are similar and compare them.
- Reflect about individual experiences.
- Look for student's interests.

- Discuss beliefs and points of view.
- Ask students to draw conclusions.
- Ask students to make predictions.
- Ask students how a particular problem can be solved.
- Plan debates.
- Seek different solutions to common problems.
- Distinguish between fact and opinion.

These strategies must be integrated into lessons and become part of the teaching repertoire in every content area. Teachers should believe that all students are capable of figuring out complex ideas, expressing their subsequent insights, and developing problem-solving skills.

What is unquestionably true in special education is the proliferation of best practices. Best practices are grounded in evidence-based research. It is not uncommon to see such titles as "Best Practices for Students with Autism," "How to Teach Students with a Learning Disability How to Read," and "Classroom Practices for Students with Attention Deficit Disorders." If one wants to know which disability is most popular or of most concern to parents and schools, examine the titles of published curriculum guides. It is interesting to note that titles including students with intellectual disabilities (formerly referred to as mental retardation) seem to have disappeared from the literature altogether.

Evidence-based research practices ensure a greater likelihood of the intervention working. This is very important when it comes to students who are part of a special education program. Learning to use the best practices for students with disabilities will result in the teacher's understanding of good teaching. Best practices consist of assessments, interventions, strategies, and techniques promoting the strengths of the students.

Best practices are necessary in order to ensure that instruction is seamless and each student reaches his or her full potential. Best practice in special education provides the tools that meet the needs of each child. It links instructional strategies to assessment; it finds the strength of each student; and it helps to find the learning style of each child so that appropriate interventions can be implemented. It also links instruction toward the students' experiences, giving positive feedback and positive reinforcements, and promoting social validity (McDonald & Allen, 1990).

A successful process and a road to best practice is *Understanding by Design* discussed by Grant Wiggins and Jay McTighe (2011). This can be implemented in special education classrooms. It integrates instruction with assessment, and allows continual monitoring toward student achievement. It easily leads to differentiation where each student can be reached. Successful implementation of the understanding by design framework will result in utilizing best practices in special education. This approach, which emphasizes backward design, allows the teacher to plan instruction in a way that clearly addresses the process of learning. Begin the lesson with the result. The stages in this process include identifying the desired outcomes first, then looking for appropriate evidence and finally including experiences in the instruction (Wiggins & McTighe, 2006).

Successful strategies and techniques that place emphasis on critical thinking skills and motivation for learning become important tools for the classroom teacher. A crucial tool is the lesson plan.

Lesson plans should provide the systematic evidence that demonstrates and records the teaching and learning interactions in a classroom. Lesson plans represent what a teacher wants to do, has done, is doing, and will do as well as determine the expectations the teacher holds for each student in terms of learning and understanding. One approach toward a successful lesson plan focuses on effective decision-making. The lesson plan should reflect the decisions, goals, and instructional objectives noted on the IEP for the child with special needs.

The delivery of instruction includes developing critical thinking skills, and should be an integral part of every classroom because it allows for genuine and relevant inquiry into the big ideas of the core content, provokes deep thought, lively discussion, sustained inquiry, and new understandings. Critical thinking requires students to consider alternatives, weigh evidence, support their ideas, and justify their answers. It also stimulates vital ongoing rethinking of big ideas, assumptions, predictions, and prior lessons and, if done correctly, can spark meaningful connections to prior learning and personal experiences. In addition, thinking critically can create opportunities for knowledge transfer to other situations, and help "students effectively inquire and make sense of important but complicated ideas and knowledge" (Prins, Veenman, & Elshout, 2006, p. 73).

Alter and Gottlieb (2010) and Vaughn, Klingner and Hughs (2000) have all pointed out that, regardless of the proliferation of research conducted with students with disabilities, there is a lack of application, usage, and sustainability of that research into practice. Thirty-five years after the passage of comprehensive landmark federal legislation designed to protect the rights of students with disabilities, and 10 years after the passage of federal legislation requiring that students be taught using "evidence-based" approaches and that progress for subgroups, that is, students with disabilities, be reported separately, we still know very little about the effects of special education services on the everyday lives of students with disabilities.

In the years since the passage of the Education For All Handicapped Act (1975) and its reauthorization as IDEA (1990, 1997, 2004), neither parents nor school boards have routinely pushed to create a climate in which basic instructional evidence is collected to monitor and evaluate the efficacy of special education implementation and special education reform. However, there has been some progress. Venables (2014) showed that student performance is measurable through a systematic process. First, the teacher must decide if there are gaps in learning. (What are the areas of deficiency? What are the areas of strength? What are the causes for failure? How are the successes, weaknesses and failures monitored?) The benchmark assessments will show the evidence of mastery. If mastery has not been obtained, new instructional designs and strategies may be implemented.

The literature has identified three major factors that influence the sustainability of, and connection between research and practice:

1. Teacher knowledge and learning is not woven into the fabric of the research, and contextual factors including classroom environment, paperwork, and opportunities to collaborate do not support implementation of best practices (Malouf & Schiller, 1995).
2. Research-based practices do not tend to adequately reflect the realities of classroom teaching (Gersten, Vaughn, Deshler & Schiller, 1997).
3. The consequences of implementing a research-based practice may not be obvious to the teacher immediately. It seems that most teachers perceive their own teaching to be "moderately" effective, and believe their way of teaching is best and there is little consensus in the research regarding best practice that would warrant giving up their own approach.

Without regard to evidence, many practices and programs lose popularity. Programs that become popular because of marketing strategies, word of mouth, and political pressure often do not seem to work. In order to increase student achievement, and more importantly, develop skills for critical thinking, existing programs require reform as well as setting the standard for instructional accountability.

TOWARD AN INSTRUCTIONAL APPROACH

Considering the current state of instructional research in special education and its sustainability, our approach to instruction is based on two considerations. First, the absence of a national data base that demonstrates that special education classes (e.g., self-contained, resource room, consultant teacher) are more effective than general education classes on valued outcome measures, that is, academic performance.

In 1984, Gottlieb and Alter first reviewed the voluminous literature on classroom and teacher effectiveness and found four major variables that can affect student learning:

1. Background of the student and socioeconomic status.
2. Operational contexts in the classroom and the whole school, such as the type of grouping practices employed, percentage of time spent in academics, etc.
3. The nature of teacher interactions with all students.
4. The type of interactions pupils have with each other. Although these four categories do not exhaust the possible influences on student performance, the literature at that time was inconclusive as to what is an appropriate education in the least restrictive environment.

Swanson and Sachse-Lee (2000) did a meta-analysis to identify effective instructional models that yield high effect sizes as well as components that make up those models. They found that strategies implemented within small-group instruction, direct instruction and/or both models yielded significant differences. However, the instructional components that made up those models were not analyzed.

Second, although there are aspects of the data that suggest special classes or inclusion classes are more (or less) effective in supporting academic and/or social behavior, we find the data are ignored especially in urban school systems. The urban systems are driven by litigation, compliance, and fiscal issues, and thus favor a reduction in the number of students referred to and placed in special education.

There is a constant search for more efficient ways to deliver special education rather than a focus on effective instructional approaches. For example, dismantling a self-contained classroom or a resource room and integrating the students into a general education class gives the school principal a much-needed classroom but does not address the instructional conditions in the classroom or the school. Ultimately, analyzing the CCSS and finding a reliable way to identify the skills and weaknesses that students have in order to master the standards requires instructional plans, collaborative decisions, and collaborative actions by teachers.

Instruction is initiated, nurtured, and maintained by the classroom teacher, based on ongoing and dynamic transdisciplinary assessment, and in collaboration with related service providers. A teacher needs to gather and synthesize information (clinical as well as instructional) that will allow for the development and implementation of an individualized and group instructional program.

The primary task facing teachers of students with a disability is to identify and specify how a particular student should be involved in a general education classroom. From this perspective we have made several assumptions regarding instruction and the student in special education. Just as inclusive practice is an approach to teaching, *special education should be viewed not as a "place" but rather as a resource that incorporates a set of instructional, curricular, environmental, and resource options intended to facilitate more appropriate student outcomes.*

Reducing placements in special education is not an important goal in its own right. What is important is providing the best possible instructional services to students who are performing poorly in school, and using school resources to maximize the effect. As discussed, if instruction is a dynamic interaction of teaching and learning then prevention and *early* intervention of learning problems must be planned and implemented throughout the delivery of instruction. Then, reliance on remediation can be eliminated.

The way in which instruction is approached through the Common Core Standards is often scripted. However, teachers of students who have special needs have a complex instructional task. Their students may need more repetition, differentiated instruction, greater exposure to the content, modeling, or a personal graphic organizer in order to process information. Presenting students with options for learning the content and solving problems that promote understanding will inevitably increase the success rate in the classroom.

The literature regarding instructional strategies, interventions, and curriculum innovations is rich with perceived successes. However, when we take a closer look at the data, we find wide variability in teacher implementation, and most importantly, we find dissemination almost entirely absent from the literature. In other words, what works in one setting under specific guidelines and resources for implementation is difficult to replicate in other settings. Studies in special education have provided instructional approaches, strategies and techniques for children with needs ranging from being exceptionally gifted to those with multiple disabilities. However, it is clear that there is no approach that consistently works in all schools with all students.

Planning and implementing instructional programming for all students needs to be a school-wide commitment. Boyer (1995) outlines many of the basic components of a school devoted to being a community for learning. The community is built on sets of priorities, with several components contained in each priority

The first priority is School as a Community. The school should have a clear mission, sense of purpose, a collaborative environment, respect among students and staff, and an organized instructional climate that is also nurturing. Teachers should be empowered to work in teams and have time and resources for physical and mental renewal. Teachers should be the instructional leaders who serve as mentors and scholars and there should be partnerships and collaboration between home and school which begin in pre-school years.

The second priority is Curriculum with Coherence where literacy is the first and most essential area. All children are expected to become proficient in the written and spoken word. Language needs to be defined broadly to include words, numbers, and the arts, the essential tools of learning which, taken together, help create a curriculum with coherence. Curriculum design is successful when it includes at least eight themes based on shared human experiences that integrate the traditional subjects and help students see connections across disciplines. These include the life cycle, use of symbols, membership in groups, sense of time and space, response to the aesthetic, connections to nature, producing and consuming, and living with purpose.

Additionally, there needs to be a commitment to authentically interpreting and measuring of the results. Assessments would measure literacy, core knowledge, and personal growth. They would center on portfolios that include written materials, student products and performances, teacher feedback and observations. Assessments are necessary early in a child's school life in order to make decisions about the adjustments needed, and the design, delivery and implementation of instruction. The adjustments and delivery are bound to help students raise the bar.

A realistic and accurate analysis of the skills that a student lacks will result in more accurate preparation and better results. Assessments help the teacher to tailor instruction so that the diverse learner reaches appropriate goals and accomplishments. These are important decisions about students. Teacher accountability is closely tied to an acute understanding of assessments.

Third, a Climate for Learning must be facilitated through small class size, flexible teaching schedules, and student grouping patterns that vary to account for differential learning styles among students. It would also include bringing members of other generations into the school. In every classroom, there must be resources available to enrich learning, such as a large variety and supply of books, access to field trips, computer network connections, and other technology including Wi-Fi technology and a smart board in every classroom. The school must be committed to serving the whole child, including their physical, emotional, and social well-being. However, Boyer proposes a middle ground where schools are not social service centers addressing every student's need, yet still provide basic health and counseling services, as well as afternoon and summer programs.

A fourth priority is a Commitment to Character. Students will develop personal and civic responsibility, based on seven core virtues. Boyer also says that these virtues (which include honesty, respect, responsibility, compassion, self-discipline, perseverance, and giving) are those on which there is substantial consensus. Theses virtues are taught through school climate and curriculum, and service is strongly encouraged.

Boyer's priorities would enhance instructional accountability in two ways. First, it would require schools to have a system to evaluate its instructional environment and, second, it requires a school-based platform for lesson plans as the best evidence of instructional accountability.

CONCLUSION

To effectively incorporate critical thinking skill development into lesson plans and classroom environment, Rosenshine (2012) identified key principles that all teachers should know. The ten research-based principles of instruction come from the following three sources:

1. Research in cognitive science which focuses on how our brains acquire and use information. This cognitive research also provides suggestions on how we might overcome the limitations of our working memory; the mental "space" in which thinking occurs when learning new material.
2. Research on master teachers comes from teachers whose classrooms made the highest gains on achievement tests. In a series of studies, a wide range of teachers were observed as they taught. Investigators coded how they presented new material, how and whether they checked for student understanding, the types of support they provided to their students, and a number of other instructional activities. By also gathering student achievement data, researchers were able to identify the ways in which the more and less effective teachers differed.
3. Research on cognitive supports to help students learn complex tasks such as thinking aloud, providing students with scaffolds, and providing students with models—come from this research.

Rosenshine's list of some of the instructional principles that have come from the above-mentioned three sources is as follows:

1. Begin a lesson with a short review of previous learning. Establish a base-line and access prior knowledge. Children with learning challenges require repetition.
2. Present new material in small steps with student practice after each step. Willingham states that "it is virtually impossible to become proficient at a mental task without extended practice" (Willingham, 2009, p. 107).
3. Ask a large number of questions and check the responses of all students. Ask open-ended questions that encourage problem-solving, for example, What are the primary causes of World War II?
4. Provide models. Demonstrate how to solve a problem. Provide the steps necessary to complete the task.
5. Check for student understanding. Match the questions to the instructional levels of the students.
6. Obtain a high success rate. Through measurable assessments and reliable data, teachers can provide change and proficient understanding of instruction.

7. Provide scaffolds for difficult tasks. As children learn how to solve problems, the teacher supports and guides the steps toward completion.
8. Require and monitor independent practice.
9. Engage students in weekly and monthly review.
10. Provide appropriate and effective feedback. A teacher must provide input that is meaningful. The student can then decide what is needed and where they will go next (Brookhart, 2008).

Effective feedback leads to the process of knowing how to think rather than what to think, and it has become an important issue in special education. Rather than expecting students to recite the facts about a topic or content by memorizing or retaining facts, the key to helping students apply information and knowledge goes along with the ability to analyze, evaluate, make inferences and comparisons, and, finally, to solve problems (Willingham, 2009).

The approaches for children with special needs must be considered carefully. The inclusive classroom should cultivate a collaborative, safe, and secure environment. The tools that teachers use must provide the children with a community and a structure that supports the students' needs.

In summary, key elements planning for critical thinking and collaboration for the students with special needs should include:

1. A wide array of preventative, treatment-based, and support services that are comprehensive in scope, available at a single point of contact (i.e., school) and designed to meet the needs of the student, teacher, and family.
2. The "outcomes" of the services in terms of their impact on student and family must be measured.
3. A program grounded in evaluation (formative and summative assessments). Program evaluation would include the effectiveness and efficiency of implementation; student progress as it relates to instruction; and parents involvement and satisfaction with the program.
4. A valid and reliable decision-making model that guides the instructional program. For example, the basic components of an instructional program could include questions like: (a) What behavior does the teacher intend for the student to perform? What does a teacher intend to teach? (b) How does a teacher intend to teach the behavior? (c) How can the teacher verify that the behavior has been learned? Or has been taught? (d) Can the student/does the student generalize the behavior across content areas? (e) Can the student perform the behavior in an efficient and effective manner?
5. Reorganization that should start from a best practices perspective. For example, Wasik and Slavin (1990) reported the results of a best-evidence

synthesis of research on the use of one-to-one tutoring delivered by adults to students in the primary grades who are learning to read. Research on five programs was synthesized: Reading Recovery, Success for All, Prevention of Learning Disabilities, the Wallach Tutorial Program, and Programmed Tutorial Reading. All five programs showed substantial positive effects on student reading achievement. Two studies found cumulative effects of one-to-one tutoring and one study found lasting but diminishing effects. The five programs showed substantially more positive effects on student reading achievement than other similarly expensive programs on reduction of class size and provision of aides in the classroom.

6. An instructional approach that can be used by all schools. Models could be presented as illustrations of approaches. For example, a framework for classifying educational models was developed by The Center for Educating Students with Handicaps in Regular Education Settings. The framework is based on two approaches: instructional (e.g., the content of what is taught, the strategies and methods of teaching) and organizational (how schools are structured and the procedures to administer the educational programs).

7. An instructional approach that can be used by all teachers. It is necessary for teachers to construct interventions that focus on meaningful instructional objectives. Emphasis must be placed on proactive decisions that include early diagnosis. Looking at each individual student rather than the entire school will help to act as an "agent for change" (Lewis & Sugai, 1999; Walker et al., 1996). Teachers must learn how to draw accurate conclusions about their students and ensure that interventions are designed and implemented for positive outcomes.

8. Instructional approaches that include collecting data for each student in order to evaluate progress. Eventually students must to able to monitor their own accomplishments and progress. Self-monitoring produces greater motivation as well as greater success in developing practical skills (Shapiro & Cole, 1994). When teachers understand and recognize the major concepts in the core standards, they are better equipped to make instructional decisions and design strategies for children with learning challenges. Teachers must encourage their students to solve and apply sophisticated problems in a variety of areas. Having a strong foundation and an understanding of the standards will foster the instructional decisions and instructional choices that promote critical thinking, strong problem-solving techniques and analytical skills that are necessary for success.

9. Children need to demonstrate evidence of their knowledge. Teachers must learn to modify curriculum materials in order to reach the student with special learning challenges. Simply reviewing a set of specific ideas and skills may not be enough for all students to really understand the material. In order for all students to achieve performance objectives,

accommodations and modifications must be built into the design of instruction.

10. Critical thinking skills which develop the framework for objective-driven instruction. Cognitive conditions have to be right in order for children to become good thinkers (Willingham, 2009).

There is no doubt at all that attempts by teachers to instruct all students, and especially students with disabilities, are sincere. However, the Common Core alone will not solve the instructional problems in special education that have existed for so many years. It appears that the issue of how to develop appropriate instructional programs capable of being effectively delivered by the classroom teacher is still a crucial question.

Only when we ask and answer the questions that focus on planning and delivery of academic and social instruction that enables a student to think critically will we be able to talk meaningfully about appropriateness of education. Effective education is characterized by preventing failure, implementing instructional interventions, and a sincere concern for every child. The teacher must connect to the instructional gaps that exist in the curriculum and plan rather than identifying the deficiencies in the student's learning; in other words, connecting to the student's needs even as instruction is occurring is a step that is often missing (Venables, 2014).

In conclusion, this chapter has identified current concerns and strategies with regard to instructional programming for students with disabilities. A major issue has been identified in terms of teaching to and for a label. Instructional delivery must respond to collaborative team decisions that respond to the strengths and talents as well as the possible obstacles to learning. The question that is increasingly being asked, namely, "Does special education make a difference?" and a first step in demonstrating that it does make a difference is for the special education and general education community to show that together all students can learn.

REFERENCES

Alter, M. & Gottlieb, J. (2010). Sisyphus & the Problems in Special Education. *Education Update.* www.educationupdate.com/archives/2010/NOV/html/spec-sisyphus.htm academia.edu

Beals, K. (2014). The Common Core Is Tough on Kids with Special Needs. Retrieved September 16, 2015 from http://www.theatlantic.com/education/archive/2014/02/the-common-core-is-tough-on-kids-with-special-needs/283973/.

Boyer, E. L. (1995). The basic school: A community for learning. *Carnegie Foundation for the Advancement of Teaching*

Brookhart, S. (2007–2008). Feedback that fits. *Informative Assessment, 65*(4), 54–59.

Ennis, R. H. (1987). A taxonomy of critical thinking dispositions and abilities. In Baron, J. B. & Sternberg, R. J. (Eds.). *Teaching Thinking Skills: Theory and Practice.* New York: W. H. Freeman, 9–26

Friend, M. & Bursuck, W. (2009). *Including Students with Special Needs Fifth Edition.* Boston, MA: Pearson.

Gersten, R., Vaughn, S., Deshler, D., & Schiller, E. (1997). What we know about using research findings: Implications for improving special education practice. *Journal of Learning Disabilities*, 30, 466–476.

Kurth, J. & Gross, M. (2015). *The Inclusion Toolbox. Corwin.* Thousand Oaks, CA: Sage.

Lewis, T. J. & Sugai, G. (1999). Effective behavior support: A systems approach to proactive schoolwide management. *Focus on Exceptional Children*, 31(6), 1–24.

Malouf, D. B. & Schiller, E. P. (1995). Practice and research in special education. *exceptional children*, 61(5).

McDonald, J. & Allen D. (1990) *Turning Protocol.* Bloomington, IN: National School Reform Faculty.

McMillan, J. H. (2007). Formative classroom assessment: The key to improving student achievement. In J. H. McMillan (Ed.), *Formative classroom assessment: Theory into practice* (pp. 1–7). New York: Teachers College Press.

Peterson, J., Hittie, M. & Mishael M. (2010). *Inclusive Teaching: The Journey Towards Effective Schools for All Learners.* Boston, MA: Pearson.

Prins, F., Veenman, M. & Elshout, J. (2006). The impact of intellectual ability and metacognition on learning: New support for the threshold of problematicity theory. *Learning and Instruction,* 16, 374-387

Rosenshine, B. (2012). Principles of instruction: Research-Based strategies that all teachers should know. *American Educator*, 36(1), 12–19, 39.

Shapiro, E. S. & Cole, C. L. (1994). *Behavior Change in the Classroom: Self-Management Interventions.* New York, NY: Guilford Press.

Swanson, H. L. and Sachse-Lee, C. (2000). A meta-analysis of single-subject design intervention research for students with learning disabilities. *Journal of Learning Disabilities*, 33, 114–136.

Vaughn, S., Klingner, J., & Hughes, M. (2000). Sustainability of research-based practices. *Exceptional Children*, 66, 163–171.

Venables, D. R. (2014). *How Teachers Can Turn Data into Action.* Alexandria, VA: ASCD.

Walker, H. M., Horner, R. H., Sugai, G., Bullis, M., Sprague, J. R., Bricker, D., et al. (1996). Integrated approaches to preventing antisocial behavior patterns among school-age children and youth. *Journal of Emotional and Behavioral Disorders*, 4, 194–209.

Wasik, B. A. & Slavin, R. E. (1990). *Preventing Early Reading Failure with One-to-One Tutoring: A Best-Evidence Synthesis.* Paper presented at the annual convention of the American Educational Research Association, Boston.

Wiggins, G. P. & McTighe, J. (2006). Examining the teaching life. *Educational Leadership*, 63, 26–29.

Wiggins, G. and McTighe, J. (2011). *The Understanding by Design Guide to Creating High-Quality Units*. Alexandria, VA: ASCD.

Willingham, D. (2009). *Why Don't Students Like School? A Cognitive Scientist Answers Questions About How The Mind Works And What It Means For The Classroom*. San Francisco, CA: Jossey-Bass.

Chapter 8

Creativity and Motivation in the Teaching and Learning Process

Bettina Steren dos Santos, Carla Spagnolo,
and Caroline Buker

We will not succeed in navigating the complex environment of the future by peering relentlessly into a rear view mirror. In order to be successful, we must free our creative power.

—*Robinson, 2012*

This quote reveals the purpose of this study, which is the result of personal concerns about the teaching methodologies and pedagogical practices that permeate educational environments, and perspectives resulting from reflective moments that originate from our experiences as teachers.

The teaching profession today increasingly requires attitudes that develop specific skills and competencies in order to attend to the demands of social reality. Faced with this reality, how can we think of pedagogical practices that stimulate creativity and motivation in the classroom? This question instigates us to think about the teaching and learning process from the perspective of creative methodologies as a possibility of recreating the classroom environment with creative and motivating actions that promote student learning. This chapter establishes relationships between creative methodologies and the motivational theory of self-determination.

Creative methodologies refer to the five stages that are considered relevant to all people involved in the teaching and learning process: discovery, interpretation, ideation, experimentation, and evolution. These steps are based on the principles of Design Thinking (DT) (Brown, 2010; Nitzsche, 2012), though adapted to the educational context. It is a process that requires constant participation, authorship and a proactive stance of all those involved in the classroom environment, which consequently promote the empowerment of the creative teaching and learning processes. Nonetheless, the use of this methodology is not an end in itself. Its premise is complete human development, since it triggers relations that enhance autonomy, competence, and belonging, which are basic factors in the motivational theory of self-determination (Deci and Ryan, 1996).

With this discussion, we intend to approximate theory and practice, in order to provide opportunities for students and teachers to feel stimulated to develop autonomy, authorship/ownership, and citizenship in relation to choices for a better classroom, school, and society.

ACADEMIC EDUCATION AND PEDAGOGICAL PRACTICE IN THE CURRENT CONTEXT

The rhythm of change accelerates every day. The digital technologies of information and communication transform our way of behaving, thinking, studying, working, and relating to one another. In response to the intense changes in the world, we will have to find new ways of dealing with situations that are affecting society. Faced with this challenge, innovation, and creativity can effectively affect the process of readapting to the new world, which requires a nonlinear view of development.

According to Perez Gómez (2015), the educational activities in schools cannot aim only to assimilate that which the community has already rectified abstractly and in a de-contextualized manner. In order to increase our capacity to interact with people and uniquely face challenges and problematic situations, it is essential to develop an understanding of real problems and assume responsibility for getting adequately involved in each situation.

In this sense, teaching institutions need to be open and prepared to act differently according to each reality and emerging needs. However, the linear position that many educational environments still maintain is notorious, and regrettably only maintains a reproductive and repetitive system. Robinson (2012) claims that producing meaning in the teaching and learning process, in these cases, remains in a vacuum. The big problem is that the current systems of mass education are a catastrophe in themselves. Far from looking to the future, they remain stubbornly fixed in the past, as it is clear that "current educational systems were not designed to meet the demands that we face today. They were created to satisfy the needs of an era that has already passed. Reforms are not enough: we need to recreate these systems" (p. 59).

This is why the purpose of schooling should not only be about teaching, but also about creating learning conditions. This means that the teacher should no longer be a mere transmitter of content but rather become the creator of learning environments and the mediator of the intellectual development process of the student.

Perez Gómez (2015) claims that relevant teaching and learning require the activity of the subject in a continuous process of construction and reconstruction. Student involvement must be seen as an active process of questioning, investigation, and intervention. What makes school relevant is not the content, which can be acquired by other means and through other sources in the digital era, but the nature of the experience of learning that results in the formation of personal identity in relation to the learning community.

Students must be able to invent themselves, express their desires, and recognize their potential. They need to be given opportunities to learn to think and to create and recreate alternatives to learning with more meaning. Learning should be redefined in a more complex and profound way, starting with questions related to real situations, and interconnected with experiences that can unite theory and practice.

Hargreaves (2003) claims that the academic curriculum today needs to involve the cultivation of skills that develop deep cognitive learning, and the incentive for creativity and inventiveness among students. Moreover, it needs to use the research findings from working in networks and teams, and the pursuit of continuous professional learning as teachers. It should also include the promotion of problem-solving, the willingness and confidence to take risks, trust in cooperative processes and the ability to deal and adapt to change as a possibility of improvements for education and society.

Schools in the future will have little resemblance to those of the past. Teachers will have to teach in a very different way. According to Earl, Hargreaves & Ryan (1996), it is not enough for schools to provide students with basic skills. Students will need to achieve more complex skills like critical thinking, creative problem-solving, independent and collective work.

For these reasons, it is necessary to prepare students not only for the basic reading and writing, but to get involved with the world, which encompasses understanding the intricate, connected nature of contemporary life. Moving in this sense requires ethical and innovative actions, which are conducted by specific and creative methodologies.

CREATIVE METHODOLOGIES: DESIGN THINKING IN EDUCATION

Creative methodologies refer to the process of redefining and capturing the concept of education, and broadening the pedagogical activity based on more open and interdisciplinary conceptions. The school envisioned in these methodologies is based on complete human development and creativity. In them, teachers, students, administrators, and parents are encouraged to constantly think about the commitment of the academic institution to the development of learning and also to reconsider pedagogical practices from distinct perspectives. We should admit that the convergent thought, within the divergent thought, constitutes the bases of a problematizing education. A creative school educates for change, prepares for the unknown, and develops the ability to learn how to learn. The creative process is that which mobilizes qualities that are in opposition, though reciprocal, as in connotations and denotations, passivity and productivity, awareness, and lack of awareness. Still, it integrates intelligence, thinking, language, perception, symbolization, motivation, emotions, and all the historical cultural baggage coming from coexistence in the process. Essentially, creativity is the integrative synthesis of all of these processes and mechanisms inherent to human beings (Bellon, Isabela & Alvarez, 1984).

Creativity is not entertainment for idleness, but an attitude that is as vitally necessary as breathing and eating. Therefore, the educational process in schools should have the purpose of developing the potential in individuals so that they can use resources beyond the acquisition of knowledge, and establish self-awareness. It is necessary to consider the overall education of the students, and so the school should be prepared to provide students with an environment of freedom, which allows for expressive creative skills.

Drawing principles from Design Thinking (DT) to education, we can pursue innovative subsidies for the educational environment, which favors broader development, through creativity, autonomy, authorship and a proactive stance. It means thinking about the education of the future, aimed at current needs, and, therefore, "education of the future must be primary and universal teaching, centered on the human condition. [Learners] must recognize themselves in their common humanity and at the same time recognize the cultural diversity inherent in all that is human" (Morin, 2006, p. 47).

Education should favor the natural ability of the mind in formulating and solving essential problems, stimulating the full use of general intelligence, which refers to the free exercise of curiosity. These considerations allow us to use the DT approach in schools, by taking the human being as the central objective. These principles can offer a more collaborative and fun teaching and learning process, with more confidence in creativity, and distinct ways of engaging students in problem-solving.

It is also important to point out that the specified choice of DT is due to its flexibility in thinking and acting, and to its premise of involving different views regarding an issue. As Santos (2003) claims, for the evolution of man as well as for his survival, networks for exchanging energy are necessary, as they enable the establishment and development of connections that are essential for life and human coexistence, especially in learning.

Education needs to move away from the closed, fragmented, authoritarian Cartesian–Newtonian model that is disconnected from context

(Moraes, 1997). In many schools, children are still limited to the reduced space of their classes, immobilized in their movements, silenced in their speech, and prevented from thinking. When children are "reduced in their creativity and in their possibilities for expression, [they] also find themselves limited in their social interactions, unable to attempt new flights and achieve new spaces" (p. 50). Education can be different when it is developed around motivation, which is based on experience and curiosity, and which awakens students.

In order for DT to be adequately applied, modified stages are used based on DT material for educators. DT in education provides greater belief in creativity and in the purpose of transforming challenges into opportunities. Some characteristics are fundamental for understanding their meaning in education and specifically in the teaching and learning process.

As previously claimed, DT is centered on the human being, since it begins with empathy and understanding the needs and motivations of people (students, teachers, parents, administrators). It is collaborative, since it involves everyone; and optimistic, since it believes in the creativity and action by everyone. It is experimental, because of the freedom to make mistakes and learn from those mistakes by reconsidering the ideas themselves in collaboration with other people. DT allows one to learn by doing, that is, to combine theory and practice, with positive expectations for actions that lead to innovation and the possibility of doing better.

This adaptation took place as it was first considered to be coherent with the educational proposal. Therefore, the stages of DT in education have the following labels: discovery, interpretation, ideation, experimentation, and evolution:

1. Discovery: Being open to new opportunities, being inspired, and creating new ideas. Discoveries build a solid foundation for ideas. It involves challenges, research, knowledge of the content and classroom environment, and the observation of daily life in schools. In this stage, it is important to identify the needs and desires of those involved in the process. It is the moment of learning by interacting with people in the environment, by considering their experiences and by observing their peers. Overall, it is related to the general and broad understanding of a situational reality, and it incorporates some subject or topic to be studied.

   It is the stage for analyzing reality and for detecting existing problems. Solutions can be pursued through dialogue, research, divergence, and convergence until one obtains the desired answers to solve these problems.

   Empathy is not related only to factors and content; it is also related to approximations between people, since the development of knowledge and perception is directly related to the world of affection and curiosity.

Affection enables a different perspective of others and brings people together, leading to greater engagement for solving problems, or other situations related to learning. On the existing relation between affection and cognition, Vygotsky (1993) claims that achievements on the affective level are used on the cognitive level and vice versa, highlighting the relevance of others in the process of building knowledge, and the constitution of subjects and their ways of acting.

Converging with the theory of Vygotsky, Piaget (1977) states that affection and cognition complement one another and one offers the support necessary for the development of the other. In the absence of affection, there is no interest, desire, need, and motivation for learning. Moreover, there is no questioning and curiosity and, without them, there is no intellectual development. Academic education needs to be committed to complete human development and this means that life should be guided by principles of autonomy and cooperation.

Maturana (1998) claims that, in the educational process, we need to first value what people know in order to guide "our children" toward action related to their daily lives. To this end, it is necessary to learn to look at what they do and listen carefully.

2. Interpretation: The stage of interpretation is connected to the sense and meaning of something; it is the explanation of what is not clear. It transforms stories into *insights*, observations, visits, and conversations into actions. However, this is not a simple task. It involves telling stories, choosing and condensing thoughts, until we find a clear direction. The perception (insights) of information that sparks interest is fundamental and serves as a basis to raise issues and ask questions. The challenge is in transforming observations or current needs into questions and figuring out how to do so effectively.

It is essential to recognize the thought process as a kind of insight for a way of seeing reality and all its forms. Our conceptions are always transforming, providing forms to experiences, but not as true knowledge. Since our way of thinking is limited, insights represent our way of seeing and interpreting everything as a result of our experiences, and ways of thinking and knowing.

In the middle of so many uncertainties, education needs to anticipate individuals' needs to learn continuously. Students need to learn how to investigate, understand the different forms of access to information, and develop the critical need to evaluate, gather, and organize the most relevant information. As Moraes (1997) claims, students need methodologies that help develop skills to manage and produce knowledge leading to questions, manifestations of curiosity and creativity to their positions as subjects in life.

This is what Demo (2005) calls "educating through research," that is, the urgency to promote research as a learning tool in education. Students take command of their learning by becoming subjects, without the intention of having ready-made recipes dominate the classroom. The author defends the proposal that the foundation of academic education is research since it always includes the emancipatory perception of the subject. It aims to create and generate opportunities, to the extent in which they begin to rebuild themselves through the systematic questioning of reality.

A fundamental measure will be to make sure that it exists in the desirable school environment in order to make students participate actively and get involved (Demo, 2005). The school needs to represent a collective workplace. This presumes that there is interest between teachers and students in the pursuit of motivation, respecting the cultural contexts of each participant in a relationship of mutual trust. Demo explains that "it is always about learning together . . . what is learned in school should appear in life" (p. 17).

3. Ideation: This is the stage of the generation of ideas. It is the level that encourages thinking in an unrestricted way, or "out of the box." In this phase, generated ideas are displayed in a visual way, whether through drawing, sketches, outlines, etc. It is considered that information presented visually causes more impact in the process. The focus is also on courage, divergence of ideas, and to subsequently converge and describe concepts.

For Robinson (2012), human consciousness is molded by ideas, beliefs, and values that result from our experiences and meanings. Therefore, ideas can free as well as imprison us. We create worlds and personal realities that we experience and there is always the possibility of recreating them. The great ideas generated through history transformed the view of the world in their time and helped reform culture. As such, we build the universe in which we live and we can rebuild it constantly through different technological and social experiences and evolutions.

The ideation process is a creative process, which starts with a thought, an outline, an initial project due to the need to find a solution to a problem. Robinson (2012) explains that "creativity is a dialogue between ideas and the means chosen" (p. 149). It is related to the perception of learning to see things differently, to explore without the fear of failing or making mistakes. Being creative in this sense involves investigating, exploring new horizons, and using one's imagination to make personal choices that contribute the means with other people.

Collaboration and mutual respect occupy a central role in this stage. Collaboration encompasses the joint work of people on common processes, in which the interactions affect the nature of the work and its results. For Robinson, collaboration involves two processes: first the acceptance of all ideas and offers that appear, and second, making people feel good. This means that it is not about judging, but helping create something that is beneficial to everyone.

When talking about acceptance of others, we must cite (Maturana, 1998) who talks about the biology of love: "The core of human coexistence is love, the actions that constitute the other as a legitimate other, in the realization of the social being who lives in acceptance and respect for himself as well as in the acceptance and respect for others" (p. 32). This way, it is necessary to take on a reflective position in the world and understand that the acceptance and respect for oneself and for others is indispensable. Responsibility and freedom emerge in the reflection that exposes our thinking (doing) in the scope of emotions, with the awareness that the world that we live in depends on our desires and actions.

4. Experimentation: This stage of experimentation gives life to ideas. This is the moment of building prototypes to make ideas tangible and obtain answers in order to understand and learn how to improve and refine an idea. Prototypes enable the sharing of the ideas with other people. Moreover, they stimulate creativity, since prototypes can be created through the use of stories, announcements, models, role plays, digital technologies, and so on. Feedback, through frank and open dialogue, is given to the different prototypes and this is essential for understanding other points of view and for giving continuity to the refinement of ideas. Based on the evaluation and considerations of other people, it is possible to reflect on aspects that need to be reviewed in pursuit of alternatives for the necessary changes. This stage provides the first step toward the construction of a plan of action so that ideas can really be put into practice.

Imagination is the fundamental gift of human awareness (Robinson, 2012). Creativity, however, goes beyond. Being creative involves doing something, putting imagination to work. For Robinson (2012), "creativity is imagination put into practice" (p. 140). The space for creativity is a continuum in all stages. However, in this phase, there are interferences of evaluations during the whole process. It is a period in which ideas through practical and visual paths are shared simultaneously and people and groups receive feedback.

5. Evolution—Action: This stage is characterized by the concrete action of ideas and prototyping that emerged in the previous stages. It is the moment of mobilizing more people and resources so that the intentions planned up until this point are executed. If in this stage, the factors involved are related to concrete actions, then the means and alternatives to make things happen are pursued. If the stage is directly involved with classroom learning, one can think about the practical application of theory, whether in the classroom, in individual and/or social life.

The theory of chaos by Colom (2004) aims to establish a connection between theory and practice. Knowledge must be extracted from practice, and practice must be the source of knowledge, creating a confluence between thinking and doing. The author also discusses perspectives of the future in academic education, referring to an open school attentive to the social reality that is definitively prepared for change and innovation. He defends forms of learning that, in some way, simulate situations that the students extract from disorder, the new orders that will serve as a platform to begin another creative and constructive adventure of knowledge.

The methodology of DT in education can be used in daily academic life, in all situations, from finding solutions to existing problems at school as a whole to learning content in the classroom environment.

The important thing about this methodology is that it can lead the people involved in the process to think about and question the value and the objectives of the teaching and learning processes, without limitation or fear of making mistakes. It can also motivate learning due to the fact that it enables involvement with real-life problems that are of interest to students and teachers. In other words, to the extent in which there is space for students and teachers to actively participate in the planning and discussions about the school curriculum and organization, it is based on this space that we can understand "who we are" and "what we want," stimulate and aid in the development of autonomy, belonging, and competence—the basic principles of the self-determination theory (SDT).

This creates a space to not only actively engage students and teachers in active participation and discussion about the school's curriculum, but also serves as a place for students to understand their identity (who they are) and objectives (what they want) in life. DT stimulates and aids in the development of autonomy, belonging and competence, and demonstrates the basic principles of the SDT.

WHAT IS THE SELF-DETERMINATION THEORY?

The SDT was proposed by Eduard Deci and Richard Ryan, in the mid-1970s. It has become widely accepted and pervasive in various fields of knowledge, especially in the academic context. The focus of their analysis resides in the guidelines of motives that drive behaviors, and establishes internal and external *loci* of causality for these behaviors. From this binomial emerges the two main motivational guidelines that form the foundation of the theory: intrinsic and extrinsic motivations.

Intrinsic motivation corresponds to a typically self-determined behavior, in which interest in an activity is guided by free choice, spontaneity and curiosity. The effort dedicated to the realization of an activity is not linked to external contingencies and rewards, but to the characteristics inherent in the activity itself. In this context, in which tasks have purposes in themselves, these theorists report that intrinsically motivated behavior is more associated to feelings of satisfaction, achievement, and pleasure (Deci & Ryan, 1985, 1991).

Regarding extrinsic motivation, the activity or task is subordinate to obtaining a goal or result. According to Deci & Ryan (1995), in this situation, accomplishing actions is very much related to rewards, evaluations, deadlines, punishments, and compliments, among other aspects. What determines behavior is much more associated to control, moved by external wishes, in which the individual acts under pressure, in detriment to free will and autonomy. In this controlled behavior, the subject tends to perceive activities/tasks as instrumental for obtaining a determined objective. However, what appears in the forefront is the final objective and not the task/activity itself.

For Ryan, Deci & Grolnick (1995), self-determined behavior is governed by meeting three basic characteristics, which the authors define as "innate psychological needs": the needs of "autonomy," "competence," and "relatedness" (p. 68).

Autonomy is understood as an exercise of free will, choosing and conducting behaviors, without much regulation or external control. The subject experiments with the behavior itself, which is initiated and continued based on his choices. The authors point out that subjects are autonomous when they perceive a *locus* of internal causality, a high level of freedom, a low level of external control and the possibility of choice in carrying out these actions.

Meanwhile, competence resides in nurturing perceptions of personal effectiveness through experiences that lead to determined objectives. In this theory, people are likely to get involved in activities that are adapted to their current needs and levels of knowledge, thus maintaining the need to be perceived as effective in social interactions. This reflects on the natural desire to exercise one's own skills to develop new competences.

Finally, relatedness refers to the need to establish significant interpersonal relationships in specific contexts, generating the perception of relatedness and support from a determined group. Together with the perception of autonomy and competence, the need for relationships constitutes the determining element of intrinsically motivated behavior.

According to Ryan and Deci (2000), these three basic needs "seem to be essential to facilitate the natural tendencies for growth and integration, as well as for a constructive social development and personal well-being" (p. 68). They also claim that "healthy development requires satisfying all three needs," in a way that meeting "one or two are not enough" (Deci &

Ryan, 2000, p. 229). According to them, there is no optimal development in which some of these needs have been neglected. The basic needs are constituted as interdependent and integrated needs in such a way that "satisfying each one of them reinforces and strengthens the others" (Deci & Ryan, 2000, p. 244).

Frequently, intrinsic and extrinsic motivations are reported in the literature as disconnected and antagonistic phenomena. To address this problem, Deci and Ryan (2000) propose an organization denominated *continuum*, in which they suggest different motivational levels. They range from *amotivation* (demotivation), which represents the absence of intentionality, going through four levels of extrinsic motivation (external regulation; internal regulation; identified regulation; introjected regulation) until reaching the highest motivational level, which coincides with intrinsic motivation and self-determined behavior. In this sense, SDT specifies the characteristics and processes inherent in each one of these levels, highlighting that they should not be understood as disconnected mechanisms.

Brazilian researchers present different aspects that lead to the understanding that external motives can contribute to the internalization of intrinsic motivation (Santos, Antunes & Schmitt, 2011). According to these authors, social demands can favor the construction of intrinsic motivational processes, configuring, according to SDT, the most solid, long-lasting and balanced motivational level when compared to the other levels that the theory distinguishes.

SIMILARITIES BETWEEN DT AND SDT FOR MOTIVATIONAL PROCESSES IN THE CLASSROOM

There are significant similarities between DT and SDT: the two theories seem to contribute to questions aimed at the development of teaching and learning processes in educational environments. At the same time that there is effective and creative participation of all people involved in the process, one can observe the presence of self-determined behaviors that elevate intrinsic motivation, as illustrated in figures 8.1 and 8.2.

The educational context should be by nature a motivational context with possibilities of developing creativity. Students need to engage in a continuous process of cognitive, affective, and social growth and expansion. Motivation can affect new learning as well as the execution of skills learned, strategies, and behaviors: "Students who are motivated to learn a topic are willing to commit to any activity that they like and that will help them learn how to understand any teaching with determination" (Pintrich & Schunk, 2006, p. 6).

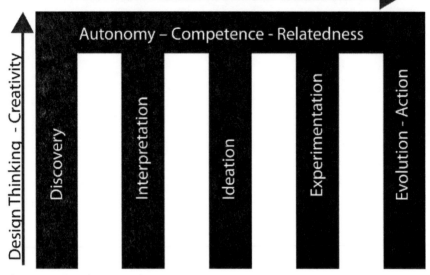

Figure 8.1   Development of DT Stages.

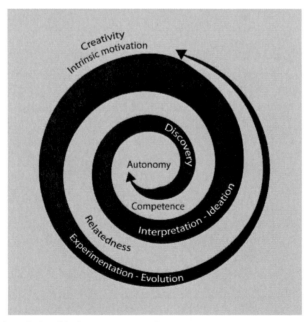

Figure 8.2   The relationship between DT and SDT.

In the classroom, the immediate effects of student motivation consist of being actively involved in the tasks pertaining to the learning process. Motivation in school implies quality of involvement. If a student is motivated to learn something, surprising results may be achieved.

It is important to point out that motivation is a process that exists in individuals. The pursuit of accomplishing personal goals is directly related to the motives that make people act and to social issues that represent the establishment of connections and affection. Motivation and learning are interconnected learning are interconnected since the motivation to learn gives direction and intensity to human conduct in the educational context.

Creative methodologies offer subsidies for the student to be an active subject in the teaching and learning process. It opens space so that students can develop autonomy and creativity, for the possibility of pursuing new ways of learning, at the same time that they interact with peers and teachers. Deci and Ryan (1996) have claimed for some time that people need autonomy, the feeling of belonging to the environment, as well as competence to feel more motivated.

Thus, DT is a pedagogical methodology that enables creativity and practices that aim for thinking together with the aid of different resources. It can spark greater interest in students and teachers to strengthen learning and to aid in the motivational processes. Based on these premises, the roles of the teacher and student need to be reconsidered. In order to make the learning process an objective for both the student and the teacher, it should not be primarily focused on the teacher, as it is believed and established in the traditional processes of education.

Therefore, we use the similarities between DT and SDT as processes that move people to action, based on relations that are established between the environment, needs and the object of satisfaction. They are dynamic and personal processes. As such, it is essential to understand the motivational processes in every person, because it is by observing and understanding people with unique characteristics and subjectivities that we can conceive development and learning as a process that is not impervious, but that happens over the course of everyone's lives.

Perhaps with time, there will no longer be a need to think of alternatives for answering questions such as: what can we do to spark interest, stimulate effort, and thought and strengthen learning? Perhaps by accepting the changes of a hybrid society and allowing the construction to involve all those interested, we can live with more motivation and happiness.

APPLICATION IN THE SCHOOL CONTEXT

The experiences using DT in the education are undoubtedly challenging and meaningful. DT stimulates learning, both professionally and personally, and engages participants actively in the process. The development of each of the stages happen through workshops that offer constant feedback based on the DT stages.

As an example, we describe one of the experiences, which was accomplished with a team of teachers, administrators, students, and their parents in an elementary school in Porto Alegre, Brazil. In a number of meetings, the group went through the different stages of DT with the aim to rethink the school, especially by proposing initiatives to improve the processes of teaching and learning in that school.

First, we presented the goals and the theoretical concepts of DT to the group. To carry on the development of each stage, we put participants in groups. In the first moment (observation and empathy moment), participants identified themselves and formed groups based on categories: students, teachers, parents, and administration. The stages of the proposal are presented in Table 8.1.

In the course of the meetings, the groups began to collaborate and interact in more dynamic and meaningful ways in order to address the needs of their school. Besides the different needs expressed by each person and group, there was as a common goal, which was to address the identified problems: to improve the quality of the teaching and, consequently, the students' learning through more interdisciplinary practices and with more dialogue among

Table 8.1   Overview of Workshops

	Subject	Action
Workshop 1	Initial presentation	– Integration and introduction of the group. – Presentation: What is Design Thinking? – Initial questions and interactions: Who am I? What is my problem today?
Workshop 2	Stages 1 and 2: Understand and observe	– Map of empathy. – Presentation of the map to the groups by the other groups.
Workshop 3	Stage 3: Define	– Defining the problem: what is the problem facing the school community?
Workshop 4	Stage 4: Ideation	– Brainstorming ideas and actions to solve the problem. – Delimit one or two ideas.
Workshop 5	Stage 5: Prototyping	– Make the idea visible. – Develop and create a prototype of the idea.
Workshop 6	Outlines to Stage 6 (Testing)	– Planning to continue the workshops in order to put the projects into practice. – Evaluate the meetings. – Personal accounts. – Fraternization.

all the stakeholders (administration, teachers, students, and parents). After identifying the problem, participants brainstormed suggestions and created prototypes of an interconnected school, which was connected to the outside world by distinct bridges, and another one linked by direct connections between one classroom and another, bringing together the distinct subjects and fields of knowledge.

The results of this experience were extremely satisfactory. By engaging in the DT stages and creating a prototype of the school they envisioned, participants came up with possibilities to improve the school environment and established more meaningful connections between students, teachers, administration, and parents.

The pedagogical practices that use DT can promote creativity and enable the motivational processes in a classroom environment, through inquisitive and dialogical interactions. The critical eye of the participants served as a kind of conducting wire to the necessary changes. By problematizing the pedagogical practices of the school, participants were able to come up with ideas for new pedagogical activities and plans. The real meaning of the changes in the school methodology is in the conjuncture between the concepts and the people, the meanings and directions developed according to the interests and needs of each member and each reality.

In this sense, we believe that the use of DT methodology promotes the development of a motivational environment based on dialogue, which brings about change by finding elements that make the classroom more creative and welcoming, giving students and teachers higher autonomy and a feeling of ownership of the teaching and learning processes.

CONCLUSION

In this chapter, innovations in methodologies in the educational context were presented as possibilities for dealing with the contemporary challenges emerging in the teaching and learning processes. Design Thinking in education can contribute directly to changing the position of teachers and students, as it emerges as an alternative for solving problems with creativity and development with autonomy, competence, and relatedness. As a result, it triggers greater motivation and involvement of educators and learners to teach and learn.

For Santos (2010), people learn when they are secure, when they are given support and affection, when there are goals, low external control and high personal recognition. In other words, we really learn when relationships are established.

Essentially, these theories and methodologies exemplify the idea that without learning there is no motivation, and without motivation there is no learning. However, for these processes to happen, it is necessary to assume a creative and innovative methodological position. Teachers and students need to be epistemologically curious, in constant pursuit of knowledge, moving through stagnant models, through understanding and building practices that spark the desire to know, to want to know, giving due meaning to learning. As Robinson (2012) has said, education is not a linear process, since it involves the cultivation of talents and sensibilities that enable people to live better in the present to create their own future. To transform education, it is essential to change, and to change, we need attitude, knowledge, and initiative.

REFERENCES

Bellon, F. M., Isabella, O. M. D., & Alvarez, J. M. (1984). *La creatividad em la edu-cacion.* Barcelona: Editorial Escuela España.

Brown, T. (2010). *Design Thinking: uma metodologia poderosa para decretar o fim das velhas ideias.* Rio de Janeiro: Elsevier.

Deci, E. L., & Ryan, R. M. (1985). *Intrinsic motivation and self-determination in human behavior.* New York: Plenum.

Deci, E. L., & Ryan, R. M. (1991). A motivational approach to self: Integration in personality. In R. Dienstbier (Ed.), Nebraska Symposium on Motivation: Vol. 38. *Perspectives on motivation.* (pp. 237–288). Lincoln: University of Nebraska Press.

Deci, E. L., & Ryan, R. M. (1995). Human autonomy: The basis for true self-esteem. In M. Kemis (Ed.), *Efficacy, agency, and self-esteem* (pp. 31–49). New York: Plenum

Deci, E. L. & Ryan, R. M. (1996). Need Satisfactions and the self-regulation of learning. *Learning & Individual Differences,* 8(3), 165–184.

Deci, E. L. & Ryan, R. M. (2000). The 'what' and 'why' of goal pursuits: Human needs and the self-determination of behavior. *Psychological Inquiry,* 11, 227–268

Demo, P. (2005). *Educar pela pesquisa.* Campinas, SP: Autores associados.

Earl, L., Hargreaves, A. & Ryan, J. (1996). *Schooling for change: Reinventing education for early adolescents.* New York: Routledge

Hargreaves, A. (2003). *Replantear el cambio educativo: un enfoque renovador.* Buenos Aires: Smorrortu.

Maturana, H. (1998). *Emoções e Linguagem na Educação e na Política.* Belo Horizonte: Editora UFMG.

Moraes, M. C. (1997). *O paradigma educacional emergente.* Campinas, SP: Papirus.

Moraes, M. C. (2003). *Educar na biologia do amor e da solidariedade.* Petrópolis, RJ: Vozes.

Morin, E. (2006). *Os sete saberes necessários à educação do futuro.* Brasília, DF: UNESCO.

Morin, E. (2000). *A cabeça bem-feita: repensar a reforma, reformar o pensamento.* Rio de Janeiro: Bertrand Brasil.

Nitzsche, R. (2012). *Afinal o que é design thinking?* São Paulo: Edições Rosari. 207.

Pintrich, P. R. & Schunk, D. H. (2006). *Motivación en contextos educativos: teoría, investigación y aplicaciones*. Madri: Pearson Educación.

Piaget, J. (1977). *Psicologia da Inteligência*. Rio de Janeiro: Zahar.

Portal design thinking para educadores. O que é Design Thinking. Retrieved from: http://www.dtparaeducadores.org.br/site/?page_id=7.

Robinson, K. (2012). *Libertando o poder criativo: a chave para o crescimento pessoal e das organizações*. São Paulo: HSM Editora.

Ryan, R. M., Deci, E. L., & Grolnick, W. S. (1995). Autonomy, relatedness, and the self: Their relation to development and psychopathology. In D. Cicchetti & D, J. Cohen (Eds.), *Developmental psychopathology: Theory and methods* (pp. 618–655). New York: Wiley

Ryan, R. M. & Deci, E. L. (2000). Self-Determination theory and the facilitation of intrinsic motivation, social development, and well-being. *American Psychologist, 55*(1), 68–78

Santos, B. S. (2010). *A motivação em diferentes cenários*. Porto Alegre: Edipucrs.

Santos, B. S., Antunes, D. D., & Schmitt, R. E. (2011). Teorias e indicadores motivacionais no ensino superior. In: Morosini, M. C. *Qualidade na educação superior brasileira: indicadores e desafios*. Porto Alegre: Edipucrs.

Vygotsky, L. S. (1993). *Pensamento e linguagem*. São Paulo: Martins Fontes.

Chapter 9

Critical Second Language Pedagogy

Lessons Learned from Teaching Students in Poverty

Fernando Naiditch

Many generations of educators in Brazil have learned to teach and approach classroom instruction through the lenses of critical pedagogy. This approach is largely based on the work of Brazilian educator Paulo Freire, particularly through his most well-known book, *The Pedagogy of the Oppressed* (1970). In it, he called for a pedagogy of transformation based on social responsibility. As such, the pedagogy of the oppressed is not only *of* or *for* the oppressed. It is also a pedagogy *of* and *for* the non-oppressed who are truly committed to social transformation and who will work together with those whose voices have been silenced.

Freire believed that no form of education could be neutral and that all pedagogy is a call to action. He recommended pedagogical approaches that recognized the experience and dignity of students and their culture and that called into question the assumptions which lay at the base of their social systems.

Freire's (1980) pedagogy also sought to question and revisit our understanding of curriculum, grasping that the not-always seamless fabric of learning is made alien by teaching methods that split it into irrational pieces. Freire's (1992) approach involved mapping the problems or issues that affect a particular community and working from within that community to come up with creative solutions and possible courses of action by engaging in dialogue and questioning. Therefore, he criticized "banking" educational methods, which see students as empty accounts to be filled with deposits of knowledge.

Knowledge was a result of an examination of social understandings, not a doctrine determined by testing services. Motivation came from demonstrations of how education is linked to power. Perhaps most importantly, for the process to work, the educator-leader had to be deeply involved in the daily lives of the students.

The pedagogy proposed by Freire (1970) is one in which dialogue leads to freedom, humanism leads to subjectivity, and, ultimately, results in social transformation. In this chapter, I explore some of the basic ideas suggested in Freire's pedagogy—namely the process of finding one's voice, developing social responsibility, and moving toward social transformation. The project described in this chapter was developed with a group of pre-service teachers of English as a foreign language (EFL) in Porto Alegre, southern Brazil, and aimed at helping new teachers develop the necessary skills in order to serve the population and the communities in which they would be inserted as educators and citizens.

Given that language and language teaching are never neutral endeavors, educators must address questions of linguistic and cultural identity especially in the context of the spread of English language teaching and learning. Therefore, this chapter examines the experiences of a teacher educator of preservice EFL teachers, in Brazil, as the prospective teachers learn to understand and try to negotiate their classrooms. Finally, the importance of a political awareness of teaching English in indigenous classrooms is discussed, and a number of suggestions are made to facilitate pre-service teachers' skills to better serve underprivileged students.

In order to examine the importance of infusing the education of EFL teachers with a critical view, I will start by describing the incident that prompted my student teachers to reflect on issues of equity and social justice and to develop a curriculum that provides for a critical dialogue and addresses questions of linguistic and cultural identity.

THE SCENARIO: UNDERPRIVILEGED STUDENTS IN A BRAZILIAN *FAVELA*

As the end of the year approached, a new group of pre-service EFL teachers was about to graduate and begin their careers. They had one last requirement before graduating—their student teacher observations. My student teachers were all placed in similar educational contexts: public schools located in the outskirts of the city or community centers that served poor populations living in *vilas* or *favelas* (slums or shanty towns). Vilas and favelas are seen in almost every Brazilian town. They are built in poor areas and lack basic public services. Its inhabitants may or may not have jobs and the community suffers from problems with public services, crime, and hygiene, to name a few.

Most teachers in our group felt that if you could teach in the most extenuating and difficult circumstances, you could teach anywhere. This was both challenging and exciting. My student teachers wanted to make a difference in the lives of the students they were about to teach, but did not necessarily understood what "difference" could actually mean in practical terms. Like many educators, they wanted to change the world and believed that education was the only way of doing so—one classroom at a time.

The student teacher that I was going to observe that day—Maria—had been particularly enthusiastic about her work in a poor area of the city. Maria understood how difficult it was for both her and her students to be there in that "pretend" school environment, a room with broken windows, not enough chairs or desks for everyone, no supplies, no chalk. Technology did not exist in their vocabulary and whatever they came to use in that class was what Maria had gladly purchased or managed to borrow from a colleague or a friend to bring to class to share with her students.

Maria spent hours planning her classes, creating beautiful handouts, and selecting materials to help her sixth-grade students understand and use English as a foreign language. Learning to use a foreign language for them was like being in one of the *telenovelas* (soap operas) they watched every night on prime-time. You could be anyone you wanted to be. For almost an hour, twice a week, those students belonged in a different world, the world of the English-speaking people. In this world, they could create their own rules and play by them.

One of the advantages of teaching a foreign language is that you can transport your students to a different reality and the classroom becomes a stage where the players can assume new identities and new lives, and that seems to be one of the main reasons these students were so motivated and seemed to enjoy studying English so much.

In fact, much of the work developed by my student teachers in foreign language education involved elements of Boal's *Theatre of the Oppressed* (1979), where the audience (students) take an active role and participate in the process of developing the lesson and deciding on its direction based on the way they react to it and respond to the content, activities, and materials.

Boal coined the term *spect-actor* (espect-atores, in Portuguese) which refers to the fact that in theater (or in our case, in the classroom), audiences (students) would transform their roles from mere spectators (observers) to actors who engage, participate, and decide on the courses of the action taking place. This process empowers students by making them active interlocutors who not only imagine change, but who can actually work toward generating social action that will bring about change.

For that day, Maria planned a lesson on careers, professions, and occupations. Her carefully prepared handouts had pictures of workers in action and the instruments they use in their jobs. She brought crayons, markers, scissors, glue, and a bunch of other supplies with different shapes, textures, and colors to illustrate the lesson and make it fun for the students. She was ready to embark in the world of the working people, from carpenters to engineers, from florists to dentists, from doctors to teachers.

Then, all of a sudden, a boy yelled from one of the corners in the room:

• How do you say *rapist* in English?

He was followed by two other boys who also wanted to contribute to the series of questions:

• How do you say *pickpocket*?
• And *drug dealer*?

My student teacher, Maria, was paralyzed. Suddenly, all the time spent preparing the lesson, and all those beautifully created handouts and carefully selected materials were not going to help her. She had been confronted with questions she had not anticipated and may not have been ready or prepared to face. The model that she had for the class was based on normative assumptions of work and career—ones that clearly did not translate to that community.

Maria stared at me looking for an answer. Our quick exchanges prompted me to just tell the students the words in English. They already knew them in Portuguese, so it was just a matter of using a different code. Whether in Portuguese, English, Chinese, or Farsi, the actual words are just a code. The meaning they carry and what we associate them with is what mattered to me, to her, and what should matter to all of us.

As the teacher educator and Maria's supervisor, I was also surprised with the students' reactions to the lesson and to the meanings expressed through their comments. No matter how experienced a teacher is, teaching is always a challenging endeavor. We are always questioning and learning through the interactions and the dialogues we engage in with different and diverse student populations. The scenario described here, as well as, the issues it raised became a matter of curriculum.

This story is also an example of what happens when teachers are just handed down a curriculum and told to simply follow it because it reflects what students need to know at that grade level. Rarely is there a discussion about who decides what is appropriate or necessary and what the bases are for developing a curriculum. My student teacher faced the challenge of not only learning how to become a classroom teacher, but also how to become a curriculum developer, how to take charge of the education of the students she was teaching, how to empower her students and herself, and how to assess her responsibility as an educator.

Because education is deeply implicated in the politics of culture, curriculum is never simply a neutral assemblage of knowledge. It is always part of a selective tradition, someone's selection, and some group's vision of legitimate knowledge. It is produced out of cultural, political, and economic conflicts, tensions, and compromises that organize and disorganize people. As Apple (1993, 2014) argues, the decision to define some groups' knowledge as the most legitimate, as official knowledge, while other groups' knowledge hardly sees the light of day, says something extremely important about who has power in society.

CRITICAL PEDAGOGY AND SECOND LANGUAGE TEACHING: A THEORETICAL FRAMEWORK

Paulo Freire (1992) felt that for the learner to move from *object* to *Subject*, he or she needed to be involved in dialogical action with the teacher. Dialogic action has two basic dimensions: reflection and action. Freire (1970) believed that education either functions as an instrument which is used to facilitate integration of the younger generation into the logic of the present system and bring about conformity, or that it becomes the practice of freedom, the means by which men and women deal critically and creatively with reality and discover how to participate in the transformation of their world.

My student teachers and I chose to abide by the latter—education as a means of empowering and thus transforming. Not only did we believe in the principle of a public education system, but also in the role public schools serve in a democratic society. Democracy has to be learned and the schools are the vehicle through which we empower citizens to understand, to listen, and to be listened to, to consider possibilities and alternatives that may not have been their initial choice, to learn to question, and to search for satisfactory answers.

To engage in critical reflection requires "moving beyond the acquisition of new knowledge and understanding, into questioning [of] existing assumptions, values, and perspectives" (Cranton, 1996, p. 76). Four elements are central to critical reflection: assumption analysis, contextual awareness, imaginative speculation, and reflective skepticism (Brookfield, 1988). Assisting adults in undertaking critical reflection is a frequently espoused aim of adult education (Bright, 1996; Brookfield, 1994) but it is a goal that is not easily achieved. However, you can only develop this kind of critical thinking and teaching in the classroom if you learn to embody it as part of your regular practice as an educator and citizen. Moreover, you also need to learn to lead in the classroom so that your pedagogy leads to some kind of social action that has social impact (Preskill & Brookfield, 2008).

The development of democratic practices in the classroom also serves the purpose of preparing students for the democratic practices of society, which ultimately means that one of the purposes of schooling is to prepare for citizenship. Giroux (2005) points out that "citizenship, like democracy itself, is part of a historical tradition that represents a terrain of struggle over the forms of knowledge, social practices, and values that constitute the critical elements of that tradition" (p. 5).

Being a "socially constructed historical practice," citizenship, as well as democracy, "need to be problematized and reconstructed" (p. 6). In that sense, the role of schools is crucial to empowering learners because schools build knowledge upon which power is gained. Moreover, they provide the ideal environment for students to develop the critical skills needed in order to build and develop their roles as social and political agents.

For Freire (1970), literacy is a political act. In and outside the classroom, the political awareness that one gains through assigning meanings to the knowledge one brings into the school leads to the dissemination of that knowledge and to the production of new knowledge. When faced with pedagogical decisions in the classroom, teachers need to know that their decisions are not merely pedagogical; they have serious educational, political, and societal implications.

Preparing teachers for the challenges they will face in their classrooms requires reconsidering the notion of quality (O'Cádiz, Wong & Torres, 2002). As opposed to quality being associated to competitiveness, as in neoliberal education, quality within a critical framework requires access to knowledge and social relationships. Freire's political-pedagogical discourse reveals an interconnectedness between the social and the political being. His problem-posing framework is in fact a result of this concern of quality being associated with people learning how to solve daily problems collectively and collaboratively.

Problem-posing was a central notion in my student-teacher seminar and in the action plan described later in this chapter. The example of a problem-posing approach to classroom practices emphasizes this notion of the need for practice resulting from a solid theoretical basis. A pedagogical practice that focuses on identifying and discussing problems that affect a certain community will only result in transformation if accompanied by some kind of action (Freire, 2006). The power of knowledge and the ability to question and reflect should be seen as an essential tool in order to intervene in the world (Gadotti, 2005).

Through cooperation, dialogic subjects are able to "focus their attention on the reality which mediates them and which—posed as a problem—challenges them. The response to that challenge is the action of dialogical subjects upon reality in order to transform it" (Freire, 1988, p. 149).

The program content of education is neither a gift nor an imposition—bits of information to be deposited in the students—but rather the organized, systematized, and developed "re-presentation" to the individuals of the things about which they want to know more. This is expressed through the Freirean notion of "generative themes," common issues that a community identifies that need to be discussed and that may help develop their critical consciousness. Another principle that has contributed to this project is the notion of *transcurriculum*, that is, a curriculum which is developed based on an interdisciplinary intercultural approach (Cortesão, 2002).

Curriculum is political text and discourse to be transformed into political practice. In order to do so, we need to broaden the idea of what a second language classroom is and borrow from other disciplines and areas of study in order to elaborate on wider issues and develop a more solid and comprehensive understanding of the issues at hand. We need to encourage our foreign language learners to bring knowledge from outside the traditional school resources and to search for different means of communication and different perspectives. Another way of seeing this practice is to define curriculum as a *multifaceted pedagogical act* (Naiditch, 2008).

Foreign language learning was the means through which we first started communicating with the learners described above, what brought us together, but by developing skills in the second language, our learners were also developing more general critical skills for life. Studies in critical second language teaching have generally focused on the relationship between language learning and social change (Norton & Toohey, 2004).

Learning a language is learning to use a powerful tool. By learning how to communicate or express their meanings via language use, learners end up developing a deeper understanding of their social environment, their histories, and themselves. Through the pedagogical practice of language teaching, learners also develop their social visions (Simon, 1992) and explore possibilities.

The use of a second or foreign language may facilitate this process of discovery and exploration because by engaging in the learning of a different code and culture, learners experiment language learning from a different perspective and are faced with a different way of organizing and interpreting the world. The foreign language classroom allows learners to distance themselves from their reality by engaging in a different reality. In other words, by transporting learners to a different context, the learning process toward understanding their own reality and uncovering their own environment may be facilitated. It is a kind of *detachment* that sometimes is needed for *reattachment*, that is, learning about the other in order to learn about yourself more clearly (Naiditch, 2008).

Critical pedagogy provides both the tools and the procedures which are necessary in order for teachers to engage with the experiences of marginalized learners (Luke, 2004). Moreover, critical second language education may help learners develop an even more elaborate sensitivity to cultural, linguistic, political, and socioeconomic diversity among students by focusing on power relations and how they operate in different cultures and how they emphasize and sustain inequality.

Learning a second language can also cause learners to become ambivalent and develop *subversive identities* (Canagarajah, 2004). While in the process of negotiating their identities, learners may resort to *pedagogical safe houses* (Canagarajah, 2004) in the language classroom. This means that learning a second language (or a second dialect) is a process of identity construction in which learners need to understand and negotiate the tensions they face by being members of diverse communities. The second or foreign language classroom provides learners with an opportunity to develop *multivocal literacies* (Canagarajah, 2004) and enables them to cross both discourse and community boundaries.

ANALYSIS: QUESTIONS ASKED AND LESSONS LEARNED

Within the theoretical framework described above, I now discuss the action plan that Maria, the other student teachers, and I developed as a result of reflecting on the classroom incident. Maria admitted she had never asked her students what they wanted to be when they grew up, or what their dreams and aspirations were. Her lesson was about what she considered to be widely recognized professions or occupations.

According to Maria, the decision about which vocabulary items to teach those students was based on two simple reasons. First, she had been using a variety of ESL textbooks to take ideas from. Those textbooks presented an imaginary world where anyone could be anything, but, more importantly, a world where professions reflected middle class aspirations and represented a desired or an imaginary, even utopian world—one in which everyone has a salary that pays all the bills, one in which everyone is employed, everyone can make a decent living and, above all, the houses are warm and comfortable and people are always happy.

We decided that choosing an appropriate textbook is only part of the issue because the textbook is not the curriculum. Unfortunately, for many teachers who teach second, especially foreign, languages, the textbook becomes the only resource in the classroom and dictates the content to be studied. Many recent graduates assume that if a well-known publisher is endorsing a certain publication, it could only be the result of carefully planned and extensively conducted and validated research. Thus, many teachers tend not to question authors' choices and pedagogical decisions in their textbooks.

One of our tasks in the student teaching seminar was to learn how to choose, evaluate, and adapt textbooks. Many new teachers believe that textbooks are good because they have been pilot-tested and reflect the newest research and methodological approaches in language teaching. This is not only false, but misleading (Loewen, 2007). Teachers may choose to adopt a textbook as a tool or a teaching aid, but they need to be able to develop critical lenses in order to understand what textbooks represent, whose world they reflect, and whose purposes they serve.

Another reason why Maria chose to talk about what she referred to as "common professions" in society had to do with presenting the students with a variety of professions that represented different social universes. She realized how distant these students were from the reality of becoming a doctor, but she considered it relevant for students to know what a doctor is, what he does, and how important being a doctor and being any of the professions mentioned in that class were.

To be fair, Maria had a plethora of possibilities. There was a doctor, but there was also a teacher, like her, a carpenter and a painter, like some of the men who lived in that *favela*, among others. So it would be unfair to say that Maria did not take into account social and economic values attributed to different professions. Although not extensively developed, there was some discussion on the social value of each profession.

The extent to which her students' universe was represented in that class remains an issue to be addressed—and it was. Some of these students' parents had jobs. They were maids and security guards; they worked in supermarkets or did some odd jobs. Maria claims to have tried to address her students' world. What she did not address nor consider as part of lesson planning was the fact that some of these students were also being raised in such extreme poverty that talking about professions as part of the curriculum may have even been considered by many as offensive. Some of those students were also exposed to verbal and physical violence and were being brought up in a world where abuse, negligence, abandonment, drugs, alcohol, and violence were all too common.

Maria could never have predicted—in fact no one could have—that some students would not only use those words (rapist, pickpocket, thief, etc.) in the classroom, but would also refer to them as being "professions." In our discussion and dialogues with the students, we came to understand that they were not necessarily associating being a rapist or a pickpocket with having a profession or a career, but that they understood them as identities.

In other words, they did not aspire to be any of those things, but were mentioning them because they were part of the world these students knew and had been exposed to from an early age, and they also fit part of the definition brought up in class of what people do and activities they engage in. More importantly, this classroom situation reflects a reality that most of us would certainly try to ignore bringing up in our classes, whether we teach a foreign language or mathematics or anything. No teacher I know would like to believe or accept that children would ever make such relationships or that they would even consider becoming any of those things.

In order to address these questions, we need to take a deep look into what we do as teacher educators. It is amazing to see how much emphasis is placed on methodology in second and foreign language teacher education programs. In fact, we have become so technique-oriented that the "art of teaching" may be seen by many as a collection of easy recipes to be applied in any classroom, in any situation and that, if given the "appropriate" tools, anyone can teach (see Selinker and Naiditch, 2004, for a discussion).

Historically, knowledge bases of teacher education have focused on the content and pedagogical knowledge of the teacher (Shulman, 1987). This issue of content knowledge versus pedagogical knowledge is ripe with debate. Many times student teachers are so concerned with learning about the managerial aspects of the classroom that they do not always analyze the meaning of teaching or consider their sociopolitical responsibility (Shor, 1992) as educators or "an awareness of the forces that affect the micro- and macro-level conditions within which we acquire knowledge and of how we view the uses and meaning of knowledge" (p. 290).

Critical pedagogy is an approach that attempts to help students question and challenge domination, and the beliefs and practices that dominate. In other words, it is a theory and practice of helping students achieve critical consciousness. Shor (1992) defines critical pedagogy as "habits of thought, reading, writing, and speaking which go beneath surface meaning, first impressions, dominant myths, official pronouncements, traditional clichés, received wisdom, and mere opinions, to understand the deep meaning, root causes, social context, ideology, and personal consequences of any action, event, object, process, organization, experience, text, subject matter, policy, mass media, or discourse" (p. 129).

Pedagogy reflects the knowledge, dispositions, and practices the instructor brings to his or her teaching. An instructor's teaching and learning experiences, his or her intercultural experiences, and awareness of broader sociopolitical contexts shape his or her conceptualization of and practices within a course of study. The instructor's content and pedagogical content knowledge also act to inform the course pedagogy and the opportunities afforded to teachers as they learn to teach diverse students.

Research substantiates that teachers' content knowledge and their capacity to adapt that content in pedagogically powerful ways is critical to providing students with high-quality learning opportunities (Grossman, 1990). Finally, the instructor's disposition toward inquiry, assessment, and change play an important role in how he or she adapts the pedagogy to the continuously shifting terrain between him and herself, the content, and the prospective teachers. Cochran-Smith (2001) suggests that "inquiry as stance is a process that involves learning to raise new questions, and, at the same time, unlearning long-held assumptions, and beliefs that are often difficult to unroot" (p. 3).

This stance supports the instructor to question and reassess his or her pedagogy, teachers' learning, and the course content.

While we often speak of developing student-centered classes as essential for promoting learning, how about a student-centered curriculum? My student teachers realized that even though they had been given the necessary tools to become teachers and had had some classroom experience, they were not responsible for some of the most important educational decisions in their classrooms, that is, the curriculum.

As student teachers, they had more freedom and voice, especially because they were teaching in communities where there was not much oversight from governmental agencies or offices. However, after their student teaching period, they did not know where they would end up teaching and most, if not all, schools decide a priori what the curriculum is (or should be) and require that teachers implement it thoroughly. Maria developed her curriculum based on a set of assumptions and routines, and even materials that were available to her at the time. She was learning how to become a teacher by experimenting, taking risks, and by learning through her mistakes, but she knew that after graduation, this may not be an option anymore.

In order to distance ourselves from the *hidden curriculum* (McLaren, 2006), develop a new curriculum in some form of *cultural politics* (McLaren, 2006), and truly address issues of social justice and equity brought up by the foreign language students, Maria, the other student teachers and I decided to take ownership of the curriculum and negotiate it with the students in that community. If the student teaching experience is supposed to be the moment in which pre-service teachers experience and experiment with language and pedagogy, this was the moment in which my student teachers needed to step up and develop a course of action.

This was not an easy task. In analyzing his experiences as a classroom teacher in Toronto, McLaren (1997) points to Freire's role in helping him recognize and express his own complicity in the oppression he was trying to help his students fight against. As he puts it, Freire's writings helped him to "unlearn the influences of [his] liberal heritage which puts white teachers in the position of 'missionaries' among the unprivileged" (p. 13). Freire's words, echoed by McLaren, were also the basis of the action plan described in the next section. In order to teach for democracy, and educate for equity and social justice, we need to recognize our own privileges and work hard to unlearn our neoliberal heritage so as not to become "missionaries."

As a teacher educator, my aim was to help Maria and my student teachers to develop pedagogical practices that would reflect the words they had read in *The Pedagogy of the Oppressed* (Freire, 1970). We developed a learning community based on an understanding of social condition mediated by a dialogic act. This group of pre-service teachers developed not only an awareness

of their and their students' social condition, but tried to transform that awareness into practice by focusing on a curriculum that would integrate theory and
practice, learners and community, citizens and society.

DISCUSSION: AN ACTION PLAN

The critical classroom incident described before was what prompted my
student teachers and me to question the curriculum and to create an action
plan in order to address the issues their learners had brought up. Not only
did Maria's lesson promote change, it helped us all question and develop a
new understanding of curriculum, particularly one that would speak to the
students and would explicitly address issues of social justice and equity.

The questions raised about curriculum, textbooks, teaching materials,
and classroom management, among others, became our first step toward the
development and implementation of a new curriculum, a curriculum that was
negotiated with the students and that was open to revision, assessment, and
change.

The learners in that *favela* were studying English as a foreign language
(EFL) for the first time in their lives, and their motivation toward this "different" and truly foreign language was such that we thought about developing
a bilingual curriculum focusing on biliteracy. Why not take advantage of
their enthusiasm to build on literacy skills on both their first language (L1),
Portuguese, and the second language (L2), English? Because of their limited
proficiency in English and their inability to express complex thoughts and
write about them in the L2, we thought we could work together with the Portuguese teacher in order to have students develop their skills first in the L1
and then transfer the skills developed to their use of the L2 (Cummins, 2001).
These students had been studying English for a short period of time and the
little they knew was basically vocabulary items and simple conversational
exchanges with some colloquial expressions, such as those used in greetings
and introductions.

The English lessons involved a lot of translations and students communicated mostly in the L1. It was only natural that they would express themselves
in Portuguese first, especially if they were to tackle issues that even in the L1
were not that easy for them to verbalize. Given their level of motivation about
working with us, they were all excited about having a bilingual classroom in
which they would express themselves in their mother tongue first and then
try to use the L2 to express some of the ideas or the vocabulary used in order
to talk about those topics.

The basis of the new curriculum was the community those learners
belonged to and how that community was affected by and in turn affected
larger social, economic, and political circumstances. The lesson about

professions in English was discussed with the students and they came up with ideas of things they wanted to learn and write about, from professions to workplaces, from their families to the other families they saw on the television or they heard about from their parents' descriptions. By looking into their communities, exploring their surroundings and examining their social condition, those students from a *favela* in a large urban area in southern Brazil learned about the environment they had been brought up in and discussed possible ways of promoting change by becoming literate in (possibly) two languages.

The first thing we needed to consider was the reason why the students went to school. We engaged in true dialogical action with these students. Students and teachers came up with questions and issues that they wanted to include in the curriculum. Our conversation about the role of schools in society, for example, enlightened us to what it was that motivated or forced those students to be in the classroom.

Not all the students understood the real purpose of going to school. Nor can we—or anyone—simply state what the real purpose of schooling is, as there are many different perspectives which are also socially, historically, politically, economically, and culturally constructed. The point here, however, is to try and understand the purpose of schooling from the learners' point of view.

Some of those students admitted to being there just because they needed a place to be while their parents were at work, while others thought of the school as a social place where you "make friends" and "meet boys." Some students did mention "getting an education," "learning," and even "becoming intelligent," but their understandings of what these all meant varied immensely. Once Maria understood the vast array of possibilities and reasons her students came to class, it was easier for her to communicate with them and to also introduce new meanings and new reasons for them to attend classes, keep coming to school, and not to drop out.

The same kind of procedure—problem-posing—was used to understand why some students had asked about and mentioned the professions they did. We needed to be able to understand what students understood by a "profession" and what kinds of aspirations they had for themselves. A profession, for most of the students represented an occupation; something you do every day and get paid for. However, there are so many people in their environment who do not have jobs that these students also related having a profession to having some kind of education.

The discussion on education focused on going to college and finishing school and the types of jobs available depending on how much education you have. The students also showed familiarity with the informal sector of the economy: people who clean houses, sell food on the streets, wash and iron, sell artifacts, and drugs. The students showed some awareness about what goes on in the world outside their community, but their awareness sometimes also translated into hopelessness, after all they understood that they did not have the financial conditions to pursue further education; they understood that the education they received lacked in quality and credibility, and that they needed to find some work in order to help their families and survive.

This is the feeling that I refer to as hopelessness and that was what helped us to understand their associating certain activities that we did not consider professions as being professions. They knew people who stole for a living; they knew people who did it regularly. Their description of a profession fit in so well with the semantics of what one would define as a profession that one would find it hard to argue against their logic.

So why does it still shock us so much? Because our logic does not accept or accommodate their definitions; because what we know as a profession is what is socially accepted as such, and whoever does not fit into that category is an outlier. This is what most children who grow up in *favelas* seem to see themselves as outliers. As educators and citizens, we wanted to show them a world of possibilities. Their hopelessness was also a way of demanding those possibilities. The pedagogy of the oppressed (Freire, 1970) is also the pedagogy of hope (Freire, 1992) and the pedagogy of possibility (Simon, 1987).

If they wanted to become a drug dealer or a thief; that would be their choice, but as educators it was our responsibility to present alternatives, to show different sides and perspectives, to help create a better future for themselves by introducing students to a world of possibilities.

Apart from the teachers they knew and saw every day, there were other people working in their community that we decided to focus on. We were not willing to simply accept the fact that they did not know about professions that were not part of their universe, especially because there were people working in that community whose jobs or professions affected those children's lives daily. The basic rule was to start from what they knew and then build on their knowledge.

Sometimes people do not even know what they know or they just decide to be selective for specific reasons, which was what these students were trying to tell us. In fact, we seem to have been the ones who listened to them. We showed them that what they had to say mattered and that they indeed had something to say. Moreover, in order to decide on what it was that they wanted to talk and write about, they also needed to learn to observe.

These were needy children and what could have been interpreted as aggressive behavior in the class, especially given their language use and lexical choices, was a mere reflection of the way they were treated by the people in and outside their community. It is not that this is the only way they knew how to communicate their meanings or needs, but it seems to have been the only way they knew how to draw attention to themselves, to be listened to. Once we responded to their needs, their attitude changed, their manners and language use changed and, what is more, they demonstrated an ever-increasing interest in learning about what we had to share with them.

In order to learn about your own condition, you need to learn to observe— carefully and attentively. A simple exercise like walking around their community and focusing on the people they saw, what they looked like, what they were wearing and carrying, where they lived, how they spoke, who they spoke to and what about was enough to show them that they not always paid attention to their surroundings. Being able to observe and reflect on what you see around you proved to be an extremely difficult exercise for these students, but they also reported on things they had never really noticed before: sounds never really identified, smells that had been ignored, colors that reflected the reality they lived in.

When asked what people they knew in their community and what professions or jobs they had, the students were able to not only mention the professions they knew in the community, they could also describe what the people looked like, where they worked, and even what days and times they were around. The professions mentioned included the ones some of their parents and relatives had, such as maids, security guards, handymen, and some informal occupations like street vendor and paper boy, but they also included the nurse and the doctor that visited their community on a regular basis, the various city workers who did work in and around their community, and, of course, all of us who worked at the school. Many of the professions mentioned by the students were actually included in Maria's initial lesson.

Once we had established the professions we knew in the community and had put faces on them—real professions represented by real people the students knew and could relate to, our next step was to spend some time with these people in order to learn more about who they were, what they did and how they felt about their work.

Our classes included field trips to the community health center, to some of the homes in the community, and to the areas surrounding it. In class, students prepared questions they wanted answers for—and their questions even included how much money people made and where they kept it. Students organized themselves in small groups and each group interviewed different people in and around the community. After collecting the information, they had to select and organize it to be then presented in class where we would also write about the experience. Students chose the topics, the words, and the facts they wanted to talk and write about.

By engaging in this activity, students realized that not only are there many possible occupations, jobs, and careers, but also that the meaning of what a profession is may vary according to social and economic standards. The professions people in their community have may not be as socially valued as those had by the people they work for, but, as they concluded, many "rich people could not do their professions well without us." This was particularly important because it taught students about how things are interdependent and interrelated in society.

Finally, it is also important to recognize that even though some students may still think that the "professions" they had initially mentioned in class may be recognized or accepted as professions within their universe, there are other possible professions available and that education is a powerful vehicle to achieving something better, or at least different from what they know. These students' struggle is the wider struggle of classes and power in society. They understand their role as the "oppressed," but they also recognize the importance of not simply accepting this role as part of human condition or as fate.

This discussion led to a wider discussion on the importance of staying in school for the reasons they already knew and for the reasons they had just started to realize. Schooling seems to have achieved a new meaning for these students. The fact that they had been empowered had indeed broadened the meaning of schooling within their universe.

Learning to read and write, especially when you become better equipped to decide what you want to read and write about, becomes a powerful tool to expressing yourself, your views, and your ways of seeing and interpreting the world. By developing this curriculum jointly, my student teachers and I learned how to observe classrooms with different lenses and how to truly learn about the students and the lives we affect day after day.

Their responsibility was shared with their language learners who also found their voice and learned to express it. They talked, shared, and wrote about their experiences in their L1 and after that the foreign language classroom was also taken to a new level. It was the English language teacher who had taken the time to work with them, to listen to them, and to guide them through the process of discovering language and society.

It was not as surprising to me when I went back to that classroom and saw those students trying to talk and write about the people they had interviewed using and writing words such as doctor, garbage truck, school, and teacher.

CONCLUSION

Education is going through a standardization process that goes against basic principles of critical pedagogy that focuses on the local characteristics of the community and the population that a school serves. In times when educational systems worldwide have become extremely measurement-oriented, the tendency toward globalizing education is eliminating cultural local differences and neglecting student populations with specific cultural and ethnic makeup and particular needs.

In this context, second and foreign language educators are at an advantage. For many learners, the foreign language classroom may be the only contact they will have with another language—let alone another culture—while at school. Therefore, learning a foreign language may also represent a concrete possibility for learners to think critically about their own culture.

The story described in this chapter to illustrate principles of critical pedagogy in practice is an example of what happens when a foreign or second language is used as the medium for instruction. Through experiencing a different language and by being exposed to a different culture, these learners managed to verbalize issues that affected and afflicted them in the first language, in their first culture. Their subsequent interest in expressing their voices in their first language and the need to develop further literacy skills in order to make their voices heard show that first and second language teaching and learning can actually complement and enhance each other.

The project described in this chapter was an attempt to transform concepts and principles of critical pedagogy into classroom practice. Our approach was rooted in the experiences of the marginalized learners we were working with and focused on the structural socioeconomic, political, and racial oppression. Through dialogic interactions between students, ourselves, and the community at large, we believe we have managed to empower learners to become agents of social change—and that only happened because of our belief in education as the way toward citizenship.

Education is a long-term process, though, and we should not expect immediate results. Some of the people who criticized us at first for teaching English to children who could "hardly speak or write" in their first language, probably did not consider some important factors. Foreign language learning should not be a privilege exclusively destined to the elite. It should be the right of every child to demand foreign language classes and the study of foreign cultures and people. Moreover, the excuse that one should have mastered one language before starting studying another one has already been disproved (Krashen, 1999; Cummins, 2001; Crawford, 2004). In fact, learning a foreign or second language supports the development of first language literacy (Garcia & Kleifgen, 2010; Naiditch, 2003).

Literacy is the right of every citizen and no one should have his or her rights denied or neglected. Teaching learners how to use language(s) should be a major concern for both first and second foreign language teachers who believe in education toward liberation. The development of literacy skills (and of literacies) is a powerful tool for learners to communicate with the world, to understand it, and, ultimately, to transform it.

Maria and the other student teachers most certainly learned how to make more educated and well-informed pedagogical decisions, taking into account different perspectives, weighing all different sides of an argument or an issue, exhausting all possibilities, searching for new answers and even thinking of solutions for problems that have not yet been confronted.

REFERENCES

Apple, M. W. (2014). *Official knowledge: Democratic education in a conservative age.* (3rd edition). New York: Routledge.

Apple, M. (1993). The politics of official knowledge: Does a national curriculum make sense? *Teachers College Record,* 95(2), 222–241.

Boal, A. (1979). *The theatre of the oppressed.* New York: Urizen Books.

Bright, B. (1996). Reflecting on "reflective practice". *Studies in the Education of Adults,* 28(2), 162–184.

Brookfield, S. (1988). Developing critically reflective practitioners: A rationale for training educators of adults. In: Brookfield, S. (1988). (ed). *Training educators of adults: The theory and practice of graduate adult education.* New York: Routledge.

Brookfield, S. (1994). Tales from the dark side: A phenomenography of adult critical reflection. *International Journal of Lifelong Education,* 13(3), 203–216.

Canagarajah, S. (2004). Subversive identities, pedagogical safe houses, and critical-learning. In: Norton, B. & Toohey, K. (Eds.). (2004). *Critical pedagogies and language learning.* Cambridge: Cambridge University Press.

Cochran-Smith, M. (2001). Learning and unlearning: Educating teacher educators from an inquiry stance. Paper presented at the American Educational Research Association, Seattle, WA.

Cortesão, L. (2002). *Ser professor: Um ofício em risco de extinção.* São Paulo: Instituto Paulo Freire/Cortez.

Cranton, P. (1996). *Professional development as transformative learning: New perspectives for teachers of adults.* San Francisco: Jossey-Bass.

Crawford, J. (2004). *Educating English learners: Language diversity in the classroom.* Los Angeles, CA: Bilingual Education Services.

Cummins, J. (2001). *Language, power, and pedagogy: Bilingual Children in the Crossfire.* Clevedon: Multilingual Matters.

Freire, A. M . A. (2006). *Paulo Freire: Uma história de vida.* Indaiatuba, SP: Villa das Letras Editora.

Freire, P. (1970). *Pedagogia do oprimido.* São Paulo: Editora Paz e Terra S/A.

Freire, P. (1973). *Education for critical consciousness.* New York: Continuum.

Freire, P. (1978). *Pedagogy in process.* New York: Seabury.

Freire, P. (1980). *Pedagogy of the oppressed.* New York: Continuum.

Freire, P. (1985). *Politics of education.* New York: Bergin and Garvey.

Freire, P. (1992). *Pedagogia da esperança: Um Reencontro com a pedagogia do oprimido.* São Paulo: Paz e Terra.

Freire, P. (1994). *Pedagogy of hope.* New York: Continuum.

Freire, P. (1998). *Teachers as cultural workers.* Westview: Boulder.

Freire, P. & Horton, M. (1992). *We make this road by walking.* New York: Continuum.

Freire, P. & Macedo, D. (1987). *Literacy: Reading the word and the world.* New York: Bergin & Garvey.

Gadotti, M. (2005). O Plantador do futuro. *Memória da pedagogia 4: Paulo Freire.* São Paulo: Segmento-Duetto.

Garcia, O. & Kleifgen, J. (2010). *Educating emergent bilinguals: Policies, programs, and practices for English language learners.* New York: Teachers College Press.

Gibson, R. (1999). Paulo Freire and pedagogy for social justice. *Theory & Research in Social Education,* 27(2), 129–159.

Giroux, H. (2005). *Schooling and the struggle for public life: Democracy's promise and education's challenge.* Boulder, CO: Paradigm Publishers.

Grossman, P. (1990). *The Making of a teacher: Teacher knowledge and teacher education.* New York: Teachers College Press.

Krashen, S. (1999). *Condemned without a trial: Bogus arguments against bilingual education.* Portsmouth, NH: Heinemann.

Loewen, J. W. (2007). *Lies my teacher told me: Everything your American history textbook got wrong.* New York: Touchstone Publishers.

Luke, A. (2004). Two takes on the critical. In: Norton, B. & Toohey, K. (Eds.). (2004). *Critical pedagogies and language learning.* Cambridge: Cambridge University Press.

McLaren, P. (1997). Um legado de luta e de esperança. *Pátio Revista Pedagógica.* Ano I, No. 2, 10–14. Porto Alegre: ARTMED.

McLaren, P. (2006). *Life in schools: An introduction to critical pedagogy in the foundations of education.* London: Allyn & Bacon.

Naiditch, F. (2003). *Bi-literacy development in the classroom: Examples from the South Bronx.* Paper presented at the 2003 NYSTESOL Annual Conference. Rye: New York.

Naiditch, F. (2008). *Interculture development and the second language classroom.* Paper presented at the 2008 AERA Annual Meeting. New York: New York.

Norton, B. & Toohey, K. (Eds.). (2004). *Critical pedagogies and language learning.* Cambridge: Cambridge University Press.

O'Cádiz, M. P. & Wong, P. L., & Torres, C. A. (2002). *Educação e cidadania: A práxis de Paulo Freire em São Paulo.* São Paulo: Instituto Paulo Freire/Cortez.

Preskill, S. & Brookfield, S. D. (2008). *Learning as a way of leading: Lessons from the struggle for social justice.* San Francisco: Jossey-Bass.

Selinker, L. & Naiditch, F. (2004). Reframing grammar and grammar teaching: A Talmudic approach. *Rivista di Psicolinguistica Applicata,* 4(1), p. 13–39.

Shor, I. (1992). *Empowering education: Critical teaching for social change.* Chicago: University Of Chicago Press.

Shulman, E. (1987). Knowledge and teaching: Foundations of the new reform. *Harvard Educational Review,* 57(1), 1–21.

Simon, R. (1987). Empowerment as a pedagogy of possibility. *Language Arts,* 64(4). 370–382.

Simon, R. (1992). *Teaching against the grain: Texts for a pedagogy of possibility.* New York: Bergin & Garvey.

Afterword

Encouraging Teachers' Growth and Development Using Practitioner Research

Kathryn Herr

While many of the chapters in this book were about fostering critical thinking with and among students, this chapter moves the focus to supporting teachers as they cultivate critical thinking and reflection about their own teaching practices and the broader contexts of education. In particular, practitioner research is presented as one approach for teacher development and professional growth as teachers reflect upon and desire to make changes in their classrooms and beyond.

While known by a variety of terms—teacher research, action research, practitioner research—what they hold in common is a number of key assumptions: that the inquiry process can deepen an educator's understanding of problems of practice, that is, address everyday puzzles to improve teaching, students' learning and educational structures; that the research question is generated by the teacher herself or in an inquiry group of colleagues; that inquiry is done through systematic data gathering, moving it beyond everyday problem-solving; and, that the knowledge generated through the inquiry process is valuable for the local site—a teacher's own classroom or school—but that it can also inform the field of education more broadly.

The process positions teachers as researchers in their own right rather than simply as consumers of the educational research of others. It also underscores the value of insider knowledge and the unique contribution of on-the-ground educators to the knowledge base of education. An insider perspective and questioning of current practices and policies is a valuable resource toward continuing to refine them toward the best interests of students. In this sense then it recognizes the expertise and insight that teachers bring to the further development of knowledge relating to the real world of education.

Educators problem-solve all the time. Practitioner research moves beyond this to systematic inquiry. While traditional social science research frowns on intervening in any way in the research setting, practitioner research assumes action is an integral part of the process. It is commonly described as a spiral of action cycles. In his now classic work, Kemmis (1982) described this spiral as an undertaking in which (1) a plan of action is developed to improve what is already happening; (2) action is taken to implement the plan; (3) the effects of the action in the context in which it occurs are observed; and (4) further planning and subsequent action is based on reflecting on this initial observation of the effects. The process is carried out in a succession of these cycles.

While seemingly a fairly clean, and clear process, many of us find it messier than it initially appears. Practitioner research is often without a clear beginning or end. We can enter the spiral at any point along the way. That is, typically we have been thinking about an issue for some time and have probably even tried some interventions. Informally, the action research cycle has begun. And while we commit to reflecting on what we have learned so far, the tempo of schools is a fast-paced one. Often we are called upon to formulate a plan of action before we have had much time to really reflect.

Part of the goal though is to slow things down a bit, we can be more deliberate. We move from informal planning, observing, and meaning making to more systematic data gathering that will inform further actions. The inquiry process is designed to lead to more complex understandings of issues so that any remedies or interventions can be constructive and on target. Common starting points are frustrations, problems, irritants, or brick walls. Practitioner research can be a way into viewing these puzzles in new ways so that effective solutions may be more possible.

In my own case, I was working as a middle school teacher and counselor at a well-endowed private school. Originally an all boys' school, designed for sons of affluent families, had gone co-ed a decade earlier. When I was hired some years later, part of my job was to support the school's next evolution and help it move toward further socioeconomic and racial diversity. Benefiting from a sizable endowment, the school was positioned to offer full tuition scholarships to foster these goals.

If students could perform well on the rigorous battery of admission tests and handle the screening interview, they had an opportunity for a free ride at what was considered a premier educational institution. With high hopes the school began recruiting and admitting the more diverse student population it sought. A few years after starting this process, a large number of the recruited students were gone, with many not invited back due to poor academic performances. Those who remained often seemed to be hanging by a thread. The discourse in the school was one of "Well, if the kids can't take advantage of the opportunity, there are plenty in line who will."

As one of the school counselors charged with supporting the diversity efforts, I was uncomfortable with these analyses of individual failure and the idea that somehow the kids didn't measure up or weren't trying. Knowing that they had shown their readiness for the rigors of the academic environment via solid performances on entrance exams, I struggled to offer a different story line of what was happening, but I frankly wasn't all that sure myself. I knew that within the confines of my counseling office, with the protection of confidentiality, the students told tales of being miserable and feeling out of place. While, actively problem-solving with them and intervening on their behalf our efforts fell short.

Frustrated and discouraged, I resolved to step back a bit and see if I could get a different view of the issue. While at that point, I had never heard of practitioner research, I did know the tenets of research more generally and "equipped" with that knowledge, bumbled my way into studying my own school. I ultimately documented that journey and my growing understanding in a book written with two professors from a local university (see Anderson, Herr & Nihlen, 2007).

Teachers do not necessarily consider themselves researchers although they may have been exposed to teacher research during their pre-service or graduate school educations. For those who were acquainted with the process, the task is to now move it from a discrete assignment in a class to an ongoing practice in their classrooms and schools. For those who have not done practitioner research at all, it can seem like a leap to embrace a researcher identity as well as the skills necessary to do it. Many though have found great professional rewards in studying their own schools and practice.

In reflecting back on an action research project in which she had been involved, one teacher researcher offered:

> Being a part of this research has been life changing. I've spent time reflecting on my teaching practice but more so on the students. The overall experience has impacted me on many levels and I know I will never teach the same, think the same about students, and I will stop and listen a lot more to what is being said by my students. Although challenging and personally revealing, I'd still do it all over again. (Kane & Chimwayange, 2014, pp. 52–53)

THE ABCS OF PRACTITIONER RESEARCH

In the following section, the basics of practitioner research are laid out along with some examples. There is no one right way to go about practitioner research but what it does demand is a willingness to be open to new understandings through systematic inquiry. New insights that challenge everyday understandings are a common part of the process. To safeguard the potential of practitioner research, the researcher or the inquiry group should be quizzing themselves throughout the process, asking questions such as: *How is it we "know what we know?" How have data challenged our assumptions? Shifted our understanding?*

*Is our understanding growing more complex? Whose voice has been heard?
Have multiple perspectives been taken into account? Has the process helped
resolve the issue? Resolved for whom?* This is not an exhaustive list, but when
held in mind they will be helpful in retaining the promise of the process.

THE RESEARCH QUESTION

The initial question to be considered via the research process is often one
borne of problems or frustrations. In my case, frustrated by my practice,
I asked, "How might I better support the students we had recruited?" Posing
a question for research is simply a starting point. Initial data gathering helps
further refine the question as we come to better understand the issues surrounding it. It is expected that the initial research question will be reformu-
lated multiple times as the inquiry is pursued. Our growing understanding
helps us pose the next iteration of the question.

Many iterations of my question later I came to ask, "How might this school
support the students it recruits beyond the granting of scholarships?" The
importance of this iteration indicated a better understanding of the issue. The
focus moved from holding individual students solely responsible for their
struggles and failures to a questioning of the broader school environment and
its practices. This insight led us to work toward more fundamental changes in
school structures and climate, moving beyond the simplistic solutions often
offered of asking the students to "try harder."

In another example, a novice special education teacher in an elementary
school posed an initial question of "how do I take my students on field trips?"
The question was posed in a graduate class I was teaching at the time and
I remember thinking how boring this question sounded—how hard was it to
take a field trip? But I had often reminded students that research questions are
embedded in the larger context of their school sites and districts, something
I needed to remember myself as it came into play with her study.

At first, she spent a lot of her time on the nuts and bolts surrounding field
trips—the forms to be filled out, how to arrange transportation, etc. Our
graduate class, myself included, idly listened to these ongoing updates of
her data gathering—mostly district forms and budget sheets. Confident that
she had got it right, she submitted her request—and it was turned down.
She returned to her forms, double-checked them all and was puzzled as to
what had happened with her request. After several rounds of the request being
denied, she began to wonder what else was at work. Now she was beginning
to get our attention as well.

As her inquiry unfolded, she became concerned that her students were
marginalized from many of the routines of the school and were denied

opportunities that other students seemed to have. She began to focus on how they might be better integrated into the life of the school and be offered opportunities similar to those of the other students. Her puzzles became ones of wondering how to shift attitudes toward her students, helping others to see them through a lens of what their strengths could offer the school community. As a class we avidly followed her week-to-week explorations, now completely engaged in what she was undertaking.

She realized that her question was less about how to take a field trip and more about exploring the limitations being imposed on her students and how the limiting beliefs of others rendered her students' strengths invisible. What initially looked like a fairly easy question to pursue—the logistics of field trips—had evolved into a more complex undertaking.

She worked to devise an experience that would be affirming for the students but that would also capitalize on what they had to offer to the larger community. Her inquiry became a careful study in how she might best advocate for them and how she could support her students in becoming their own advocates. Her students were eventually allowed to go on a field trip. But the teacher also realized that her overall work in addressing the limiting conditions imposed upon them went beyond this small but important success.

DATA GATHERING

One ongoing tension for practitioner researchers is the issue of time and data gathering. The intent is not to create additional work; rather the goal is that insights from the inquiry process will inform professional practice, allowing us to work in more gratifying and effective ways. Because educators are doing research in their "spare" time, data-gathering approaches work best when incorporated into the daily routines of teachers.

A starting point for inquiry is to ask what data already exist, what information is already available and whether it can be helpful for the questions now being posed. Teachers often have hunches regarding the questions they are posing and these hunches can sometimes be "tested" via existing data. Rather than reinvent the wheel and start from scratch, it is sometimes possible to analyze existing data in new, helpful ways.

For example, in my own study trying to better understand the failing performance of capable students in my school, I first systematically checked their attendance records. I wanted to be sure they weren't missing more school than other students. I thought this was plausible since students and their families had to find their own transportation to the school. Many students traditionally car-pooled with others. Informal networks of parents, drawing on relationships built while volunteering at school events or whose homes were clustered in affluent areas of the city, organized these efforts among themselves.

Students we had recruited were more often plucked out of their neighborhoods, one or two here or there, spread out across a sprawling city without much public transportation. There were no apparent natural networks for them or their parents to tap into these car-pooling arrangements. They were new to the school community and ways in were not easily accessible. For example, while the school had recruited a more diverse student body, much of the life of the school was built around the idea of parents, mostly mothers, who were available to volunteer, often during traditional work hours. Any parent employed out of the home, without flexible hours, was immediately out of this loop of informal, but important, connections.

I could easily access the daily sign-in sheets used in the school to record whether a student was in school and what time they arrived each day. I checked to see whether the students about whom I was concerned were missing more frequently or arriving late. I could also access the network of carpools, checking to see how many of the recruited students were linking into these kinds of arrangements. I saw the latter as a symbol of their connection informally to the larger school community.

This kind of data allows a practitioner researcher to see whether the data support her working theories or hunches that might help explain our area of concern. It is not at all uncommon that these first efforts demonstrate that we need more data. The explanations we tell ourselves are often off, do not hold up in the light of data or do not tell the whole story.

In calling for "inquiry as stance," Cochran-Smith and Lytle (2009) describe it as a worldview we develop, a critical habit of mind where we learn to view the everyday in new ways. Growing into the mindset of a researcher in our own sites, then, implies that we move through that space with a questioning eye, that inquiry becomes a way of being (Alvesson, 2003). It implies that business as usual is open for interrogation, particularly if not all in a community are well served by current arrangements of schooling and practices.

Returning to the earlier example of the novice, special education teacher demonstrates this notion of an inquiry stance. Walking to her classroom one day, she began to think about where she and her students were located in the school. A self-contained special education classroom, they were in a portable, that is, a detached building, separate from the rest of the school. Portables were pre-fabricated buildings used by her district when it faced overcrowding in the original school building.

Beginning to think more metaphorically, she began asking herself what other ways her students were held separate in the school. As she went about a routine school day, she consciously observed when and where her students were included as part of the school and when they were held separate.

She jotted these observations down in a small notebook she carried through that week. She watched for the opportunities they had to interact with the larger school body and began to question, when they were held separate, the rationale or the why behind that decision. She mulled through these observations in her research journal, asking how the imposed boundaries limiting her students' interactions with the rest of the school limited their learning opportunities. She also wondered about what the school community was losing in its exclusion of her students.

Important in this example is the systematic recording of her observations as well as her reflections about them. Practitioner researchers commonly utilize a researcher journal to record their ongoing thinking and observations. This becomes a practice in noticing the everyday in new ways and systematically reflecting on these observations. These possible insights then can be pursued through further data gathering or in actions based upon them that are then studied for effect.

Unlike some other forms of research, the assumption in practitioner research is that an initial data-gathering step is devised and then begun. A complete roadmap to the inquiry is not expected since the idea is that the strategy for data gathering and action will continue to unfold in light of the ongoing spiral of inquiry and reflection. At the same time, it is expected that the research question itself will continue to develop as it is informed by what is learned.

Data gathering is often a mix of available data that can be analyzed for its relevance to the research question coupled with data gathered specifically for the inquiry underway. I intentionally started interviewing the students who had been recruited to better understand their experiences in the school. Some I knew well already, but others I approached specifically for the inquiry. I was particularly curious about the students who were doing well and wanted to learn more about their experiences. Unfortunately, what these interviews captured were narratives of what the students termed "learning to be white" and alienation from their own cultures.

Other data gathering can be serendipitous, where since we are in the sites on a day-to-day basis in multiple capacities, we simply come across data that is relevant to the inquiry. This is part of that inquiry stance referred to earlier, working to view the setting with fresh eyes even as we participate in routine events. For example, I was at the monthly meeting of the faculty when a key administrator addressed the group, talking at length about the diversity efforts and the mission of the school. I took notes during the meeting and later turned these notes into a lengthier transcription. In the process I was acutely aware of the goals and the rhetoric of the diversity effort and the lived reality of the students.

Moving ahead, this observation was useful as we worked to change the culture of the school. Invoking that mission, sometimes reminding the administrator himself of the original vision he had espoused was useful in the change process even if it meant facing difficult changes in the school. Essentially we were asking him to consider moving beyond scholarships toward the creation of a truly welcoming environment for diverse students.

Any question a teacher poses is asked in a specific context so simply raising an issue to explore already begins to send ripples through the environment. As questions for inquiry are raised and refined, and particularly as the complexity becomes apparent, the inquiry may appear to be more political than originally thought. Others become interested, threatened or intrigued. "The questioning stance seems to lend itself to asking why we carry out business as usual and provoke new conversations about the status quo" (Anderson, Herr, and Nihlen, 2007, p. 126).

It is not unusual to encounter other vested interests or exhume unexamined beliefs manifest in a school's structure or culture during the inquiry process. Seeing what is possible in terms of solutions within particular contexts is part of practitioner research. It is assumed that everyone works within constraints yet this awareness is balanced with a sense of not wanting to acquiesce too quickly to the idea that "things will never change." As a teacher begins to question her own practices or the practices in her site, others begin to get interested as well. So while initially starting as an individual researcher, others may begin to gradually join the change process.

INDIVIDUAL OR COLLABORATIVE INQUIRY?

Because insider researchers are so immersed in their sites of study—their students or classrooms or an issue in their own school—there is often great benefit in doing the research collaboratively. A major hurdle for insider researchers is to interrogate their own tacit knowledge—what it is they think they "know" and to submit this knowledge to questioning.

It helps to have others involved in this process of "trying to make the familiar strange" and acting as "critical friends." Critical friends are those who agree to pose questions about the data. Whether one other person or an ongoing small group, the critical friend arrangement is designed to ensure that someone is playing the devil's advocate, pushing on understandings that are taken for granted. They challenge the researcher to newly re-examine their understandings based on the research data rather than relying on unquestioned assumptions (Anderson, Herr and Nihlen, 2007).

Working with others in different positions in the same site (teams of administrators, teachers, students, community members, etc.) often offers differing vantage points and understandings on the same issue. Because they are also invested in the issue under exploration, motivation and interest is often high. Democratic validity in practitioner research refers to the extent to which research is done in collaboration with parties who have a stake in the issue under investigation (Anderson, Herr and Nihlen, 2007). It allows the researcher to ask whether proposed solutions benefit some at the expense of others. Collaborative inquiry teams can often anticipate these kinds of possible conflicts of interests.

Some form inquiry groups beyond their own work sites, where they meet regularly with others to discuss their own research and a larger change agenda. Again, the group members can act as critical friends for each other, pushing on assumptions about "the way things are done there" and challenging the researcher to consider alternative explanations. This questioning of the taken-for-granted understandings is probably one of the more difficult tasks in practitioner research so to invite others into the process is usually a helpful path to take whether inside one's site or beyond.

Because any change process is a challenge, and since practitioner research typically questions the status quo, it can be helpful to approach the inquiry with other willing collaborators. Cochran-Smith and Lytle (2009) describe the work of education and inquiry into it as a social and political undertaking. In this view, when working from a stance of inquiry, educators move beyond simply figuring out how to get things done.

Instead they deliberately ask what to get done and why, who decides and whose interests are served. They suggest that this stance involves a continued process of rendering problematic current arrangements of schooling that benefit some at the expense of others. Cochran-Smith and Lytle (2009) assume that the work of practitioners is to participate in educational and social change. With this in mind then many practitioner researchers look to partner with others in the process.

CONSIDERING ACTION

Educational or social science researchers typically make recommendations for change or further research when they complete a study. Practitioner research differs from this approach, in that action is built into the process of inquiry. It is assumed that researchers will intervene in the issue of concern and then study the intervention.

Often the intervention is somewhat effective but most commonly needs ongoing adjustment based on further understanding. Because of this, it is important to study each intervention along the way, with the assumption of a need for further development based on initial and ongoing analyses. Whether something "works" or not, it is regarded as information useful in moving forward.

For example, in my own study, the students I was initially studying eventually became collaborators in the inquiry and change effort. After ongoing discussions, they decided to ask for time with the school's curriculum committee, to see if more diverse authors could be incorporated into the curriculum. When they were not successful in changing the formal curriculum, the students decided to try a Plan B. They instituted an after-school film and book forum, essentially offering a parallel curriculum to the more formal one offered during the school day.

While not what they originally were looking for, the after-school offerings did attract a large number of students. It also attracted a wider range of students who became interested in the efforts to change the school culture to be more inclusive. This larger coalition resulted in a student group being established to take up issues of diversity and work with administrators and teachers to influence decision-making.

The novice special education teacher referred to earlier was not able to initially arrange much of a field trip for her students. But she did connect with a local nursing home within walking distance of the school. She and her students volunteered there to be companions to some of the residents, sitting with them and keeping them company.

Since a number of the residents were fairly isolated, the nursing home welcomed these young volunteers. While there, the teacher and her students took pictures of themselves with the residents; often these included residents reading to the students, with looks of pleasure on both sets of faces. The teacher used these to create a bulletin board display back in the school.

In doing this she brought documentation back into the school environment and demonstrated to the larger teacher and student bodies that her students could function well in a larger slice of the environment. She also showed that they could be active contributors whose efforts enhanced the school's reputation in the community positively. The nursing home residents were gratified to embrace the reality that they could serve in a useful role with the next generation.

THE POTENTIAL AND CONTRIBUTION
OF PRACTITIONER RESEARCH

Blumenreich and Falk (2015) make the case that when teachers are encouraged to think and act like researchers they build a capacity for learning, for themselves and their students. The inquiry process helps "teachers generate new knowledge from examining how they work with the children in their care" (Blumenreich and Falk, 2015, p. 47). This can be particularly useful when teachers are asked to incorporate new standards and approaches to curriculum into their classrooms.

Studying one's own classroom or school helps address the question of how effectively a teacher is managing to integrate new standards into her ongoing work as an educator. Critical thinking is seen as a vital component that students will need in the future for success. Common Core Standards place front and center the ability to enact higher order thinking skills—problem-solving, application, synthesis, and evaluation, to name a few of these skills.

These are congruent with many of the skills necessary to carry out practitioner research. As teachers enact these for themselves, Blumenreich and Falk (2015) suggest that their students benefit. This occurs from teaching practices that are improved while studying them. But this chapter asserts that there is additional benefit in seeing their teachers apply critical thinking skills to their own context of schooling toward its improvement.

Some practitioner research projects ultimately involve students as collaborators in critically examining their environments. For example, Kohfeldt, Chhun, Grace, and Langhout (2011) report on a project with fifth-graders where the students carried out research in their school and presented their findings and recommendations to the school principal. Later they presented their research at a school-wide assembly and involved a broader audience in taking up consideration of possible interventions.

Work by Ozer and Wright (2012) studying youth-led action research in two urban high schools demonstrated that the opportunity to do research enhanced key areas of growth in the students. In particular, their study indicated that the inquiry process conducted by the students allowed them to exert more influence on policies and practices in the school by critically examining them in their research. And finally, Zaal and Terry (2013) reported that students engaged in participatory research had opportunities to develop skills that they otherwise might not have acquired.

As teachers themselves become more comfortable with the research process and experience its benefits for their own growth, they are more likely to involve their own students in it as well. There is a fundamental shift in relationships of schooling as educators and their students become co-researchers for positive change and co-learners. They critically examine their own contexts with an eye toward changing them. These skills obviously prepare students to take their places as future citizens who are committed to positive change practices for issues of concern to them.

CONCLUSION

There has been a long-standing struggle in education to consistently acknowledge and affirm that teachers are generators of knowledge, not simply consumers of research that outsiders generate (Christianakis, 2010). But through the increasing number of venues to disseminate this work to larger audiences, the rich contributions of teacher research are becoming increasing visible (see, for example, websites such as teachersnetwork.org).

In addition, there is a growing plethora of resources for educators who want to learn more about practitioner research. Two books commonly consulted include *Inquiry as Stance: Practitioner Research for the Next Generation* by Marilyn Cochran-Smith and Susan Lytle and *Living the Questions: A Guide for Teacher-Researchers* by Ruth Shagoury Hubbard and Ruth Miller Power. Teachers are also writing book length accounts of their own practitioner research. See Cynthia Ballenger's *Puzzling Moments, Teachable Moments: Practicing Teacher-Research in Urban Classrooms* for an excellent example of a teacher publishing her classroom inquiry.

As the teacher researcher movement grows, Cochran-Smith and Lytle (2009) assert that it is creating a push-back against schooling practices that are not seen as beneficial to student learning. Many teachers enter the field of education with a passion and commitment to teaching and the possibilities of education to benefit the larger society. In what can sometimes be discouraging circumstances for teaching, practitioner research is one method to both engage in critical learning for themselves and work for positive changes on a larger scale in the educational landscape.

REFERENCES

Alvesson, M. (2003). Methodology for close up studies—struggling with closeness and closure. *Higher Education, 46,* 167–193.

Anderson, G.L., Herr, K. & Nihlen, A.S. (2007). *Studying your own school: An educator's guide to practitioner action research.* Thousand Oaks, CA: Corwin Press.

Blumenreich, M. & Falk, B. (2015). Research and teacher self-inquiry reawaken-learning. *Phi Delta Kappan, 96*(5), 47–51.

Christianakis, M. (2010). Collaborative research and teacher education. *Issues in Teacher Education, 19*(2), 109–125.

Cochran-Smith, M. & Lytle, S. (2009). *Inquiry as stance: Practitioner research for the next generation.* NY: Teachers College Press.

Kane, R.G. & Chimwayange, C. (2014). Teacher action research and student voices: Making sense of learning in secondary school. *Action Research, 12*(1), 52–77.

Kemmis, S. (Ed.) (1982). *The action research reader.* Geelong, Victoria, BC, Canada: Deakin University Press.

Kohfeldt, D., Chhun, L., Grace, S., & Langhout, R.D. (2011). Youth empowerment in context: Exploring tensions in school-based y-PAR. *American Journal of Community Psychology, 47,* 28–45.

Ozer, E.J. & Wright, D. (2012). Beyond school spirit: The effects of youth-led participatory research in two urban high schools. *Journal of Research on Adolescence, 22*(2), 267–283.

Zaal, M. & Terry, J. (2013). Knowing what I can do and who I can be: Youth identity-transformational benefits of participatory action research. *Journal of Ethnographic and Qualitative Research, 8,* 42–55.

About the Editor

Fernando Naiditch holds a PhD in multilingual multicultural studies from New York University. He has been teaching for over twenty-five years and has taught not only in his native Brazil and South America, but also in Europe, the Middle East and the United States. He holds a BA in linguistics, a diploma (DOTE, Dip. TESOL) in second language teaching from Cambridge University, England, and an MA in second language acquisition from Universidade Federal do Rio Grande do Sul (UFRGS) in Brazil. Fernando is also a certified public school teacher in New York State and is the recipient of the 2003 James E. Weaver Memorial Award given by New York State TESOL for his work with and contribution to with English language learners in the New York City public school system.

Fernando has specialized and published in the fields of TESOL, multicultural/bilingual education, culturally and linguistically responsive teaching, and critical pedagogy. As a teacher and teacher educator, Fernando has worked in different parts of the world and has conducted research in different educational settings under various political, social, and economic contexts. His research focuses on the use of critical pedagogy as a tool to achieve equity and social justice in education and on addressing the needs of culturally and linguistically diverse student populations. His dissertation, a study on the pragmatic features of Brazilian ESL learners, received the Outstanding Dissertation Award at NYU in 2006.

Fernando Naiditch is currently an Associate Professor in the Department of Secondary and Special Education in the College of Education and Human Services at Montclair State University in New Jersey. Apart from teaching undergraduate and graduate students, Fernando also provides professional development for a number of school districts in teaching English language learners and in developing culturally responsive curricula.

About the Contributors

Mark Alter is professor of educational psychology at New York University and was the founding chair of the Department of Teaching and Learning, having served as chair for fourteen years. He has an extensive record of publications, national and international workshops, and funded grants in the fields of teacher education and special education. He was granted a Fulbright senior specialist award in special education to Viet Nam, and was awarded the NYU Distinguished Teaching award. Alter has an extensive background in the classroom, as well as a PhD from Yeshiva University in special education.

Kathryn Herr is professor in the Department of Educational Foundations at Montclair State University in New Jersey. She teaches qualitative and practitioner action research. She is the co-author of two books on action research, *Studying Your Own School: An Educator's Guide to Practitioner Action Research* and *The Action Research Dissertation: A Guide for Students and Faculty.* Prior to her university work, Kathryn was a social worker, school counselor, and middle school teacher.

Olivier Michaud is professor of educational foundations at the Université du Québec à Rimouski (UQAR) at its campus of Lévis (Québec, Canada). He holds a PhD in philosophy for children with a focus on qualitative studies from Montclair State University. He has been studying and practicing philosophy for children in Canada, Mexico, and the United States. He has led philosophical communities of inquiry with elementary school children and practices it now with his students in education at UQAR. His research focuses on how the practice of philosophy fosters the democratic education of students in different settings and in grades K–12.

Elizabeth Quintero has worked as a teacher (Pre-K to grade 2), curriculum specialist, and university teacher educator. She is currently professor and coordinator of early childhood studies at California State University Channel Islands. She brings critical perspectives to her work with programs that serve young children and families from a variety of cultural and historical backgrounds in multilingual communities, including Mexico, Turkey, Macedonia, asylum-seekers in the United Kingdom, and many areas of the United States. She is the author of numerous publications including *Storying Learning in Early Childhood: When Children Lead Participatory Curriculum Design, Implementation, and Assessment* (2015) and co-author with Mary K. Rummel of *Storying: A Path to Our Future—Artful Thinking, Learning, Teaching, and Research* (2014).

Joan Rosenberg is clinical professor at New York University. She received her doctorate from Columbia University, Teachers College. After her twenty-five-year career as a teacher, counselor, and administrator at the New York City Department of Education, she went to NYU to teach curriculum and methods courses at the graduate and undergraduate levels and to supervise student teachers for the programs in special education. Currently, she is the program leader for programs in special education and collaborates with parent groups, education attorneys, and advisory groups in order to evaluate special education programs. In addition, she serves as a member of the Board of Trustees at Young Adults Institute. Her professional interests focus on children with emotional challenges.

Mark Russo is supervisor of mathematics for the Pascack Valley Regional High School District, where he works to support effective instruction in mathematics. Previously, he served as a high school mathematics teacher, where he focused on developing students' quantitative reasoning skills and improving their attitudes toward mathematics. Mark has a PhD in mathematics education from Montclair State University, as well as a master's degree in secondary Mathematics education from New York University and a master's degree in global development and social justice from St. John's University.

Bettina Steren dos Santos has had extensive experience both as a teacher and a teacher educator in Brazil. She has a PhD from the University of Barcelona in educational psychology and has also completed postdoctoral work at the University of Texas at Austin. Bettina is currently associate professor in the College of Education at Pontifícia Universidade Católica do Rio Grande do Sul (PUC-RS), where she teaches both undergraduate and graduate level courses. Her current research focuses on motivational processes in educational contexts. Her chapter in this book was co-written with two of her doctoral students, Carla Spagnolo and Caroline Buker.

Jean Ann Bianchi Slusarczyk received a BA in early childhood and elementary education from the College of St. Elizabeth and earned her MA from Nova Southeastern University in teaching and learning. During her thirty-four years as a practitioner, she was a classroom instructor for all primary grades as well as a literacy coach and basic skills interventionist. During her public school tenure, Jean Ann received several awards including the New Jersey Governor's Teacher Recognition Award and the Montclair State University Teacher in a Democracy Award. In 2014, she retired from the Bloomfield School Public School system in New Jersey and began to work for Montclair State University as a professional development consultant and university education mentor.

Lucia (Lucy) Villaluz is an experienced classroom teacher with an MA in teaching and learning and a BA in psychology. She is a first grade inclusion teacher in Bloomfield, New Jersey and an adjunct professor for Montclair State University where she mentors clinical students and also serves as a cooperating teacher. She received the New Jersey Student Teacher of the Year Award in 1995 and the New Jersey Governor's Teacher Award in 2005. In 2015 she received the Teacher in Democracy Award from Montclair State University. In addition to her twenty years of experience in the first grade classroom, she also provides professional development for educators on coaching and mentoring novice teachers.